LIMITED WAR
The Challenge to American Strategy

BY ROBERT ENDICOTT OSGOOD

LIMITED WAR | The Challenge to American Strategy

THE UNIVERSITY OF CHICAGO PRESS

CHICAGO AND LONDON

International Standard Book Number: 0-226-63779-4
Library of Congress Catalog Card Number: 57-5275

THE UNIVERSITY OF CHICAGO PRESS, CHICAGO 60637
The University of Chicago Press, Ltd., London

*To My Mother
and the Memory of My Father*

FOREWORD

The Center for the Study of American Foreign Policy was established in 1950 under a grant from the Lilly Endowment and is now supported by a grant from the Carnegie Corporation. Its general purpose is to contribute to a better understanding of the principles, objectives, and probable results of American foreign policy and contemporary problems of United States foreign policy.

The Center has previously published Robert E. Osgood, *Ideals and Self-interest in America's Foreign Relations* (1953), Gerald Stourzh, *Benjamin Franklin and American Foreign Policy* (1954), and Leon D. Epstein, *Britain—Uneasy Ally* (1954).

The present volume deals with a problem that goes to the very heart of American foreign policy. How can the United States protect and promote effectively its interests on the international scene without running the risk of an all-out atomic war? How is it possible to conduct foreign policy in the shadow of the atomic deterrent without making of that deterrent a reality? It is on these fundamental questions that this book reflects, and it is to them that it attempts to give at least tentative answers.

HANS J. MORGENTHAU
Director

PREFACE

The purpose of this book is to bring theoretical and historical insights to bear upon an urgent practical problem in contemporary American foreign policy. In the broadest sense, the problem is this: How can the United States utilize its military power as a rational and effective instrument of national policy? This is an old problem, but it has never been so acute. In its present form it is complicated by the existence of weapons of such massive destructive power as to render the deliberate, scrupulous limitation of warfare an indispensable condition of American security and, perhaps, of the survival of civilization itself.

I have not tried to "solve" this problem by prescribing a detailed defense program or precise courses of action to be employed under the full range of possible contingencies. Rather, I have sought to illuminate the general principles and basic requirements of an over-all national strategy, without which the most comprehensive planning cannot produce sound military policies. This approach is rooted in the conviction that before there can be an American strategy enabling the United States to employ military power rationally and effectively within a framework of feasible political objectives, there must also be a fundamental rethinking of traditional American attitudes concerning the nature of war and the relationship between force and policy. To be sure, a correct understanding of the nature of war and the relationship between force and policy will not of itself produce sound military policies; the wisest conceptions are useless if they are not translated into successful concrete programs and courses of action. On the other hand, in the absence of such an understanding, the most brilliant technical proficiency in military planning and organization is likely to be not only ineffective but positively disastrous.

The major part of this study is a venture in the risky business of interpreting contemporary history. In full recognition of the lack of information it must reflect, I nevertheless undertook it in the belief that we can learn enough about this crucial postwar decade to discern some indispensable lessons concerning the substance of American strategy and, equally important, concerning the American approach to national strategy. A critical examination of the evolution of American strategy in this decade shows that insofar as the United States has failed to anticipate and counter the Communist military and political threat as effectively as objective circumstances might have permitted, it has failed, fundamentally, because of a deficiency in American attitudes and conceptions rather than because of a lack of native intelligence, technical competence, or material power. But although this deficiency is deep-rooted and, one might say, almost inevitable, considering the nature of American predispositions and experience in international politics, it is not irremediable, and it need not be fatal. On the contrary, America's astonishing adjustment on an *ad hoc*, almost instinctive, basis to a radically new political and military environment suggests that the nation is perfectly capable of responding to the vexing requirements of a sound strategy with a measure of maturity and wisdom that will be commensurate to the challenge, if its leaders can only muster the perception, the foresight, and the courage to present that challenge in its real image and its full dimensions. Therefore, in a sense this book is as much a call for leadership in the urgent process of public education as it is an attempt to illuminate the perplexing problems of force and policy that make such leadership imperative.

I am especially indebted to Hans J. Morgenthau, director of the Center for the Study of American Foreign Policy, at the University of Chicago, for painstaking, stimulating, and incisive guidance at all stages of this manuscript. My colleagues Gerald Stourzh and Tang Tsou have given me the benefit of their fund of knowledge and their sensitive judgment, and I deeply appreciate their contributions. I am grateful to Henry Kissinger for his conscientious reading and appraisal of the manuscript while he was engaged in his own project at the Council on Foreign Relations. Finally, I am happy to thank my wife publicly for fostering common, as well as academic, sense in some of the more difficult passages.

TABLE OF CONTENTS

INTRODUCTION

How can the United States employ military power as a rational instrument of foreign policy when the destructive potentialities of war exceed any rational purpose? To answer this question resolutely is the supreme task of American foreign policy.

The rational use of military power requires a strategy capable of achieving two primary objectives: (*a*) the deterrence of such major aggression as would cause total war; (*b*) the deterrence or defeat of lesser aggressions, which could not appropriately be met except by means short of total war. To deter total war, the United States must convince potential aggressors of two things: first, that it can subject them to destruction so massive that they could not possibly gain any worthwhile objective from a total war; second, that it will employ this kind of retaliation against aggressions so threatening as to be equivalent to an attack upon the United States itself. To deter or defeat lesser aggressions the United States must convince potential aggressors—and demonstrate if necessary —that it is willing and able to conduct effective limited warfare.

America's capacity for total war is a prerequisite for the restriction of warfare, but unless the nation can also wage limited war successfully, Communist aggression may force the United States to choose between total war, non-resistance, or ineffective resistance. Such a three-pronged dilemma would be disastrous for America's military security and her diplomatic position. Yet the United States cannot avoid the dilemma under its present policies. Therefore, the only rational course is to develop a strategy capable of limiting warfare and fighting limited wars successfully. Such a strategy is within America's material and spiritual resources, but it demands revision of the country's traditional approach to war and to the use of military power. That is the thesis of this book.

Limited, Unlimited, and Total War

At the outset, let us understand what we mean by limited war. A limited war is one in which the belligerents restrict the purposes for

1

which they fight to concrete, well-defined objectives that do not demand the utmost military effort of which the belligerents are capable and that can be accommodated in a negotiated settlement. Generally speaking, a limited war actively involves only two (or very few) major belligerents in the fighting. The battle is confined to a local geographical area and directed against selected targets—primarily those of direct military importance. It demands of the belligerents only a fractional commitment of their human and physical resources. It permits their economic, social, and political patterns of existence to continue without serious disruption.

It is apparent from this definition that limited war is partly a matter of degree, in that war's limitation or lack of limitation depends upon the scope of the objectives for which the belligerents fight and upon the dimensions of force they employ in order to achieve their own objectives and deprive the enemy of his. Nevertheless, that degree makes a substantial difference. In practice, it is not difficult to identify limited wars as a distinct historical phenomenon.

Limited war, however, is not a uniform phenomenon. Such a war can be limited in different ways; it can be limited in some respects and not in others, depending upon its physical characteristics and the perspective of the belligerents. Thus, conceivably, a war can be limited in geographical scope but virtually unlimited in the weapons employed and the targets involved within the area of combat. On the other hand, a war can range over an extensive geographical area and involve a large number of belligerents and yet, like the Seven Years' War (1756–63), remain limited in the scale of its battles—though this is not likely under conditions of modern military technology, transportation, and communication. Furthermore, a war may be limited from the perspective of one belligerent, yet virtually unlimited in the eyes of another. Thus a war involving a limited commitment of the resources of two major powers within some peripheral strategic area, like the Korean peninsula, may be a matter of life or death to a third power that is unfortunate enough to inhabit the area.

By the same criteria that define a limited war, an unlimited war is fought with every means available in order to achieve ends that are without objective limits or that are limited only by the capacity of the belligerents to destroy the enemy's ability to resist. In unlimited war the belligerents either fight for no well-defined objectives at all, other than the destruction of the enemy, or else fight for objectives which threaten values so important as to be beyond compromise and which, therefore, compel the belligerents to exert their utmost military capacity toward breaking the enemy's will and securing an unconditional surrender.

Although the distinction between limited and unlimited war is partly a matter of degree, the distinction is clear enough in practice to have immense significance for national policy. To be sure, it is easy to point to many historical examples of limited war but difficult to adduce examples of completely unlimited war, which, like Rome's annihilation of Carthage, are devoid of any restriction whatsoever upon their determining aims and the means employed to achieve these aims. In the most extreme instance of unlimited war all major nations would be belligerents. The belligerents would strive to appropriate or annihilate everything of value to themselves and their enemies. They would use any and every means available to achieve that end. No area of importance to any belligerent would be exempt from hostilities. No target would be immune from obliteration. Such a war would end only with unconditional surrender or mutual exhaustion. Before it had ended, all segments of society would have felt its shattering impact, and all normal patterns of national life would have been destroyed. A completely unlimited war of this nature is difficult to imagine. And yet, if we apply the definitions of limited and unlimited war relatively and according to the rules of common sense, it is clear enough that the Religious Wars of the sixteenth and seventeenth centuries, the French Revolutionary and Napoleonic Wars of the eighteenth and nineteenth centuries, and the two World Wars of the twentieth century were, in all essential respects, unlimited wars; whereas the other wars of the eighteenth century, the greater part of the nineteenth century, and, more recently, the Greek civil war, the Korean War, and the war in Indochina were, just as clearly, limited wars.

In this study the term "total war" refers to that distinct twentieth-century species of unlimited war in which all the human and material resources of the belligerents are mobilized and employed against the total national life of the enemy. Because in the history of warfare extreme means and extreme ends tend to go together—since a war of great intensity, scope, and destructiveness encourages extravagant aims, as well as the other way around—the totality of warfare seriously militates against its effective limitation and control. However, this does not mean that a total war must be beyond all limitation. Even in the case of total war it is essential that men recognize and exploit a significant margin within which political policy and military operations can be conducted so as to control the results of war for limited, rational ends. However, the absolute prerequisite of such control is the deliberate formulation and pursuit of political objectives that will permit the belligerents to end the war short of total defeat or exhaustion.

In the final analysis, the nature and significance of a war must be judged by its material, political, and psychological consequences taken as a whole rather than by an attempt to fit all the conceivable character- istics of warfare neatly into self-contained categories. However, there is one characteristic of overriding importance in distinguishing among wars: the nature of the objectives for which the belligerents fight. The decisive limitation upon war is the limitation of the objectives of war. Thus it is possible that a war ranging over a wide geographical area, drawing heavily upon the belligerents' military resources, and utilizing methods of intensive destruction could, nevertheless, be limited to some sig- nificant extent in its total impact if it were controlled and settled in ac- cordance with well-defined political objectives, susceptible to compro- mise. On the other hand, it is exceedingly improbable that a war fought for grandiose or ill-defined objectives could in this atomic age be limited in any significant sense of the term; for when the aims of war are, in ef- fect, politically unlimited, the dimensions of violence and destruction must be determined largely by the sheer physical ability of the belliger- ents to reduce one another to impotence.

The Need for an American Strategy of Limited War

The extraordinary significance of limited war today is apparent in the light of two decisive political and military conditions that determine the nature of the threat to American security. The political condition is the existence of a powerful Communist bloc of nations, which is bent upon seizing every opportunity to extend its sphere of control. The military condition is the existence of incredibly destructive nuclear, biological, and chemical weapons—more specifically, the fact that both the Soviet Union and the United States possess, and each knows that the other possesses, the capacity virtually to destroy each other, with the result that both governments realize that a total war would be a national catastrophe.

It seems safe to assume that so long as the United States and the Soviet Union maintain their capacity for mutual destruction and neither can be sure of preventing the other from exercising it, then neither government will rationally and deliberately choose to fight a total war, except as an act of desperation. Undoubtedly, this situation greatly reduces the danger of total war resulting from major Communist aggression, although it by no means eliminates the possibility of total war resulting from accident, miscalculation, or the actions of other nations. However, the full significance of this military condition must be seen in the light of the decisive political condition of the cold war: the Communist leaders retain their expansionist ambitions, in direct conflict with American security; and no moral scruples inhibit them from employing military force where military force is expedient. Therefore, if the Communists can minimize the risk of precipitating total war, we must assume that they will use limited military force as a means of attaining their ambitions. Actually, they can readily minimize that risk by confining their aggression to places and circumstances in which war would not jeopardize objectives of sufficient immediate importance to warrant all-out retaliation, in which the fighting could be kept within narrow geographical bounds, and in which discrimination in the use of weapons and selection of targets would be practicable. There are numerous places and circumstances in which these conditions exist. Primarily, they exist in the arc of nations contiguous or nearly contiguous to the Sino-Soviet perimeter from Iran to Korea.

Depending upon the place and circumstance, there may be a variety of feasible methods for resisting the kind of aggression that does not warrant America's assuming large risks of total war. But only methods compatible with limited war will enable the United States to avoid the choice of precipitating total war, resisting ineffectively, or foregoing resistance altogether. If this nation lacks recourse to the methods of limited war, it will face a fatal dilemma in the event of limited Communist aggression or threat of aggression. On the one hand, the immediate objective at stake will not warrant incurring the exorbitant sacrifices of total nuclear war; but, on the other hand, a series of piecemeal military or diplomatic defeats will so weaken America's relative power position and so undermine its prestige as to leave little to choose between the gradual paralysis of inaction and the sudden disaster of all-out war. One could even argue that a total war, as opposed to acquiescence in a series of piecemeal conquests, might at least leave the United States and some of its allies in a significantly more favorable situation than the Communist bloc and might relieve the Communist threat to their survival.

Of course, the Communists might not exploit the dilemma by military means. They might calculate that, since their enemy was unprepared to resist lesser aggressions except by means that would lead to total war, the risk of provoking unlimited war would outweigh the advantages of trying to obtain their objectives by an overt military venture—especially if the opportunities for political and economic penetration were promising. In that case, a bluff might succeed in deterring aggression. However, it would be foolhardy to base American strategy solely upon the most favorable contingencies. In the long run, it is unlikely that the Communist powers can be deterred from undertaking the kinds of aggression that cannot be resisted effectively. If the United States is unwilling to take the risk of total war under certain circumstances, the Communists are likely to discover it. If the United States is incapable of effective limited resistance, the Communists will probably know it. But if its bluff is called, the United States will either have to run the risk of unlimited war or compound the disadvantage of non-resistance or ineffective resistance with the even greater disadvantage of losing the credibility of its deterrent. When the American deterrent of strategic retaliation is no longer credible, the Soviet Union, believing that it can undertake aggression with impunity, may finally—like Hitler's Germany—undertake some military action which the West, out of desperation, will be driven to counter at the cost of total war. Certainly, the penalty of having one's bluff called makes it prohibitively dangerous to rely upon a deterrent that does not reflect the reality of national power and will.

However, even if a strategy of bluff should succeed in deterring military aggression, the penalties of America's inability to fight limited wars successfully are not confined to the consequences of outright military defeat; for the Communists will exploit by diplomacy a situation they may choose not to test by force. Thus Communist statesmen, aware of the unwillingness of America's allies, let alone the neutral and uncommitted nations, to entangle their policies with the policies of a nation which cannot protect them but which may be driven to precipitate an all-out nuclear war at their expense, will exert great pressure upon both groups to seek security from nuclear devastation by dissociating themselves from American policies and aligning themselves with Communist policies. A formidable and flexible military capacity will provide the Communists with tacit support for a campaign of political, economic, and psychological penetration. The Communist threat of limited aggression, coupled with the inability of the United States to contain limited aggression by limited means, will act as a powerful form of blackmail, which will tend to dissolve the political bonds of the free world and prepare the way for bloodless conquests, even while the Communists pose as the champions of peace and the United States incurs the onus of "nuclear diplomacy."

These very real possibilities point up a central assumption of this study. The problem of limited war is not just a problem of military strategy but is, more broadly, the problem of combining military power with diplomacy and with the economic and psychological instruments of power within a coherent national strategy that is capable of supporting the United States' political objectives abroad. ("Strategy" as used in this book, unless qualified by "military," is a synonym for "national strategy," which is the over-all plan for co-ordinating the nation's total resources of power, both military and non-military, so as to achieve the objectives of national policy most effectively. The adjective "political," as in "political objectives" or "political factors," pertains to the nation's general power position, which supports its interests in relation to other nations and does not exclude economic, psychological, and other non-military elements of power.) The ability to support national interests and aims with war and the threat of war under a variety of contingencies has always been an essential condition of successful diplomacy, but the United States loses that ability if its principal adversary is free to use force and the threat of force with impunity, while the United States, being unwilling to run the risk of total war and unable to counter Communist incursions by means short of total war, is reduced to mere bluff and protest. To the extent that American national strategy is supported by a diversified military capacity, capable of countering Communist aggression under a variety of contingencies, the nation will enhance the flexibility of its diplomacy and promote favorable political positions. To the extent this diversified capacity is lacking, the nation will incur the serious political and psychological disadvantages that a rigid diplomacy is bound to impose in competition with the flexible and resourceful diplomacy of an unscrupulous power.

No strategy can guarantee absolute national security. A strategy of limited war will not overcome the inherent limitations of American power, which preclude the possibility of countering Communist aggression under all conceivable circumstances by means short of total war. There will probably be situations in which local resistance will be unfeasible and other situations in which America's best efforts toward resistance will fail. And total war could break out in spite of the most prudent military and political policies. But in any of these contingencies the consequences of strategic failure will be minimized if the United States has clearly conveyed to its own people and to other peoples the firm impression that its strategy envisions only the pursuit of limited ends by limited means. In the case of non-resistance or ineffective resistance the United States would minimize its loss of prestige and of the credibility of its deterrent by having avoided the implication of an unsuccessful bluff. It would be in a much better position to capitalize politically upon its military loss by persuading allies and neutrals to join in resisting future aggression if concrete evidence of America's limited, defensive aims had left these nations in no doubt about who was the real aggressor and who was the true defender of their interests. And, no less important, the American government would have mitigated the traumatic impact of failure upon its own people by having prepared them for limited defeats as well as limited victories. Certainly, nothing could be more damaging to America's whole position in the world than to have assumed a posture of bold defiance on the basis of a military strategy it was not prepared to carry out and then to have sunk into sullen despair with the first reverse.

It is difficult to imagine a worse catastrophe than total nuclear war; but even if that catastrophe proved unavoidable, the nation might minimize losses and salvage something worthwhile if it were clear that total war had come *in spite of* all American efforts to prevent it rather than *because of* American rashness, negligence, or design. For, assuming that all life on this planet had not been extinguished, there would still be uncommitted nations and allies, not to mention recent enemies, with whom the United States would have to deal after the holocaust. Certainly, there would be vastly greater political, social, and economic problems than ever before. The United States would badly need a reservoir of good will to draw upon in order to gain the co-operation of the governments of Eurasia in restoring viable societies upon which American security would still depend no less than before the war.

The Immediate and Fundamental Problems of Limited War

We have said that American security requires finding answers to two practical questions of immediate importance: How can the United States keep war limited? How can the United States fight limited wars successfully? This study does not attempt to provide detailed and comprehensive answers to these questions. It is concerned primarily with investigating the possibilities of limiting war, with discovering the general conditions for limiting war, and with establishing the basic military and political requirements of a national strategy adapted to waging limited warfare effectively. It deals with these questions in Parts II and III, first by examining the history of war in modern Western civilization, then by appraising the evolution of American strategy since World War II, and finally by outlining an American strategy capable of achieving national security objectives under contemporary military and political conditions.

However, this study is also concerned with a more fundamental problem that underlies but transcends the immediate problems of limiting war and fighting limited wars successfully. This problem is the relation between military power and national policy. It is fundamental for three reasons:

1. War is not an end in itself; it is a means to an end. Therefore, the nature of the end should, theoretically, exercise a controlling influence over the way the war is fought. Yet, at the same time, the ends of war must be shaped in the light of the means available. Thus the problem of determining the means of war is really the problem of balancing means and ends within a larger framework of national aims, which this study calls "national strategy." However, the major purpose of national strategy is not to wage war but to realize national objectives without war, if possible. The nation's success in achieving this purpose will depend, in large measure, upon the kind of war it is prepared to fight, the circumstances in which it is prepared to fight, the objectives for which it will fight, the way it prepares to fight—in short, upon the nation's whole conception of the relation between war and national policy. This conception, in turn, will be reflected in the way national strategy utilizes military power and combines it with the other elements of power in order to attain the nation's controlling objectives.

2. Limited war raises fundamental questions of morality and expediency, which must be answered on the basis of one's conception of the proper relation between power and policy. On the one hand, men cannot regard war with moral indifference; therefore, they must be sure of the moral foundation of any strategy that employs military power as an instrument of national policy. On the other hand, they cannot be indifferent to the impact of war and military power upon national self-interest;

therefore, they must base national strategy upon a sound conception of the conditions for using military power effectively. The general questions of morality and expediency in combining power with policy transcend the practical problems of a strategy of limited war, but the practical problems cannot properly be considered apart from them.

3. A feasible strategy of limited war must be based upon a conception of limitation that is acceptable to Americans and to Communist leaders; for unless the major adversaries of the cold war observe the conditions for limiting war, an American strategy of limited war will not be feasible regardless of what the objective interests of the adversaries may require. This fact is particularly significant because the deliberate limitation of war assumes a conception of the relation between power and policy that is, in many ways, antithetical to American ideas and predispositions in foreign relations—so antithetical, in fact, that a sound strategy of limited war implies a basic revision of the traditional American approach to war.

For these reasons, before turning to the more immediate questions of how to limit war and how to fight limited wars successfully, Part I sets forth some general principles concerning the proper relation between military power and national policy, from the standpoint of both morality and expediency, in order to establish a theoretical rationale for a strategy of limited war. Then it examines the American approach to war in the light of these principles. Finally, it examines the Communist approach as compared with the American approach.

Part I | *WAR AND POLICY*

Chapter One

THE THEORY OF LIMITED WAR

The Principle of Political Primacy

In practice, the limitation of war is morally and emotionally repugnant to the American people. Yet it is in accord with America's own best principles. The explanation of this paradox lies partly in the fact that Americans have not understood the relation between military force and national policy, and so they have misconceived the real moral and practical implications of national conduct. Therefore, it is imperative at the beginning of this study to develop a sound conception of the relation between force and policy as the first step in examining the requirements of an American strategy of limited war.

The justification of limited war arises, in the most fundamental sense, from the principle that military power should be subordinate to national policy, that the only legitimate purpose of military force is to serve the nation's political objectives. This principle of political primacy is basic to all forms and all uses of military power, whether employed overtly, covertly, or only tacitly. It is as applicable to the formulation of military policies and military strategy as to the actual waging of war. In this principle morality and expediency are joined.

The principle of political primacy is essential to the nation's self-interest because military power is of no practical use as a thing in itself but is useful only insofar as it serves some national purpose. It is useful because it is a prerequisite of national security and because upon security all other national goals depend. Coercion is an indispensable feature of all human relations in which basic security and order cannot be guaranteed by the innate sympathy, reasonableness, and morality of men. The essential role of coercion is especially large in international relations, where institutional organization is anarchical or rudimentary and the bonds of law, custom, and sentiment are relatively impotent as against the intense ties of loyalty binding men to their separate and sovereign national groups.

13

The practical necessity of military power is obvious to Americans to-day, but it is not always so obvious that military power does not automatically translate itself into national security. Military power may actually be translated into national insecurity when it is employed without a proper regard for its non-military objectives and consequences. Without intelligent and vigilant political control even the most effective use of military force, by purely military standards, will not necessarily bring comparably satisfactory political results. A capricious, impulsive, or irresponsible use of military power cannot be expedient; for when military policy and strategy lack the guideposts of limited and attainable objectives and become, in effect, ends in themselves, they cease to be controllable and predictable instruments of national policy.

The individual soldier, even the commander of a battle, may sometimes promote the national interest by the kind of boldness that does not calculate the results of military action too closely, but it would be a dangerous error to apply to the whole complex problem of harmonizing military policy with national policy in accordance with an over-all strategic plan the far simpler imperatives of the battlefield. In the field of national strategy, uncalculating heroism is mere self-indulgence at the expense of national survival.

In order that military power may serve as a controllable and predictable instrument of national policy, it must be subjected to an exacting political discipline. This discipline depends upon the existence of controlling political objectives that bear a practical and discernible relation to specific policy goals. These kinds of objectives are, pre-eminently, those that envision specific configurations of power supporting the nation's security. A treaty recognizing specific international relationships; the control or protection of a certain geographical area; the establishment, recognition, or security of a particular regime; access to certain material resources—these are the kinds of objectives that must form the hard core of politically disciplined power.

One must add, because the rule is so frequently violated in practice, that the controlling political objectives in the use of military power must be not merely desirable but also attainable. Otherwise, there will be no practical and discernible relationship between ends and means. Of course, there are an indefinite number of possible objectives toward which nations may direct military power. One can easily establish a whole hierarchy of interdependent objectives, leading from the most insignificant to the most desirable objective imaginable. However, only a very limited number of these objectives will ever be closely enough related to available national power to serve as a controlling political discipline. Unless the nation's objectives pertain to specific and attainable situations of fact, they will remain in the realm of aspiration, not in the realm of policy; and, consequently, the essential condition for the primacy of politics over force will not exist. Therefore, one can describe the principle of political primacy in terms of the following rule: In the nation's utilization of military power, military means should be subordinated to the ends of national policy through an objective calculation of the most effective methods of attaining concrete, limited, and attainable security objectives.

The principle of political primacy described in this rule is as cogent on moral grounds as on grounds of national self-interest. At the outset, before examining the moral basis of the principle, one must recognize that the primacy of policy over power can be moral only if the political ends toward which military power is directed are themselves moral—or, at least, as consistent with universal principles as the ambiguities of international relations permit. But even if one assumes that this is the case (as I shall for the purposes of this book), one can hardly judge the moral validity of either political ends or military means aside from their interrelationship. The following discussion focuses upon this interrelationship, which is only one aspect of the broader problem of reconciling national policy with liberal, humane ideals that transcend purely national purposes.[1] The principle of political primacy does not embrace all the moral problems that arise in the use of military power. It does not, for example, deal with the question of when or under what circumstances a nation should employ force. However, it is of vital relevance to the question of how and for what purpose a nation should employ force.

The moral basis of political primacy is also its practical basis: the principle that armed force ought to be treated as a means and not an end. Force gains moral justification only by virtue of its relation to some valid purpose beyond its own immediate effect. Furthermore, even when it is a means to a worthy end, armed force must be morally suspect—not only because it is inhumane but because, like all forms of coercion, it is subject to the corruption that accompanies man's exercise of power over man. In Lord Acton's words, "Among all the causes which degrade and demoralize man, power is the most constant and the most active." Certainly, the exercise of military power holds extraordinary opportunities for the degradation of its user and the abuse of those against whom it is used.

But the problem of force is not so easily dismissed. Once we admit that it is morally suspect, we are involved in a moral dilemma. On the one hand, in an ideal world men would dispense with all forms of coercion and settle their conflicts by impartial reference to reason and morality; or, at least, they would channel coercion in social directions by legal controls, which receive the consent of the community. Yet, on the other hand, we know that in the real world men are not sufficiently unselfish or rational to make this ideal practicable. The abolition of force in society would lead either to the anarchy of unrestrained egoism or else to the tyranny of unrestrained despotism. Because of the imperfection of man, force is a moral necessity, an indispensable instrument of justice. Therefore, men are confronted with the fact that their own imperfection makes both force and restraint of force equally imperative from a moral standpoint. There is no way to escape this dilemma. Men can only mitigate its effects. The aim should be, not to abolish force in society, but to moderate it and control it so as to promote social purposes in a manner most compatible with ideal standards of human conduct. How can we translate this principle into the use of military power?

We commonly assume that force is least objectionable morally, as well as most effective practically, when it is exercised with a minimum of violence—preferably, as in the case of police power, when it is implied rather than directly exercised—and when it is exercised legitimately, that is, in accordance with the general consent and approval of society. This assumption suffices for the conduct of everyday affairs within the national community, because the conditions which make it practicable are present—primarily, the conditions that permit force to be exercised in accordance with the orderly procedures of law and government. These legitimate restraints not only moderate force and channel it in social directions; they also provide the individual members of a nation with the basic security they need in order to feel safe in voluntarily subordinating their self-interest to the general welfare.

However, the same procedures for moderating, controlling, and channeling force in socially sanctioned directions do not exist among nations, where the bonds of law, custom, and sympathy are frail and rudimentary. In this age national egoism has such a compelling hold over men's minds that each nation must look to its own independent exercise of power merely in order to survive. The exercise of military power among nations is subject to few of the formal and informal restraints that permit altruism to operate among individuals and groups within nations. This situation makes a vast difference between what is justifiable in the exercise of force in national society and what is justifiable in international society. It means that among nations military force becomes an indispensable means for promoting national self-interest but a thoroughly ineffective means for attaining the great universal moral goals that transcend national self-interest. This is true, in the first place, because every exercise of military power must be tainted with self-interest and, secondly, because the imperatives of national power and security do not closely conform to the dictates of universal morality.

But military force is not only ineffective as an instrument for attaining transcendent moral goals; it is morally dangerous as well. It is dangerous because the exercise of force for such grandiose goals tends to become an end in itself, subject neither to moral nor practical restraints but only to the intoxication of abstract ideals. The explanation for this tendency lies in the nature of supranational goals. Aside from the powerful tendency of national egoism to corrupt idealistic pretensions, supranational goals are too remote and too nebulous to discipline a nation's use of force. When the determining objective of force is an ideological goal, there is no way of knowing precisely when force has achieved its purpose, since the tangible results of force have no clear relation to the intangible tests by which the attainment of such goals must be measured. When a conflict of wills is put to the test of force, the final restraint and control of force must be the resolution of the conflict by accommodation, unless it is to continue until one party obtains complete acquiescence or both parties become impotent. But differences of principle, unlike conflicts of interest, by their very nature resist accommodation. Rather, they tend to arouse passions that can be satisfied only by the unconditional surrender of the adversary. Therefore, in effect, the great idealistic goals, once put to the test of force, become the rationalization of purely military objectives, governed only by the blind impulse of destruction.

That is not to say that moral principles are unjustifiable or irrelevant in a nation's use of military power or that the exercise of force, either overtly or tacitly, cannot indirectly promote ideal ends. The point is simply that universal principles must be translated into practical courses of action, directed toward achieving specific situations of fact appropriate to the nature of force, in order to constitute truly moral and rational guides for the exercise of military power. Only if the realization of these principles is conceived as the by-product of attaining concrete limited objectives can they exert a civilizing influence upon national egoism. The great idealistic goals that have traditionally provided the dynamism and inspiration of American foreign policy, insofar as they can be attained at all by military means, must be attained through a series of moderate steps toward intermediate objectives, defined in terms of national power and interest.

An important corollary of the principle of political primacy may be called the economy of force. It prescribes that in the use of armed force as an instrument of national policy no greater force should be employed than is necessary to achieve the objectives toward which it is directed; or, stated another way, the dimensions of military force should be proportionate to the value of the objectives at stake.

Clearly, this is an expedient rule; for unless a nation has a large surplus of available military power in relation to its policy objectives, one can hardly conceive of the effective use of power without the efficient use as well. Moreover, as an examination of the interaction between military means and political ends will show, the proportionate use of force is a necessary condition for the limitation and effective control of war.

The moral implications of an economy of force are no less significant. For, as we have acknowledged, the violence and destruction that accompany the use of force are an obvious, though sometimes necessary, evil. Therefore, it is morally incumbent to use force deliberately and scrupulously and as sparingly as is consistent with the attainment of the national objectives at stake.

In applying the principle of political primacy we must make allowances for the legitimate claims of military considerations upon national policy as well as the other way around. The relationship between military means and political ends should be understood as a two-way relationship, such that the ends are kept within range of the means as well as the means made adequate to attain the ends. Common sense tells us that a nation must decide what it ought to do in light of what it is able to do; that it should establish policy objectives in the light of military capabilities.

Otherwise, military power will be no more effective or politically responsible than if it were employed as an end in itself.

Moreover, we must recognize the fact that, however scrupulously we may seek to impose political discipline upon military power, military power will remain an imperfect instrument of politics. To a disturbing extent it bears its own unpredictable effects, which create, alter, or preclude the objectives for which it can feasibly be employed.

However, this does not obviate the necessity of determining the claims of military means upon political ends—so far as conscious control permits—within the general framework of national strategy; for in the absence of such a framework there can be no clear criterion for judging the validity of any claims. In other words, if military power is to serve as a rational instrument of policy, the entire process of balancing ends and means, co-ordinating military with non-military means, must be subordinated to the controlling purpose of pursuing national policy objectives according to the most effective strategic plan.

War as an Instrument of National Policy

The principles of political primacy and the economy of force apply to the whole spectrum of military power in its various uses, not just to its active use in warfare; but this book is concerned primarily with their application to war itself. There is a good reason for stressing this aspect of military power: In all uses of military power, whether overt, covert, or tacit; in all accumulation, allocation, and distribution of military power; and in all military planning there is at least an implicit assumption that the basic measure of a nation's power is its ability to wage war in defense of its interests. In the struggle for power among nations, the ability to wage war has something of the status of a common currency by which nations can roughly measure their capacity to achieve certain basic needs and desires—ultimately, if necessary, by violence.

However, the ability to wage war cannot be measured in purely quantitative terms of military power. A nation can be adequately prepared to wage one kind of war under one set of circumstances and inadequately prepared to wage another kind of war under a different set of circumstances. The utility of a nation's military power, either in diplomacy or in war itself, will depend not merely upon the size and firepower of the military establishment but also upon its suitability for countering the specific kinds of military threats impinging upon the nation's interests and objectives. Thus the effectiveness of military power depends upon the nature of the military threat, the nation's estimate of that threat, and its ability to fight the kind of war that will successfully meet the threat. It depends, equally, upon the nation's will to wage war; the way in which it combines force with diplomacy; how it enters war, how it terminates war, and how it conducts policy after a war. In other words, the effectiveness of military power depends not only upon a nation's physical and technical command of the means of warfare but, just as much, upon its whole conception of war—especially, the relation of war to international politics. And this conception of war is reflected throughout the whole spectrum of military power—in defense policies and the formulation of military strategy as well as in the actual conduct of war. Therefore, since a nation's military power depends upon its conception of war, it behooves us to act upon a conception of war that is compatible with the use of military power as a rational instrument of national policy. That conception must be based upon the principle of political primacy.

But, first, let us be clear what we mean by "war." War can be defined most simply as an organized clash of arms between sovereign states seeking to assert their wills against one another. However, it would be a mistake to regard war as a single, simple, uniform entity or as an independent thing in itself, to which one applies a wholly different set of rules and considerations than properly apply to other forms of international conflict. It is more realistic in the light of the complex and multifarious nature of international conflict to regard war as the upper extremity of a whole scale of international conflict of ascending intensity and scope. All along this scale one may think of sovereign nations asserting their wills in conflict with other nations by a variety of military and non-military means of coercion, but no definition can determine precisely at what point on the scale conflict becomes "war." In this sense, war is a matter of degree, which itself contains different degrees of intensity and scope.

Accepting this description of war, we must see how the principle of political primacy applies to the conduct of war. The primacy of politics in war means, simply, that military operations should be conducted so as to achieve concrete, limited, and attainable security objectives, in order that war's destruction and violence may be rationally directed toward legitimate ends of national policy.

On the face of it, the validity of this principle seems clear enough; and yet in its practical implications it does not meet with ready or universal acceptance. In fact, quite contrary principles of war have commonly received the applause of democratic peoples. For example, in the Kellogg-Briand Pact of 1928 the United States and fourteen other nations promised to "renounce war as an instrument of national policy in their relations with one another," thereby expressing in treaty form a widespread conviction that is still congenial to the American outlook. The principle is valid, of course, if it is interpreted merely as a proscription against unprovoked aggression; but insofar as it implies the divorce of war from the ends of national interest, it is valid neither practically nor ideally. In this sense, nations might better renounce the use of war as an instrument of *anything but* national policy.

Karl von Clausewitz, the famous German military theorist of the nineteenth century, expounded the principle of political primacy with an unsurpassed cogency. In his famous work *On War* he concluded his comprehensive analysis of the mass of factors comprising war by singling out their unifying characteristic. This, he believed, was the essential basis for apprehending all war's complexities and contradictions from a single standpoint, without which one could not form consistent judgments. He described that characteristic in the following words:

> Now this unity is the conception that war is only a part of political intercourse, therefore by no means an independent thing in itself. We know, of course, that war is only caused through the political intercourse of governments and nations; but in general it is supposed that such intercourse is broken off by war, and that a totally different state of things ensues, subject to no laws but its own. We maintain, on the contrary, that war is nothing but a continuation of political intercourse with an admixture of other means. . . . Accordingly, war can never be separated from political intercourse, and if, in the consideration of the matter, this occurs anywhere, all the threads of the different relations are, in a certain sense, broken, and we have before us a senseless thing without an object.[2]

As a description of the actual nature of war, Clausewitz' dictum that war continues political intercourse is by no means universally true; but as a statement of what war should be, it is the only view in accord with universal moral principles and national self-interest, for it is the only view consistent with the use of force as a means rather than an end. If we find this view as repugnant as the sentiment of the Kellogg-Briand Pact is congenial, then we have not fully grasped the practical and moral necessity of disciplining mass violence. On the other hand, many who can agree with Clausewitz' dictum in the abstract find it difficult in practice to accept the corollary that victory is not an end in itself. Nevertheless, the corollary is logically inseparable from the principle of political primacy. For if war is not an end in itself, but only a means to some political objective, then military victory cannot rightly be a self-sufficient end. If war is a continuation of political intercourse, then success in war can be properly measured only in political terms and not purely in terms of crushing the enemy. To be sure, a measure of military success is the necessary condition for achieving the political objectives of war; but the most effective military measures for overcoming the enemy's resistance are not necessarily the most effective measures for securing the continuing ends of national policy in the aftermath of war.

Therefore, one of the most important practical implications of the principle of political primacy is this: The whole conduct of warfare—its strategy, its tactics, its termination—must be governed by the nature of a nation's political objectives and not by independent standards of military success or glory. Statesmen, far from suspending diplomacy during war, must make every effort to keep diplomacy alive throughout the hostilities, to the end that war may be as nearly a continuation of political intercourse as possible rather than "a senseless thing without an object."

The Dimensions of War

The practical requirements of maintaining the primacy of politics in the conduct of war are not so clear as the general principle, for the general principle must be qualified in the light of the actual conditions of war. The most serious qualification results from the difficulty of controlling the consequences of war as the dimensions of violence and destruction increase. This difficulty emphasizes the importance of striving for an economy of force.

Despite the theoretical validity of the principle of political primacy, in practice we must recognize that war is not a delicate instrument for achieving precise political ends. It is a crude instrument of coercion and persuasion. The violence and destruction of war set off a chain of consequences that can be neither perfectly controlled nor perfectly anticipated and that may, therefore, contravene the best laid plans for achieving specific configurations of power and particular political relations among nations.

At the same time, the legitimate claims of military means upon political ends are particularly strong when national conflict reaches the extremity of war. The sheer physical circumstances of the military struggle may narrowly restrict the choice of military means that nations can safely employ. To subordinate military operations to political considerations might mean sacrificing the military success indispensable for the attainment of any worthwhile national purpose at all. Therefore, in practice, military necessities and the fortunes of war may determine the nature of the feasible political choices, and the subordination of certain political considerations to military requirements may be the necessary condition for avoiding defeat.

However, the need for compromising political objectives in the light of immediate military necessities only qualifies, it does not negate, the applicability of the principle of political primacy; because the wisdom of such compromises must still be judged by their relation to some superior political objective if purely military objectives are not to become ends in themselves. Clausewitz acknowledged this very qualification and reconciled it with his view of war as a continuation of political intercourse in words that are compelling today. While recognizing that the political object of war could not regulate every aspect of war, he nevertheless maintained that war would be sheer uncontrolled violence without this unifying factor.

Now if we reflect that war has its origin in a political object, we see that this first motive, which called it into existence, naturally remains the first and highest consideration to be regarded in its conduct. But the political object is not on that account a despotic lawgiver; it must adapt itself to the nature of the means at its disposal and is often thereby completely changed, but it must always be the first thing to be considered. Policy, therefore, will permeate the whole action of war and exercise a continual influence upon it, so far as the nature of the explosive forces in it allow. . . . What now still remains peculiar to war relates merely to the peculiar character of the means it uses. The art of war in general and the commander in each particular case can demand that the tendencies and designs of policy shall be not incompatible with these means, and the claim is certainly no trifling one. But however powerfully it may react on political designs in particular cases, still it must always be regarded only as a modification of them; for the political design is the object, while war is the means, and the means can never be thought of apart from the object.[3]

If, then, the principle of political primacy holds good despite the considerable claims of military necessity, the task of statesmen is to minimize the difficulties and maximize the potentialities of political control. There are three closely related rules of general application that would greatly facilitate this purpose:

1. Statesmen should scrupulously limit the controlling political objectives of war and clearly communicate the limited nature of these objectives to the enemy. The reason for this is that nations tend to observe a rough proportion between the scope of their objectives and the scale of their military effort; that is, they tend to exert a degree of force proportionate to the value they ascribe to the objectives at stake. Therefore, the more ambitious the objectives of one belligerent, the more important it is to the other belligerent to deny those objectives and the greater the scale of force both belligerents will undertake in order to gain their own objectives and frustrate the enemy's. In this manner a spiral of expanding objectives and mounting force may drive warfare beyond the bounds of political control.

2. Statesmen should make every effort to maintain an active diplomatic intercourse toward the end of terminating the war by a negotiated settlement on the basis of limited objectives. This rule rests on the following considerations. War is a contest between national wills. The final resolution of this contest must be some sort of political settlement, or war will lack any object except the purely military object of overcoming the enemy. To the extent that statesmen keep political intercourse active during hostilities, war becomes a political contest rather than a purely military contest. The immediate object of political intercourse must be a negotiated settlement, but a negotiated settlement is impossible among belligerents of roughly equal power unless their political objectives are limited. This consideration becomes especially important in the light of the fact that even a small nation that possessed an arsenal of nuclear weapons might, in desperation, inflict devastating destruction upon a larger power rather than accept humiliating terms.

3. Statesmen should try to restrict the physical dimensions of war as stringently as compatible with the attainment of the objectives at stake, since the opportunities for the political control of war—especially under the conditions of modern war, with its tremendous potentialities of destruction—tend to decrease as the dimensions of war increase and tend to increase as the dimensions of war decrease. This proportion between the dimensions of war and its susceptibility to political control is neither universally true nor mathematically exact; but as a rough generalization it finds important verification in the history of war. Three underlying reasons for this fact are especially germane to the warfare of this century:

a) The greater the scale and scope of war, the more likely the war will result in extreme changes in the configurations of national power. These extreme changes are not amenable to control; they result more from the internal logic of the military operations than from the designs of statesmen. At the same time, they tend to create vast new political problems which confound the expectations and plans of the victor and the vanquished alike. Moreover, modern war can change the configurations of power not only through the massive destruction of material and human resources but also by disrupting the whole social, economic, and political fabric of existence. On the other hand, when the destructiveness and the resulting disturbance of the configurations of power are moderate, the chances of anticipating and controlling its political effects are proportionately greater; and the whole character of warfare, in proportion as it is removed from the domination of military events, becomes more nearly a continuation of political intercourse.

b) The magnitude of a war's threat to national survival is likely to be proportionate to the scale and the scope of hostilities. But in proportion as the belligerents' very survival is threatened, they must logically place a higher priority upon immediate military considerations as compared to political considerations. For when war reaches extremities, a belligerent must calculate that even the slightest interference with the destruction of the enemy in the most effective manner possible for the sake of some uncertain political maneuver will involve an exorbitant risk of the enemy destroying that belligerent first. Military victory, no matter how it comes about, at least provides a nation with the opportunity to solve its political problems later; whereas the dubious attempt to manipulate the vast and unpredictable forces of war in precise political ways may end by placing this postwar opportunity at the disposal of the enemy. When immediate military considerations are at such a premium, political control must obviously suffer accordingly; but, by the same reasoning, when the scale and scope of a war impose no such immediate threat of total defeat, the primacy of politics can more readily be asserted.

c) As the dimensions of violence and destruction increase, war tends to arouse passionate fears and hatreds, which, regardless of the dictates of cold reason, become the determining motives in the conduct of war. These passions find their outlet in the blind, unreasoning destruction of the enemy. They are antithetical to the political control of war, because political control would restrict the use of force. Thus the greater the scale of violence, the greater the suffering and sacrifice; and the greater the suffering and sacrifice, the less the inclination either to fight or to make peace for limited, prosaic ends. Instead, nations will seek compensation in extreme demands upon the enemy or in elevating the war into an ideological crusade. Unlimited aims will, in turn, demand unlimited force. Thus, in effect, the scale of war and the passions of war, interacting, will create a purely military phenomenon beyond effective political guidance.

In the light of this proportion between the dimensions of warfare and its susceptibility to political control, the importance of preserving an economy of force is apparent. For if modern warfare tends to exceed the bounds of political control as it increases in magnitude, then it is essential to limit force to a scale that is no greater than necessary to achieve the objectives at stake. By the same token, if war becomes more susceptible to political control in proportion as its dimensions are moderated, then the economy of force is an essential condition of the primacy of politics in war.

The Rationale of Limited War

If this analysis is sound, the principal justification of limited war lies in the fact that it maximizes the opportunities for the effective use of military force as a rational instrument of national policy. In accordance with this rationale, limited war would be equally desirable if nuclear weapons had never been invented. However, the existence of these and other weapons of mass destruction clearly adds great urgency to limitation. Before nations possessed nuclear weapons, they might gain worthwhile objectives consonant with the sacrifices of war even in a war fought with their total resources. But now the stupendous destruction accompanying all-out nuclear war makes it hard to conceive of such a war serving any rational purpose except the continued existence of the nation as a political unit—and, perhaps, the salvage of the remnants of civilization—in the midst of the wreckage. Only by carefully limiting the dimensions of warfare can nations minimize the risk of war becoming an intolerable disaster.

Beyond this general reason for limiting war, which applies to all nations equally, there are special reasons why democratic nations should prefer limited war. Obviously, limited war is more compatible with a respect for human life and an aversion to violence. But apart from humanitarian considerations, we should recognize that liberal institutions and values do not thrive amid the social, economic, and political dislocations that inevitably follow in the wake of unlimited war. The liberal and humane spirit needs an environment conducive to compromise and moderation. Only tyranny is likely to profit from the festering hatreds and resentments that accompany sudden and violent upheavals in the relations among governments and peoples. The aftermath of the two total wars of this century amply demonstrates this fact.

The external interests of democratic powers are not necessarily identified with the status quo in all respects, nor do they require that the rest of the world be democratic. Clearly, neither condition is feasible. However, they do require that the inevitable adjustments and accommodations among governments and peoples should be sufficiently moderate and gradual to permit orderly change. Long-run interests as well as immediate interests of democratic nations lie in preserving an external environment conducive to relative stability and security in the world.

The mitigation of sudden and violent change becomes all the more important in a period like the present, when the most resourceful tyranny in the modern world strives to capture an indigenous revolution among colonial and formerly colonial peoples who yearn to acquire the Western blessings of national independence and economic power but who are fearfully impatient with the evolutionary processes by which the West acquired them. In these areas peace may be too much to expect, but we can anticipate revolutionary chaos or Communist domination if the world is seized by the convulsions of unlimited war.

Finally, we must add to these considerations one of even broader significance. As long as the necessary international political conditions for the limitation of armaments do not exist, the best assurance that armaments will not destroy civilization lies in the limitation of their use.

Chapter Two

THE AMERICAN APPROACH TO WAR

Dissociation of Power and Policy

Notwithstanding these general principles concerning the relation between military power and national policy, some of the strongest American traditions in foreign policy run counter to the fundamental requirements of a strategy of limited war. Although America's military policies have been revolutionized during the past decade, her basic propensities, formed during the protracted period of nineteenth-century innocence, remain in effect. Under pressure of the Soviet threat, the American people have learned that military power is an essential element of foreign relations; but they are only beginning to learn that military power must be strictly disciplined by the concrete requirements of national policy.

Dissociation of power and policy is in some measure common to all democracies. A democratic people—or the influential portion that cares what the nation does in international politics—associates itself morally and emotionally with national policies and actions, and demands that the government reflect its sentiments. This inevitably inhibits a democratic government from acting upon the kind of dispassionate calculation of ends and means that a rational adjustment of power and policy requires. For popular sentiment does not always coincide with the imperatives of power; and once the public has invested its emotional and moral capital in a particular position, it is reluctant to withdraw it—especially if this is tantamount to a defeat—even though the investment proves a bad one from an objective standpoint. These democratic propensities are especially strong when the people's spiritual commitment to their nation is heightened by the stress of war.

For many reasons it will always be difficult for modern democracies to put Clausewitz' dictum into practice. Therefore, few of the following observations apply exclusively to the United States. However, among all democratic people, Americans are bound to find it particularly difficult to use military power as a rational instrument of power. More than any other great nation, America's basic predispositions and her experience in world politics encourage the dissociation of power and policy.

This dissociation is most marked in America's traditional conception of war and peace as diametrically opposite states of affairs, to be governed by entirely different rules and considerations without regard for the continuity of political conflict. With the country at peace, foreign policy has been formed and executed with little regard for considerations of military power; but with the country at war, foreign policy has been largely suspended, and immediate military considerations have been dominant. Typically, during war the determining objective has been to obtain a clear-cut, definitive military victory in the most effective manner as quickly as possible; but when peace has returned, the determining objective has been to get rid of the instruments of victory and to return to "normal" as fast as possible. In neither case have national actions been governed by careful regard for the international political consequences. With power and policy so dissociated, America has been notoriously slow to anticipate war or prepare for it, but it has been shocked into single-minded determination to overwhelm the enemy once war has broken out. This basic propensity confirms the observation that Alexis de Tocqueville made on the basis of his American tour more than a century ago:

> When a war has at length, by its long continuance, roused the whole community from their peaceful occupations and ruined their minor undertakings, the same passions that made them attach so much importance to the maintenance of peace will be turned to arms. War, after it has destroyed all modes of speculation, becomes itself the great and sole speculation, to which all the ardent and ambitious desires that equality engenders are exclusively directed. Hence it is that the self-same democratic nations that are so reluctant to engage in hostilities sometimes perform prodigious achievements when once they have taken the field.[1]

The results of this approach to war are manifest in the record of America's foreign relations since the turn of this century. On the one hand, the United States has demonstrated an impressive ability to defeat the enemy. Yet, on the other hand, it has been unable to deter war; it has been unprepared to fight war; it has failed to gain the objects it fought for; and its settlements of wars have not brought satisfactory peace. The blame for these failures must be shared by circumstances beyond American control; but to the extent that they were avoidable, they must be attributed not to a weakness in the basic elements of national power but to a deficiency in the political management of power. And this deficiency stems not from lack of intelligence or diplomatic skill but from the faulty habit of mind that regards war as a thing in itself rather than as a continuation of political intercourse. War as something to abolish, war as something to get over as quickly as possible, war as a means of punishing the enemy who dared to disturb the peace, war as a crusade—these conceptions are all compatible with the American outlook. But war as an instrument for attaining concrete, limited political objectives, springing from the continuing stream of international politics and flowing toward specific configurations of international power—somehow this conception seems unworthy to a proud and idealistic nation.

Surveying some of the most successful American military efforts, one is struck by the extent to which the United States ignored or deliberately excluded concrete political considerations. The Spanish-American War and World War I had momentous political consequences; in both of them American intervention had a decisive effect in shaping the configurations of national power. Yet the reasons for which the nation entered and fought these wars had scarcely anything to do with the conduct of military operations or the political results. Avenging the sinking of the "Maine," liberation of the oppressed Cubans, and Manifest Destiny; the vindication of neutral rights, banishing autocracy, and the establishment of universal peace—these issues and goals excited powerful sentiments of national honor and righteousness, but they did not direct the great military power, which they generated, toward feasible political objectives serving America's vital interest amid the changing configurations of national power. In fact, Woodrow Wilson specifically proscribed such self-interested objectives as being incompatible with America's mission to serve humanity impartially. It is little wonder that, having pursued its wars in a political vacuum, the country was unprepared to assume the vast political responsibilities that followed war and that, disillusioned over the disparity between high expectations and the wars' disappointing results, America tried to withdraw from the world of conflict into an illusory isolation.

Somewhat differently, the United States entered and fought World War II primarily for the sake of its security. Yet so far as the nation as a whole and almost all its leaders were concerned, World War II was waged with virtually no consideration of the impact of military operations upon the international political conditions of American security in the postwar world, aside from the one overriding condition of destroying the Fascist powers. When the war was won, America overwhelmingly ignored the continuing need of supporting foreign policy with adequate military power and wholly neglected to prepare for the new forms that the continuing struggle for power assumed in the aftermath of war.

The same dissociation of power and policy characterizing America's approach to war has, quite naturally, infused the whole realm of military planning concerned with preparedness for war. Before World War II strategic thinking was dominated by the assumption that the only legitimate purpose of the military establishment was to protect American rights and to ward off direct attacks upon American soil. This assumption seemingly obviated the necessity of calculating military policies in terms of American interests abroad and their relation to the interests and power of other nations. Although there were repeated controversies over the size and composition of the military establishment, these controversies were almost barren of any fundamental discussion relating military policies to concrete objectives of foreign policy. In fact, they usually revolved around issues of military organization, as though these issues were unrelated to questions of national strategy. To be sure, defense appropriations were customarily justified as being necessary for "the protection and the promotion of national policy," but this stock phrase had no more practical import than "the general welfare" would have had. In effect, defense policies were formulated and legislated in a political vacuum; one of the chief criteria of their acceptability seemed to be that they should not be entangled with considerations of international politics, the very stuff of national policy.

The dissociation of military policy from political policy was reflected in the almost complete absence of collaboration, informal or organized, between military and political leaders until the eve of American intervention in World War II.[2] Military policies were formed without knowledge of their political ends or consequences. Political decisions were made without information or professional advice about military capabilities. We can hardly speak of a coherent national strategy of the United States, as opposed to a purely military strategy, until the rudiments began to appear under the pressure of the cold war. The traditional American approach to military policy is epitomized in the Chief of Staff's defense of the War Department's program for a large regular army in 1919, when in reply to Senator Hiram Johnson's futile inquiry about the nature of the international situation that required such an army, General March stoutly assured the Senate that the program "was framed on its merits, without any relation whatever to national politics or international politics."[3]

Aversion to Violence

The traditional American approach to war and, more generally, to the use of military power is a product of certain basic conceptions and predispositions concerning international relations, combined with American experience in international relations. The basic conceptions and predispositions are not peculiar to Americans; they are shared, in some measure, by all peoples under the influence of the Western liberal tradition. However, they have assumed a distinct form and emphasis in the American environment by virtue of the distinct nature of America's relations with the outside world.

The typical dissociation of military power and national policy in the American approach arises, in the first place, from a profound moral and emotional aversion to violence. This aversion springs, ultimately, from the great liberal and humane ideals of Christianity and the Enlightenment, which look toward man's progressive ability to resolve human conflicts by peaceful settlement—by impartial reference to reason, law, and morality.

Among Americans these ideals have a distinct sense of immediacy. They are not content to leave the ideals as mere aspirations. They assume that ideals have the power to transform the human and material environment in remarkable ways, if only they believe in them strongly enough. And, perhaps more profoundly than any other people, they are convinced that these ideals are an integral part of the national mission and creed. In American domestic politics the liberal and humane ideals grow somewhat ambiguous amid the competing claims upon them put forth by scores of groups and individuals caught up in the contest for power; but in the sphere of international relations, where the issues are comparatively remote from everyday experience, ideals carry great and unembarrassed conviction.

The American aversion to violence in international relations is not the sort of aversion that results in absolute pacifism. It does not prevent participation—in fact, enthusiastic participation—in war when war cannot honorably be avoided. However, it does inhibit indulgence in the enormous evil of war for limited, prosaic ends of national policy. This kind of war strikes Americans as cynical and ignoble. It is as though they conceived of war as such a denial of normal relations among states as to be beyond ordinary political intercourse among nations. In this sense, they regard war as a social aberration, in a category by itself, to which it seems incongruous to apply ordinary rules of reason and restraint. Like Prince Andrew in *War and Peace*, struggling on the eve of the Battle of Borodino to make sense out of the chaos of war, they feel, as Tolstoy himself is said to have felt, that war is too serious and too terrible to be fought with anything but war's own self-sufficient rules. "War is not courtesy," the Prince exclaims, "but the most horrible thing in life; and we ought to understand that and not play at war. We ought to accept this terrible necessity sternly and seriously. It all lies in that: get rid of falsehood and let war be war and not a game."

However, if moral sensibilities forbid the use of war as an instrument of national policy, they do not prevent the use of war as an instrument of ideology, once war has become unavoidable. In a sense they encourage this; for tender consciences find in broader, more exalted goals a kind of moral compensation for the enormity of war and a rational justification for their contamination with evil. Thus the very ideals that proscribe war become the incentive for fighting war. An aversion to violence is transmuted into the exaltation of violence.

Nothing defeats the political limitation and control of military power like the transformation of war into an ideological contest. However, we should not suppose that the aversion to war, which induces this ideological transformation, is purely an abstract moral sentiment. Quite aside from the moral odium of war, the fear of violence and the revulsion from warfare are bound to be strong among a people who have grown as fond of social order and material well-being as Americans. War not only kills and maims; it not only separates friends and families. War upsets the whole scale of social priorities of an individualistic and materialistic scheme of life, so that the daily round of getting and spending is subordinated to the collective welfare of the nation in a hundred grievous ways —from taxation to death. This accounts for an emotional aversion to war, springing from essentially self-interested motives, which is quite as compelling as the moral aversion to war. And, like the moral aversion, it tends to put a premium upon military considerations at the expense of limited, political objectives in the conduct of war. For the natural reaction to war's threat to the security and happiness of the individual is to try to end the war as soon as possible by destroying the enemy. Therefore, it is difficult to countenance any restraint or diversion of the maximum military effort for the sake of some limited, prosaic political objective, such as the establishment of a local balance of power in some remote geographical area. Moreover, because American society places such a high value on the life of each individual, Americans are disposed to demand that the sacrifice of life serve some purpose of commensurate value; and total victory seems like the minimum compensation.

Pugnacity

The more one examines the American approach to war, the more it seems to spring from contradictory motives. Certainly, the nation's moral and emotional aversion to violence is joined by a strong streak of pugnacity. There broods in the American mind a fighting spirit that recalls the days when the United States was a bumptious young nation trying to prove itself to the world, as well as the more recent days when the populace boasted that the country had never lost a war. The predisposition to exercise force to the utmost is rooted in America's consciousness of the great material power it has gained by "thinking big" and by applying all the vast resources of technology to the conquest of nature.

It is important to note that American pugnacity is not cunning and premeditated; rather it is a romantic impulse that erects boldness and initiative into patriotic tenets, but only in response to provocation. It is true that in the expansionist years the fighting spirit was strong enough to precipitate at least two wars—the Mexican War and the Spanish-American War—and to sustain a powerful strain of aggressiveness, which, but for the internal divisions created by the slavery question, might have fostered more extensive military adventures. America's profoundly peaceful instincts since her coming of age, however, have suppressed this overt aggressiveness to the point where only the strongest provocation will arouse it. Yet American pugnacity is perhaps all the more passionate for that reason, because it springs from righteous indignation rather than from design. As George Kennan has observed:

Democracy fights in anger—it fights for the very reason that it was forced to go to war. It fights to punish the power that was rash enough and hostile enough to provoke it—to teach that power a lesson it will not forget, to prevent the thing from happening again. . . . It does look as though the real source of the emotional fervor which we Americans are able to put into a war lies less in any objective understanding of the wider issues involved than in a profound irritation over the fact that other people have finally provoked us to the point where we had no alternative but to take up arms.[4]

If American pugnacity had ever been the kind that springs from the pure egoism of national aggrandizement, it might have been accompanied by a more rational and calculating approach to the use of military power. But because it was always impassioned, always tinged with outrage, moral fervor, or sheer animal exuberance, American wars have been governed less by expediency than by the kinds of broad goals and exhilarating emotions that override the rational control of force for limited objectives.

In reality, pugnacity and hatred of war, here separated analytically, are commonly fused into one explosive emotional coalescence that gives the American approach to war its characteristic preoccupation with military operations and its contempt of considerations extraneous to victory. In both words and action no one has expressed this approach to war in all its passionate ambivalence more poignantly than General Douglas MacArthur. In his congressional testimony in 1951 on his relief from command in the Far East, MacArthur went out of his way, as he has on several occasions, to stress his profound hatred of war and his belief that it should be outlawed. "I am just one hundred per cent a believer against war," he said.

> I believe the enormous sacrifices that have been brought about by the scientific methods of killing have rendered war a fantastic solution of international difficulties. In war, as it is waged now, with the enormous losses on both sides, both sides will lose. It is a form of mutual suicide; and I believe that the entire effort of modern society should be concentrated on an endeavor to outlaw war as a method of the solution of problems between nations.[5]

On the other hand, if war could not be outlawed and if the United States became involved in war, MacArthur was equally convinced that such a war should be fought all-out to a clear-cut victory; and he condemned political considerations that might hinder the utmost military effort to destroy the enemy forces quickly and effectively as being contrary to all the rules of war and the simple dictates of humanity. On this ground he severely criticized the Truman administration's restrictions upon the military effort in Korea. The administration's policy, he declared,

> seems to me to introduce a new concept into military operations—the concept of appeasement, the concept that when you use force, you can limit that force. . . . To me, that would mean that you would have a continued and indefinite extension of bloodshed, which would have limitless—a limitless end. You would not have the potentialities of destroying the enemy's military power and bringing the conflict to a decisive close in the minimum of time and with a minimum of loss.[6]

Although the American people, as a whole, were probably unwilling to follow MacArthur's specific program for achieving victory, there can be little doubt, judging from their spontaneous emotional reaction to his return to the United States and from the whole disturbing impact of the Korean War, that the General's words expressed something that is deep and compelling in the nation's attitude toward war even now.

Depreciation of Power

America's non-political approach to war must also be ascribed to a depreciation of the factor of power in international relations. In order to employ military power as a rational and effective instrument of national policy, a nation must first have a foreign policy that is defined in terms appropriate to power. But Americans have traditionally depreciated "power politics" as the tool of wicked statesmen or the last recourse during occasional crises. American policy has been preoccupied with two extreme levels of objectives: on the one hand, the level of technical performance—as in the realm of arbitration treaties or, more recently, economic aid—and, on the other hand, the level of philosophical generalities concerning the highest ideals of mankind. Too often it has left unattended the intermediate realm of politics that is concerned with the translation of national power into concrete situations of fact.

A nation that does not attend to this intermediate realm of objectives as an aspect of the continuing contest for power among nations cannot comprehend war as a continuation of political intercourse; for power is the raw material of international relations, from which the need for continual political direction arises. By depreciating the role of power the traditional American conception of international relations excludes the most important link between war and peace. Without this link, war and peace appear to be antithetical situations calling for entirely different standards of national conduct. Therefore, Americans have shown scant interest in the military instruments of national power during peace, but they have been preoccupied with them during war, to the virtual exclusion of national policy. In effect, they have identified power politics with war while dissociating it from national policy, as though they could thereby keep policy-making inviolate by excluding power politics from peace and confining it to the self-evident demands of war. Not understanding the continuity of power, they have customarily met each military contingency as a separate emergency unrelated for all practical purposes to an unceasing political process in terms of which the nation might rationally plan a continuing program of power and policy.

America's depreciation of power and hence its lack of planning spring naturally from the same ideals and sentiments that underlie the aversion to violence. Like all people, Americans tend to envision the reality of international politics in the image of their desires. Consequently, they have envisioned international society as the product of a natural harmony of interests. In this ideal society there are no lasting rivalries or deep conflicts of interests; for it is a universal society of equals, in which all members normally subordinate their special interests to the good of the whole and settle their differences by peaceful and legal means. For this reason peace is supposed to be the normal expression of the international collective interest; and the only wars are collective wars against criminal states that rebel against law and order. Power politics is therefore thought to be an abnormal state of affairs, the product of misunderstanding, faulty legal and institutional arrangements, or the exceptional wickedness of a few statesmen or particular nations rather than a pervasive and continuing element of international relations. Thus international society is cast in the image of domestic society, where the struggle for power is supposedly absorbed in the automatic processes of the free market place, which peacefully reconcile all conflicts of interest within a system of liberal values shared by everyone.

Perhaps Americans instinctively realize that the true international society does not conform to this model and that in fact their own actions do not conform to the model. Nevertheless, they are compelled to regard the struggle for power, which perverts the ideal, as wrong, abnormal, and transitory; and so they have not granted recognition to this malevolent influence by dealing with it according to its own methods. As Walter Lippmann has observed:

Our foreign policy throughout the last forty years has been dominated by the belief that the struggle for power does not exist, or that it can be avoided, or that it can be abolished. Because of this belief our aim has not been to regulate and to moderate and to compose the conflicts and the issues, to check and to balance the contending forces. Our aim has been either to abstain from the struggle, or to abolish the struggle immediately, or to conduct crusades against those nations that most actively continue the struggle.[7]

Actually, by depreciating the struggle for power, Americans have neither avoided it nor abolished it. They have simply forfeited the opportunity to use power—conspicuously military power—as an effective instrument of national policy.

Dissociation of Diplomacy and Power

Since diplomacy is the pre-eminent instrument for controlling and limiting warfare, America's approach to diplomacy is as important a source of its antipathy toward the primacy of politics as is the American approach to entering, fighting, and preparing for war. Just as the nation has traditionally approached war in a political vacuum, so it has regarded diplomacy as something apart from power. Consistent with the ideal image of international relations, Americans have commonly regarded diplomacy fundamentally as an instrument for realizing an underlying harmony of interests rather than as an instrument for directing national power toward limited objectives.

This dissociation of diplomacy and power has resulted in a certain ambivalence toward diplomacy. On the one hand, Americans have sometimes thought of diplomacy as a purely rational process whereby national conflicts are ironed out on their merits and a meeting of minds is reached. The assumption here is that all nations, whether they recognize it or not, have an equal interest in peace and the status quo and that therefore diplomacy is simply a means of making all parties aware of the common interest. It follows from this assumption that agreement in itself is a desirable thing, as evidence of reason and good will; and that agreement upon general principles of national conduct is especially valuable. This positive approach to diplomacy is exhibited in countless diplomatic ventures—for example, Cordell Hull's repeated enumerations of the articles of international virtue as a basis for resolving the conflict with Japan—and in a number of documents that have struck the nation as notable diplomatic achievements—such as the Fourteen Points, the Atlantic Charter, and the Declaration on Liberated Peoples.[8]

On the other hand, Americans have combined with this sanguine approach a profound distrust of diplomacy, as though it were incompatible with open and forthright relations among nations. The latter view is probably the obverse side of the former; for one instinctively perceives that diplomacy is in reality involved with power politics and therefore that it contravenes the ideal image. Its secrecy and deviousness are the trappings of an occult art, compatible, perhaps, with the ways of the Old World but certainly the very antithesis of the Wilsonian model of "open covenants openly arrived at." In this way distrust of diplomacy reflects the contradiction between ideals and the reality; and the distrust has seemingly been confirmed by the disparity between high expectations and the bitter results of the postwar settlements and wartime agreements of two world wars.[9]

Whichever strain—the positive or the negative view of diplomacy—has been dominant in foreign relations at different periods, both of them, consistent with their common origin in the depreciation of power, have militated against the use of diplomacy as a flexible instrument of national power—as a means of moderating, balancing, limiting, and controlling power. Instead, they have disposed Americans to envision diplomacy as an instrument for transcending power conflicts and realizing universal moral principles. Consequently, it has been difficult to countenance the compromises and accommodations which are the lifeblood of political intercourse without seeming to violate principles. And this has been markedly true when the passions of war have rendered compromise and accommodation particularly repugnant. In wartime especially, concession comes to seem like appeasement, and a limited settlement like humiliation.

Considering the premium imposed by the potential destructiveness of modern war upon limited political settlements, it is evident that the dissociation of diplomacy and power, like the dissociation of power and policy which it exacerbates, is a formidable obstacle to the control of war as a rational instrument of national policy.

The Antimilitarist Tradition

One cannot fully appreciate the American approach to war without taking into account the nation's long antimilitarist tradition. To oversimplify the matter, this tradition originated in the early fear of standing armies as a threat to democratic liberties, but it persists even though that threat is no longer a serious problem. Although the fear of military subversion or usurpation has subsided, the fear of undue military influence in the counsels of government has grown in recent decades, and Americans commonly suspect the "military mind" of being somehow antithetical to democratic principles and institutions.

To guard against undue military influence of any kind, the nation has traditionally relied upon the principle of "civilian supremacy," which is imbedded in the Constitution, implemented in legislative statutes, and reflected in the administrative structure of the federal government. However, the legal and institutional embodiments of this principle—largely originating in the fear of usurpation—have little relevance to a vast number of contemporary situations in which civilians have to make decisions that rest upon military considerations beyond the sphere of civilian competence. In practice, Americans have approached this contemporary problem with another honored principle: the principle of military supremacy over purely military matters. The military must not interfere in political matters, but the civilians should not interfere with purely military matters, the nation seems to have decided. This arrangement is intended not only to keep the military from usurping civilian functions but also to guard against civilians arrogating military authority—a contingency believed to be as contrary to democratic principles as to military efficiency. Thus the two principles together purport to define a division of labor that preserves civilian supremacy while securing the highest degree of military competence.

The trouble with this theory of separation is that military and nonmilitary considerations are inextricably entangled, and "purely military matters" have important political consequences. Therefore, as national security has become increasingly dependent upon military considerations, the theory of separation has not only exacerbated the evils of making political and military policies in a vacuum but has also tended to create such great reliance upon military considerations as to subordinate national policy to military policy. The deference of political leaders to military advice has not been matched by a corresponding capacity of military leaders to acquire political guidance, although military men have frequently been more conscious of the need for such reciprocity than the civilians. Naturally, in wartime this civilian deference to military advice is even more marked, in accordance with the view that, when the civilians have failed to keep the peace, the conduct of war becomes a purely military matter. By this devious route the fear of the influence of military personnel upon civilian affairs has contributed to the domination of national policy by military considerations.

The American Experience

It is impossible to understand America's basic conceptions and predispositions concerning foreign relations apart from her historical experience in foreign relations. When one seeks an explanation of the American approach to war and military power, the central fact emerging is that for the greater part of their national history the American people have not come to grips with the difficult problem of combining military power with foreign policy. Their prolonged enjoyment of relative isolation and security in the period from the War of 1812 to World War II spared them the necessity.

Americans were under no pressure to balance military power with political objectives, because military and political policies seemed to be in perfect harmony. Thanks to a fortunate geographic position, the protective presence of British sea power in the Atlantic, the strife among potential adversaries, and the weakness of actual adversaries, the United States was able to realize its two pre-eminent political objectives, continental isolation and continental expansion, either without resort to war or else with resort to relatively short and easy wars that involved no political complications in the conduct of military operations. The United States likewise was spared the necessity of securing its power positions through the kind of tortuous diplomatic bargains that were necessary in the Old World. Thus America's major political objectives were simple and attainable. They neither conflicted with her view of immediate military necessities nor complicated her policy with diplomatic concessions. Although the political consequences of the wars against Spain and Germany bore little relation to the nebulous and grandiose objectives for which the nation fought, this fact raised no question in American minds about harmonizing power and policy, because American security was never seriously threatened—and, after all, the United States did win striking victories. The fortunate political circumstances that made security and victory possible were concealed from America because they existed independently of any effort on her part.

American strategy began and ended with the overriding objective of continental security, conceived in the image of first acquiring and then protecting a vast fortress from enemy assault. This simple and appealing conception seemingly obviated the necessity of forming military or political policies in terms of the configurations of national power abroad. It concealed the extent to which American security was actually interwoven with the power and interests of other nations. It sustained the flattering analogy of the militiaman taking down his gun from the wall when the enemy approached and putting it back when the danger had passed. This conception seems hopelessly unrealistic to many Americans now, but pragmatically and on the face of things it was the very essence of realism until the fall of France in 1940. Although the nation did not seriously prepare for war, did not calculate the political configurations of power in waging war, and quickly abandoned its arms after war, it nevertheless won wars handily; and that seemed to be sufficient proof that a strategy of continental isolation suited American needs. Until unmistakable evidence to the contrary should arise, there was no incentive for entangling military policies with national policy or national policy with power politics.

As American experience encouraged a dissociation of power and policy, so it was equally congenial to that quality of pugnacity which overrides the political limitation of force. For America's relative isolation relieved the nation of the sobering experience of foreign occupation or defeat, which injected a note of precaution and design into the military preparations and activities of European nations. Americans could feel confident that, no matter what direction the fortunes of war might take, their security would be guaranteed so long as the insular fortress was protected. Thus instead of tasting defeat or the fear of defeat, the United States enjoyed an unbroken string of military successes, which encouraged the notion that her geographical position and her natural endowments made her invincible. There is no greater stimulus to unreasoning pugnacity than the notion of invincibility.

At the same time, America's relative isolation from the main stream of international politics also encouraged that compelling commitment to liberal and humane ideals which underlay her moral and emotional aversion to violence. If these ideals carried more weight in the American approach to foreign relations than in the external relations of other democratic nations, this must be attributed, in large part, to the circumstances that saved the nation from having to test them against the unpleasant realities of international politics. Virtue comes easily to those who do not have to put it into practice under adverse conditions. The American people were spared the education of adversity, while events confirmed their basic assurance that the national mission of bringing a universal society of peace and order to the world—even if this had to be done by a crusading war—was perfectly compatible with national self-interest.

By the same token, America's conception of an international society governed by a natural harmony of interests is a product of the circumstances that shielded her from the actual conflicts of interest. Not having experienced the immediate necessity of participating in the struggle for power, Americans found it easy, as well as gratifying, to imagine that the natural state of international politics is harmonious. Because they did not themselves have to balance the claims of universal moral principles against the claims of national security, Americans attributed the indulgence of other nations in the compromises of power politics, as well as their own abstinence, to innate moral qualities rather than to transitory political circumstances in a continuing struggle for power.

The impact of international experience upon the American approach to foreign relations becomes clearer when one compares it with the impact of internal experience upon the American approach to the domestic sphere of human relations. The same basic ideals that Americans brought to international affairs produced no comparable innocence of the role of power in national affairs. In business affairs, labor relations, or party politics Americans have taken the struggle for power pretty much for granted. The very principle of the balance of power is imbedded in the Constitution. And it is noteworthy that American domestic reformers have customarily dealt with conflicts of interest by compromise and accommodation, by moderating and controlling power, rather than by trying to abolish it. It seems likely that if America had contended with the conflicts of power among nations as intimately as it contended with power conflicts among groups and individuals within the nation, the nation would have developed a conception of international relations more compatible with the political limitation of military power.

The Transformation of the American Approach

If the American approach to war and the use of military power is so largely a product of experience, we may expect the recent radical changes in the nature of America's international experience virtually to transform her traditional approach. Undoubtedly, just such a transformation has been taking place, but it is by no means completed.

World War II destroyed America's sense of geographical isolation and produced a widespread consciousness that American security could be seriously jeopardized by disturbances in the distribution of national power overseas. This momentous alteration in America's traditional image of its position in world politics has been accompanied by radical departures in the nation's military policies and political commitments since the war. Yet World War II was fought in the pattern of America's traditional pre-occupation with military objectives. Proceeding through the cycle of un-preparedness, mobilization, overwhelming offensive, total victory, and demobilization, the nation paid little attention to concrete political objec-tives. It ended the war scarcely more conscious of the interdependence of military power and national policy than before.

It is primarily the cold war that is transforming America's traditional approach to the relation between power and policy; for the cold war con-fronted the nation, as World War II never did, with the practical neces-sity of balancing military means with political ends within the framework of national strategy. The cold war is neither war nor peace in the ortho-dox sense, but a continuing struggle for power, waged by political, psy-chological, and economic means as well as by a variety of military and semimilitary means. There is no way of fighting the cold war to a clear-cut decision without precipitating a total war; but the American people know that total war with nuclear weapons would be an incredible disaster and that the enemy may never offer the provocation for such a war. In the meantime, the United States is forced to consider the means to protect and promote its far-flung interests against unrelenting Communist pres-sure and the ever-present possibility of limited war.

Therefore, in some measure, the United States has had to alter its traditional approach to war and military policy and subordinate military considerations to considerations of high policy. In some measure, it has had to combine diplomacy with "situations of strength." In some meas-ure, it has had to harmonize military power with all the other elements of national power according to a national strategic plan for achieving its basic security objectives. The very existence of the National Security Council testifies to this fact. If it had not accomplished this much, in all probability the nation either would have precipitated a total war or suf-fered disastrous losses of positions vital to survival.

Taken as a whole, the American record in foreign policy since 1945 is a remarkable adaptation to novel and challenging circumstances. However, the most cursory examination of the evolution of American strategy in the past decade must reveal that the adaptation has been partial and on an *ad hoc* basis. The record of the United States does not show a real adjustment, either in its underlying conceptions of force and politics or in its concrete policies, to the imperatives of a strategy capable of resisting limited aggression by limited means. Such an adaptation is bound to be encumbered by the weight of traditional habits of mind resisting the pressure of unprecedented events.

Chapter Three

THE COMMUNIST APPROACH TO WAR

The Instrumental View of Violence

The Communist approach to war and the use of military power is as notable for its fusion of power and policy as the American approach is notable for its dissociation of power and policy. The explanation of this contrast lies chiefly in divergent ideologies and in different experiences with power.

The American is obliged by his basic principles and predispositions to regard all extralegal forms of social coercion with a sensitive conscience, but the orthodox Communist theoretically can have no moral inhibitions toward even the most violent forms of coercion. The liberal conscience cannot escape the moral dilemma of force, which arises, on the one hand, from abstract condemnation of force and, on the other hand, from the knowledge of its necessity in society as it is actually constituted. But this dilemma does not exist in the Communist scheme of values. Any means that promotes the ultimate goal of a classless society is morally acceptable, because the standard of acceptability is not a transcendent moral principle but only the achievement of a theoretical state of affairs. Since this state of affairs is believed to be scientifically inevitable, the only permissible question arising about the propriety of any particular means is the practical question of whether it is a scientifically "correct" step toward the predetermined end. In effect, this renders Communist morality identical with the enhancement of the Communist Party's power; for the Party is the exclusive, indispensable, and infallible instrument for achieving the classless society, and only the Party can interpret the proper means to that end. Accordingly, the propriety of violence, like the propriety of any other means, is purely a matter of its expediency as an instrument of Party power.

Thus Communist ideology, far from holding power suspect, positively sanctions it as an integral part of the inevitable process of historical evolution and, far from imposing moral inhibitions upon violence, judges it by the sole criterion of its expediency as an instrument of power. Although the Marxist utopia embodies the Christian, liberal goals of brotherly love and universal peace, it imposes no ethical restraints upon its believers; for Communist doctrine prescribes that the precondition to realizing this remote and indefinite goal is the elimination or suppression of all non-believers. In accordance with this doctrine, any "sentimental" compunctions which the early Bolsheviks may have entertained about the ruthless use of force were soon suppressed in the stress of establishing and consolidating Communist power. Lenin warned revolutionaries not to be squeamish about using force and violence, which, he declared, were essential to the creation of all new societies; and when the Bolsheviks gained power, he admonished them to remember the continuing need for merciless terror against the enemies of the Soviet regime. They followed his advice. Organized force and violence have remained the principal bulwark of Soviet society to this day.

Force and violence are just as much a part of Communist theory and practice in international relations as they are in all human relations. Here, too, the Communist approach to power was firmly established during the Bolshevik Revolution. Some of the early Bolsheviks, under the influence of the liberal, utopian element of Marxism, imagined that the revolution would supplant the capitalist system of power politics, military organization, and state diplomacy and substitute interclass politics. But when the anticipated revolutions in the advanced capitalist nations failed to materialize, leaving Russia still entangled in the world war and the sole base of world communism, the Bolshevik leaders were compelled to formulate a foreign policy, to practice orthodox diplomacy, and to look to the configurations of national power in order to preserve the revolution. Under Lenin's leadership the interests of world communism were absolutely identified with the interests of the Soviet Union and absolutely subordinated to the immediate imperatives of Soviet power. His accommodation of theory to practice determined the alliance between a rigid ideological dogmatism and a flexible, opportunistic power politics that has characterized Communist foreign relations ever since.

From the beginning of Soviet diplomacy Communist leaders have regarded warfare, hence military power, as an integral feature of international relations. Although Communist theory erects universal peace as the cardinal objective of Soviet foreign policy, it also posits warfare as the inseparable product of capitalism, which can be eliminated only by the violent overthrow of capitalism. Thus Lenin asserted:

> Socialists cannot be opposed to any kind of wars without ceasing to be socialists. We are struggling against the very root of wars—capitalism. But inasmuch as capitalism has not yet been exterminated, we are struggling not against wars in general, but against reactionary wars, and for revolutionary wars.[1]

And in his report to the Central Committee at the Eighth Party Congress in March, 1919, Lenin stated:

> We are living not merely in a state but in a system of states and the existence of the Soviet Republic side by side with imperialist states for a long time is unthinkable. One or the other must triumph in the end. And before that end supervenes, a series of frightful collisions between the Soviet Republic and the bourgeois states will be inevitable.[2]

Lenin's position was unequivocally affirmed by the Sixth World Congress of the Communist International in 1928:

> The overthrow of capitalism is impossible without violence; that is, without armed uprisings and wars against the bourgeoisie. In our era of imperialistic wars and world revolution, revolutionary civil wars of the proletarian dictatorship against bourgeoisie, wars of the proletariat against the bourgeois states and world capitalism, as well as national revolutionary wars of oppressed peoples against imperialism are unavoidable, as has been shown by Lenin.[3]

Since the death of Stalin the Party has officially abandoned the theory that war between capitalist and socialist states is inevitable, though it has by no means ruled out the contingency altogether. On February 14, 1956, Nikita Khrushchev, in an address before the Twentieth Soviet Communist Party Congress, which was generally interpreted as the authoritative restatement of Communist political doctrine, explicitly rejected Lenin's thesis concerning the inevitability of war, obliquely alluding to the deterrent effect of thermonuclear weapons. He declared, further, in a restatement of a familiar Communist position, that the transition to socialism need not come about through force and civil war, providing that the extent and form of the resistance put up by the "exploiters" does not require repression by violence.[4] Yet, however significant this reinterpretation of Communist dogma may be as the rationale for a new tactic of "competitive coexistence" and the exploitation of contradictions among capitalist states, it leaves unchanged the instrumental view of military coercion. From the Communist standpoint still, the legitimacy of war, like any other form of violence, must be judged not by universal moral principles but by its relation to concrete political goals. War may or may not serve Communist goals, depending on circumstances, but war itself is a matter of moral indifference. War, like peace, is a means to an end; therefore it must be judged by its particular political and social characteristics and its particular utility to Communist power, above all to the world base of Communist power, the Soviet Union.

Communist theoreticians have defined several different kinds of wars (imperialist, national, and revolutionary), elaborated their characteristics, and determined their legitimacy or lack of legitimacy accordingly. Stalin consolidated these classifications into "just" and "unjust" wars in the following summary of Bolshevik doctrine:

> The Bolsheviks held that there are two kinds of war:
>
> a) *Just* wars, wars that are not wars of conquest but wars of liberation, waged to defend the people from foreign attack and from attempts to enslave them, or to liberate the people from capitalist slavery, or, lastly, to liberate colonies and dependent countries from the yoke of imperialism; and
>
> b) *Unjust* wars, wars of conquest, waged to conquer and enslave foreign countries and foreign nations.
>
> Wars of the first kind the Bolsheviks supported. As to wars of the second kind, the Bolsheviks maintained that a resolute struggle must be waged against them to the point of revolution and the overthrow of one's own imperialist government.[5]

However, it is obvious from the logic of the identification of world Communist goals with the Russian national interest that the single, basic criterion for determining the justness or unjustness of a war is service to the Soviet Union.[6] Therefore, whereas America's moral and emotional aversion to violence inhibits the use of war as an instrument of national policy, communism's instrumental view of violence makes Russian national policy the sole sanction of war. And whereas the great body of America's experience in international politics encourages the divorce of power and policy, Communist experience has from the beginning dictated the fusion of power and policy.

The Image of Conflict

The Communist conception of international society contrasts as sharply with the American conception as the Communist theory of force contrasts with the American theory. Like Americans, Communists envision international society in an image compatible with their ideological aims and aspirations. But whereas the American image of the world is composed largely of implicit and somewhat nebulous assumptions, the Communist image quite explicitly purports to be a detailed and scientifically exact description of reality.

What is the Communist description of reality? Where Americans see a natural harmony of interests underlying international relations, the Communists see a natural conflict of interests. Whereas Americans regard power conflicts among nations as abnormal—the product of misunderstanding or some other remediable deficiency—the Communists regard harmony as an illusion—the product of transitory circumstances or deliberate deception.

The Marxist interpretation of history posits an inevitable and unceasing conflict between communism and capitalism (in effect, all who are not "friendly" to the Soviet Union) until the capitalists are finally eliminated and the dictatorship of the proletariat is established. Temporary coexistence between the two groups is not only possible but, until conditions for the final stage of communism are ripe, a highly desirable expedient. But permanent coexistence is unthinkable; for among states representing opposing classes, as among the classes themselves, it must always be a question of "Who will destroy whom?"

In practice, Communist leaders may be willing to wait indefinitely for the ultimate collapse of non-Communist centers of power; but as long as they retain their conviction of the unalterable hostility of the capitalist world, they cannot envision a lasting accommodation of national interests with "bourgeois states" on a basis of mutual trust and understanding. Instead, they must take advantage of every opportunity to expand Communist power and influence, even while entering into temporary accommodations; for their national security—and the legitimacy of their personal authority as well—depends upon promoting Communist power in competition with an enemy irrevocably committed to destroying them. Therefore, whereas the American image of international relations depreciates the role of power and leads to a conception of war and peace as diametrically opposite states of affairs, the Communist image envisions power as the basic element of international relations and conceives of war and peace as merely differences of degree in one ceaseless, inexorable struggle.

Rationality and Flexibility

The Communists' belief in an inexorable struggle for power and their moral indifference to force and violence should not be construed as an obsession with power or an infatuation with force and violence. They regard power, force, and violence as means to ends, not as ends in themselves. Their ideology and their practical experience in the management of power dispose them to be generally circumspect in the use of force and to abjure all impulsive or rash actions as ineffectual "romanticism" or "adventurism."

The Marxist-Leninist dogma purports to describe a necessary development proceeding according to iron laws of history. It obligates its adherents to align themselves with this development on the basis of an objective analysis of concrete situations, interpreted according to immutable principles of action. However absurd its claim to scientific validity may be, this dogma nevertheless encourages a coldly calculating approach to power. And although its claim to omniscience often taxes dialectical skill in squaring doctrine with expediency, its stress upon achieving concrete results by rational means substantially counteracts the rigidity of a doctrinaire approach.

This is not to say that the Communists' analyses of concrete situations are always accurate or that their choices of means are invariably shrewd. Communists operate under the intellectual limitations inherent in all ratiocination. Moreover, their judgment suffers from doctrinal prejudice and an astounding parochialism. The Marxist image of society distorts the Communist view of reality as much as the liberal utopian image distorts the American view; and Marxist distortion has been a major factor in a series of diplomatic blunders resulting from miscalculation of the capabilities, motives, and intentions of foreign countries. The point here is simply that the Communist system predisposes its adherents to act upon hard-headed reason rather than caprice or emotional bias, to measure costs and risks in pursuing objectives, and to keep means and ends in proportion. It is in this sense that the Communists are generally rational in their use of power.

Furthermore, the Communist system adds to rationality a remarkable opportunism and flexibility of tactics. Although Marxist-Leninist dogma theoretically commits its adherents to achieving a world revolution—an unlimited goal if there ever was one—in practice, because of a preoccupation with means, it prescribes a shrewd manipulation of power toward concrete objectives in the Party's interest. At the same time, by guaranteeing eventual fulfilment of the Marxist utopia, it relieves the manipulators of power from the compulsion to implement their program of revolution within any particular span of time. Because the end result seems scientifically certain to Communists, they can afford to wait upon events and sacrifice immediate objectives for the sake of future gains. The only rule incumbent upon them is to adapt their tactics to the existing situation on the basis of an objective calculation of realities, without regard for sentiment. Of course, they are greatly facilitated in observing this rule by their immunity to the ordinary pressures of public opinion, with which democratic statesmen must be concerned.

Communist practice has reinforced Marxist theory in sustaining the rational and flexible use of power. Bolsheviks were steeled to stealth and circumspection by the adversities of revolutionary experience, which demanded not only great ruthlessness but extraordinary elasticity in order to adapt the revolution to a variety of changing social and political conditions in Russia and throughout the world. No one was more critical of rigid and doctrinaire tactics and more insistent upon rational improvisation than Lenin. Thus he berated the "Left Communists" for permitting their contempt and hatred of the liberal reformers of Europe to interfere with their utilization of "reactionary" parliaments for revolutionary purposes.

> Of course, without a revolutionary mood among the masses, and without conditions favoring the growth of this mood, revolutionary tactics will never be converted into action; but we in Russia have been convinced by long, painful and bloody experience of the truth that revolutionary tactics cannot be built up on revolutionary moods alone. Tactics must be based on a sober and strictly objective estimation of *all* the class forces in a given state, as well as on an evaluation of the experience of revolutionary movements.[7]

The same flexibility of tactics, displayed throughout the history of the Bolsheviks' acquisition and consolidation of power within Russia, has been conspicuous in Russia's external relations under Communist control. Certainly, the outstanding characteristic of the whole history of Soviet foreign relations is the opportunistic adaptation of diplomacy and national strategy to the changing configurations of power affecting Russia's national interest. Thus in successive periods this opportunism led to an alliance with Germany as a counterweight to the victorious Allies of World War I, to joining the Allies in the League of Nations in the 1930's and becoming the outstanding champion of collective security against Germany, to an alliance with Germany during Germany's war against the Allies, to a realliance with the Allies in a war against Germany, and then after victory over Germany, to a cold war against the Western Allies, centering upon the struggle for Germany. Throughout all these tactical contortions the Soviet regime apparently maintained a complete sense of ideological consistency.

This pattern of opportunism is in accord with Lenin's advice to proceed toward objectives in zigzags and with his own exemplification of this advice in accepting the humiliating peace of Brest-Litovsk in 1918 for the sake of Russia's national interest rather than continuing the war against Germany for the sake of world revolution. Soviet conduct continues to confirm George Kennan's analysis:

> Here caution, circumspection, flexibility and deception are the valuable qualities; and their value finds natural appreciation in the Russian or the oriental mind. Thus the Kremlin has no compunction about retreating in the face of superior force. And being under the compulsion of no timetable, it does not get panicky under the necessity for such a retreat. Its political action is a fluid stream which moves constantly, wherever it is permitted to move, toward a given goal. Its main concern is to make sure that it has filled every nook and cranny available to it in the basin of world power. But if it finds unassailable barriers in its path, it accepts these philosophically and accommodates itself to them.[8]

Perhaps only those as callous as the Communists toward the use of power can subject it to the restraints of rational control with such equanimity. In any case, we must concede that their approach to power is far more congenial to Clausewitz' dictum than the American approach.

The Revolutionary Approach

It is evident from the preceding analysis that the idea of war as a continuation of political intercourse is the very essence of Communist theory and practice. It emerges inevitably from the instrumental conception of force and from the image of continual power conflict between Communists and non-Communists at all levels of social and political organization. Furthermore, it is implicit in the revolutionary character of communism. The whole purpose of revolutionary violence is political, and the whole tactics of revolutionary violence must be subordinated to political objectives and shaped in anticipation of political consequences. Therefore, the political management of force is inseparable from the revolutionary outlook. Since Communists regard war as simply one form of a continuing class struggle, they approach the largest war among states with the same political orientation that they apply to the smallest revolutionary action.

The revolutionary approach to war has its natural concomitant in the view of diplomacy as a function of power; for since the Communists look upon war and peace as continuations of political intercourse by different means, they regard military force and diplomacy as complementary instruments of power. This view facilitates the political control of war as much as the American view of diplomacy hinders it.

In Communist theory, diplomacy is just one instrument of a continuing conflict of power; it is not a means of transcending the struggle for power. In Communist practice, diplomacy is like a battle in which positions are asserted or conceded, not according to logic, truth, or the merits of the issues, but solely in response to the tactical requirements of the power situation. Hence the conduct of Communist diplomacy exhibits a formidable combination of rigidity and flexibility—of dogged persistence in pursuing an objective combined with sudden shifts of tactics when the configurations of power dictate the abandonment of one position or the pursuit of another one.

This approach is completely compatible with the moderation and control of the international struggle for power, but it absolutely precludes a permanent settlement. Because they regard diplomacy as a function of power, Communist statesmen can readily accept temporary political accommodations that reflect the reality of power. They can, undoubtedly, accept limited settlements of war more readily than the United States can. But because they believe in the inexorable hostility of capitalism, they must look upon diplomatic concessions and compromises as tactical maneuvers, not as evidence of good will and mutual understanding.

In short, the Communists bring to the conduct of diplomacy the same qualities of power-consciousness, rationality, and flexibility that they apply to the management of all forms of power. Although the moral callousness underlying these qualities is repugnant, we must concede that the Communist approach to war and diplomacy is well adapted to the limitation of military power; for it has been nurtured in a revolutionary ideology and a revolutionary experience in which the primacy of politics is the first principle of thought and action.

One does not need to posit any special influence of Clausewitz in order to account for the Communist approach to war and politics. Yet it is an interesting indication of the affinity between Communist doctrine and Clausewitz' theory of war that Marx, Engels, Lenin, and many other Communist leaders—including Mao Tse-tung—have read Clausewitz with marked approval. Lenin was particularly impressed. He made numerous marginal comments in a copy of Clausewitz' treatise *On War* and cited his views in a number of writings.[9] As Stalin correctly observed in a letter to a Soviet military historian, what impressed Lenin was not Clausewitz' military views but rather his exposition of "the familiar Marxist thesis that there is a direct connection between war and politics, that politics gives birth to war, that war is the continuation of politics by violent means . . . that under certain unfavorable circumstances the retreat is as appropriate a form of strife as the advance."[10]

Just as Clausewitz and the Communist leaders are joined in regarding war as a continuation of politics, they share the view that war is a psychological phenomenon, reflecting the social and political circumstances from which it springs, and not just a contest of material strength. Clausewitz distinguished himself from preceding students of modern war by perceiving the influence of psychological factors—particularly, the motives for which men fight—upon the forms of warfare. In the Communist view, the character of a war is determined by its social and political significance. War is not a purely military phenomenon but a form of class struggle with what Clausewitz would call an "admixture" of military means.

Consistent with this broad conception of war, communism regards the political, economic, and psychological instruments of power, quite as much as the military operations themselves, as integral parts of a single struggle that takes its form from the nature of the total human environment. As Clausewitz wrote, in a passage that Lenin underlined, "War is to be regarded as an organic whole, from which the single branches are not to be separated and in which therefore every individual activity flows into the whole." Conspicuously in the colonial and former colonial areas, this organic whole embraces the irregular forms of warfare—sabotage, subversion, political penetration, fomenting rebellion—used in conjunction with conventional means; for in these areas the social and political environment is ripe for warfare in its revolutionary form.

Mao Tse-tung has expounded the principles of revolutionary warfare more comprehensively and systematically than any other Communist writer—notably in his work *On the Protracted War* (1938).[11] His generalizations of Chinese Communist experience in the war against Japan and the Kuomintang have served as the model for the Communist movement throughout Southeast Asia. Taking Clausewitz' dictum as his point of departure, Mao writes, " 'War is the continuation of politics'; in this sense war is politics and war itself is a political action, and there has not been a single war since ancient times that does not bear a political character." Then he adds his own variation on the theme: "It can therefore be said that politics are bloodless war while war is the politics of bloodshed."[12] In Mao's view the whole purpose of war is political success, and the whole means of war must be determined by the conditions of political success. Criticizing the mechanistic theory of war, according to which "weapons mean everything," he declares: "Our view is the opposite; we see not only weapons but also the power of man. Weapons are an important factor in war but not the decisive one; it is man and not material that counts." It follows that "political mobilization is the most fundamental condition for winning the war";[13] for, according to one of his favorite similes, "The people are like water and the army is like fish."

Mao's political conception of war determines the nature of the military strategy he advocates. Because he is interested, primarily, in political results, he is not concerned about ending war quickly. In fact, counting upon the "reactionary" adversary's anxiety to end war, he would deliberately prolong it in order to provoke the enemy into rash moves, which would be the prelude to the final Communist counteroffensive. Only after political mobilization has been completed during the first two stages of guerilla warfare—the "strategic defensive" and the "strategic stalemate"—does Mao envision the final stage of the "strategic offensive," designed to overcome the enemy's forces by massive assaults against his positions. Thus, whereas Americans, fighting in defense of the status quo, are led to wage wars in a manner that will permit them to return to peace as quickly as possible, Mao Tse-tung, fighting to overthrow the status quo, is content to prolong warfare indefinitely in order to achieve his revolutionary objective.

It is ironic that an avowedly materialistic philosophy should produce such a keen appreciation of the psychological elements in the struggle for power; whereas American idealism encourages a preoccupation with the purely military aspects of that struggle. One can appreciate the true nature of the Communist threat only when one becomes as conscious of its revolutionary foundation as the Communists themselves.

The Advantages of Opportunism

A candid view of the nature of the contemporary struggle for power compels one to recognize that the Communist approach to war is as compatible with the imperatives of cold war and limited war as the traditional American approach is incompatible. Furthermore, the qualities of moral indifference, emotional discipline, rational opportunism, tactical flexibility, and power-consciousness, which account for this compatibility, give the Communists important advantages in conducting a successful national strategy.

One cannot deny that it is easier for those who are uninhibited by moral restraints to be more realistic and flexible in the management of power. Yet must we conclude that only imperialists and revolutionaries can use force rationally and effectively as an instrument of national policy? After all, every nation has power interests regardless of the ultimate purposes for which it may use power. Every nation, whatever its ideological complexion, has political policies dependent upon power for attainment. Therefore, the principle of political primacy in the use of military power is as valid for democratic as for totalitarian states. It is, in fact, as valid on moral grounds as on grounds of expediency.

Why should Communists perceive and act upon the principle of political primacy more readily than Americans? It would indeed be a sad thing for democracy if the United States could surmount its undiscriminating preoccupation with military objectives only by emulating the ruthlessness and cynicism of a totalitarian adversary.

Part II | *THE LESSONS OF HISTORY*

Chapter Four

THE DECLINE OF LIMITED WAR

Interaction between Means and Ends of War

War is not merely a physical clash of men and arms; it is a struggle of human wills. It is a product not only of the military technology and the sheer weight of material force which sustain the actual military operations but also of the political, social, economic, and cultural environment, which cannot help infusing the minds of the combatants and shaping the ends and the methods of their struggle. Therefore, one must judge the current applicability of preceding generalizations concerning the conditions for the rational control of armed force in the light of the historical relationships between war and its total environment and not merely in terms of a single factor, such as weapons.

As a general rule, it is clear enough that warfare will be more susceptible to control as a rational instrument of foreign policy when it is limited in the dimensions of force and the objectives toward which force is directed. But is it possible to limit war when the potentialities of destruction are virtually unlimited? Are there any historical lessons concerning the limitation of warfare that are applicable today? Before we judge the relevance to the present political and military situation of the general conditions of limitation discussed in chapter i, it should be instructive to examine the conditions that have sustained limited war and encouraged unlimited war in the past.

When we examine the historical conditions of limited and unlimited war, we must distinguish between general rules for conducting war, which belligerents are theoretically free to follow or not to follow at their discretion, and various features of the international environment which arise from such a complex concatenation of factors as to be largely beyond the power of states to affect. Two general rules have been stated as prerequisites for limiting war. One is that the belligerents must be prepared to conduct war in accordance with well-defined, limited political objectives, susceptible to accommodation; the other is that they must be prepared to limit the means by which they strive to attain these objectives, so that the means of war will be proportionate to the ends.

In practice, as the logic of human conflict would suggest, the limitation of the ends of war cannot be entirely separated from the limitation of the means. The history of war demonstrates an interaction between the objectives and the scale and intensity of war. The greater the value belligerents attach to the objectives of war, the greater the dimensions of force they will tend to exert against the enemy. The greater the scale and intensity of a war, the more extreme and less susceptible to compromise the belligerents' objectives are likely to be, while at the same time the consequences of war will be less subject to control and prediction. Therefore, although the deliberate limitation of political objectives has been an essential condition for the use of force as an effective instrument of policy, the steady growth in the physical potentialities of force has rendered the rational political control of war increasingly difficult. Nevertheless, despite the interaction between the ends and means of war, the ends are more fundamental in that a war in which states can draw upon the most advanced military technology is unlikely to be limited in the absence of a guiding political decision to pursue limited objectives, whereas even the most rudimentary means can lead to unlimited war when the ends of war are not limited. Rome did not need nuclear bombs to annihilate Carthage.

Two periods of modern Western history stand out as predominantly periods of limited war: the period from the Peace of Westphalia in 1648 to the French Revolutionary War and the period from the Congress of Vienna in 1815 to World War I. It is notable that in both of these periods statesmen were for the most part content to fight for limited, well-defined "reasons of state," which did not incite extreme aspirations or fears, which demanded something short of the maximum exercise of force, and which could be accommodated before military destruction passed beyond the bounds of predictable consequences. The typical limited war in Europe during the eighteenth and nineteenth centuries was fought in order to achieve marginal adjustments in the balance of power that diplomacy had failed to secure. These adjustments might concern the possession of a particular territory, the dynastic authority or succession in a state, the terms of trade between countries, or the exploitation of foreign markets, land, and resources. But whatever the objectives at stake, they were customarily accommodated in a negotiated settlement; and the sting of defeat was often soothed by compensations, which were frequently granted at the expense of weaker states or carved out from overseas territories. And so the limited value ascribed to the objectives at stake relieved statesmen of the compulsion to wage war to the utmost physical limits.

From 1721 to 1740 Europe enjoyed the longest period of peace between the Religious Wars and the Congress of Vienna. For one hundred years, from the Congress of Vienna to World War I, the Western world experienced no general war; and only during the seventeen years from 1854 to 1871 did major world powers fight one another. Yet the distinguishing feature of the periods 1648–1792 and 1815–1914 is not the low incidence of warfare but the relative moderation of warfare compared to the belligerency in other periods, notably the Religious Wars in the sixteenth and seventeenth centuries and our own period of total war in the twentieth century. To be sure, even in the eighteenth century, during which warfare was generally conducted under greater constraints than in any other period of modern Western civilization, armed conflict now and then reached extremities. Some of the dynastic wars of Louis XIV, which did not end until the Peace of Utrecht in 1714–15, were as savage and devastating as the struggles in the Germanies during the Religious Wars. The pitched battles of the eighteenth century, though not so frequent as in previous centuries, were exceedingly bloody. The three partitions of Poland were virtually unlimited wars from Poland's standpoint. On the whole, however, eighteenth-century warfare was a formal, mechanical, almost decorous operation.

The tactics of war were like the tactics of chess. The ultimate goal was the capture of a fortress or a town; but the game was often decided, almost bloodlessly, by a skilful maneuver into a superior position. To surrender a fortress with honor, after a minimum of destruction and in accordance with certain conventional formalities, was a highly developed art. Thus Louis XIV's chief engineer, Vauban, whose methods of siegecraft became the model for eighteenth-century warfare, prescribed the rules of capitulation in the following manner: "The governor of a besieged place, having no more terrain in which to retrench himself, and having destroyed the retrenchments which he will be forced to abandon, may capitulate with honor." And he concluded, "Thus our attacks reach their end by the shortest, the most reasonable, and the least bloody ways that can be used."[1] The measure of military effectiveness was not the maximum destruction of the opposing forces. Precision was more valuable than sheer force. Ingenuity was more prized than zeal. Accordingly, pitched battles were rare and indecisive. Thus the great French general Maurice Comte de Saxe, despite his impatience with some of the formalities of warfare in his time, expressed a typical preference for maneuver over direct assault: "I do not favor pitched battles, especially at the beginning of a war, and I am convinced that a skilful general could make war all his life without being forced into one." He explained that he did not mean that the enemy should not be attacked when the opportunity occurred. "But I do mean that war can be made without leaving anything to chance. And this is the highest point of perfection and skill in a general."[2]

Eighteenth-century warfare was conducted so as to interfere with the lives of the civilian population—and especially the merchants—as little as possible and so as to conserve and protect the soldiery as much as possible. Thus the burning and sacking of villages and farms, so common during the Religious Wars, became rare in the eighteenth century. Moreover, military operations were confined to half the calendar year in order to avoid the rigors of winter.

The restrictions which all these methods of warfare imposed upon military efficiency were severe indeed. Yet they were well adapted to the limited purposes for which they were employed. And perhaps most important of all, by affording the civilian population an almost unique freedom from the devastation of war, they gave maximum scope to the peaceful pursuits which were the real measure of man's progress in this era.

The limited wars of the nineteenth century were a far cry from the stilted contests of the eighteenth. By this time the sheer physical potentialities of destruction had ended forever the cumbersome tactics of maneuver and position extolled by De Saxe's contemporaries. Nevertheless, in their extent and duration and their immediate impact upon the material, social, and economic foundations of society these wars were significantly restricted in comparison to the French Revolutionary and the Napoleonic Wars that preceded them. The Crimean War (1853–56), the Austro-Sardinian War (1859), the war of Prussia and Austria against Denmark (1864), the Austro-Prussian War (1866), the Franco-Prussian War (1870–71), the Russo-Turkish War (1877), the Spanish-American

War (1898), the Russo-Japanese War (1904–1905), the Boer War (1899–1902), and the Balkan Wars (1912–13)—all these except the last involved major European powers; yet they were all relatively short and local contests (though the Spanish-American War was fought at widely distant points), which caused little disruption of society and which were settled by an accommodation of limited objectives. Only one war in this period equaled the Napoleonic Wars in its physical dimensions and the magnitude of the objectives at stake, and that was the American Civil War (1861–65), which was fought outside the main stream of world politics.

Thus both in their objectives and their physical characteristics the wars of 1648–1792 and 1815–1914 were predominantly limited wars. There were important social, economic, and cultural or moral factors that help account for this limitation, but primarily limited warfare was a reflection of the ends of war and the means available to achieve those ends. Yet neither the chosen ends nor the available means is a self-sufficient explanation; the interaction between the two is most significant.

Certainly, the wars of the eighteenth century were limited, in large part, because the means available for fighting them were so deficient and ineffective. With the disappearance of the pike, armies adapted their operations to the rudimentary instruments of firepower. The ponderous, short-range siege artillery was relatively impotent against heavy fortifications. The large-caliber, smoothbore musket was slow to fire, scarcely lethal beyond two hundred yards, and wildly inaccurate beyond fifty yards. These technical deficiencies forced the infantry to mass in tight formations, maneuver into position, and then fire a volley or two in unison in order to maximize the effect of firepower. Moreover, eighteenth-century armies were extremely expensive in relation to the limited economic resources and manpower that states could draw upon.[3] This situation reinforced the utility of tactics that avoided bloody pitched battles as much as possible, while it severely limited the weight of numbers and firepower that could be committed to a battle and the length of time a battle could be sustained. Accordingly, the whole training and tactics of armies were tailored to the requirements of a warfare of rigid maneuver and position, which precluded the kind of long-range movements, destructive pursuit, and rapid exploitation that characterized the wars of vastly increased scale and intensity in the nineteenth century.

Even in the nineteenth century the sheer physical limits upon the military potential of states minimized the scale and intensity of war. In the Crimean War the monumental incompetence of the belligerents reduced operations to a series of blunders, but one suspects that even incompetence might not have barred large-scale war—perhaps a general European war—if the belligerents could have drawn on the resources and weapons available to nations in 1914. And one wonders whether the Russo-Japanese War would have remained so limited if the combatants, rather than being forced to discontinue operations because of mutual exhaustion, had possessed the means of achieving the ambitious ends their general staffs dreamed of.

In any case, the inherent economic and technological limits to war largely disappeared between the Congress of Vienna and World War I even though the resulting military potential was not fully exploited, and this development underlay the advent of total war. It was in this period that the Industrial Revolution swept the Continent. The multiplication of goods provided nations with vast resources for war which strategists of the eighteenth century could not have imagined. It provided quantities of fuel, metal, and rapid transportation, the lack of which had previously impeded the effective use of the inventions of war. At the same time, the second half of the nineteenth century was a period of significant advances in military technology—notably the perfection of the breech-loading rifle and the percussion cartridge, the invention of a practical machine gun, and the development of wrought-iron, breech-loading, rifled artillery, with greatly extended range, rate of fire, and mobility. These technological advances, combined with the new financial and material resources and the new means of transportation and communication, created unprecedented potentialities of massive destruction. Once these potentialities became apparent to nations, it was a foregone conclusion that they would be utilized in the construction of more formidable military machines; and once they were incorporated into military plans and establishments, it was inconceivable that they would not be used when the occasion arose. The first occasion was the first total war: World War I.

Yet the existence or absence of limited warfare in any period of history cannot be entirely explained as a product of changing technology aside from the ends for which nations have fought. Thus the difference between the restricted contests of the eighteenth century and the widespread, almost continuous marauding and carnage that dominated the Religious Wars of the sixteenth and seventeenth centuries cannot be explained by material causes alone; for the technology of the eighteenth century would have been no less capable of sustaining wars of devastation had men been driven to expend their resources as lavishly and fruitlessly. Nor can the extensive and massive struggles of the French Revolutionary and Napoleonic Wars, as distinguished from the continental wars of the eighteenth century, be attributed merely to advances in military technology. Despite some tactical innovations and the development of mobile cavalry in the last part of the eighteenth century, the backbone of land warfare remained the short-range, flintlock musket and the close-ordered, disciplined infantry battalion. One may point to the genius of Carnot and Napoleon, who utilized novel tactics of mobility and concentration to achieve battles of a new scale and intensity; but these tactics cannot be understood apart from mass conscription and mass enthusiasm, which were in turn a product of novel political and ideological goals.

Historically, there has been no greater stimulus to unlimited war than the injection of highly charged ideological and emotional issues into hostilities, for these kinds of issues incite and sanction an exercise of force to the utmost physical limits for ends which cannot readily be compromised. The Religious Wars were in this sense unlimited. They were, primarily, the product of the religious passions of the Reformation. To be sure, the struggle between opposing faiths mingled with the conflict of dynastic ambitions, especially during the Thirty Years' War (1618–48); and religious strife was sustained, in part, by the opposition of monarchs to the fiscal policies and the authority of the Pope, by the struggle of the aristocracy against the growing power of the monarchs, and by the personal and political rivalries among the kings themselves. But the great religious schism of the age—the struggle for allegiance between Catholics and Protestants and among Protestants themselves—gave the wars of the sixteenth and seventeenth centuries the character of one continuous civil war extending throughout the Western world, dividing nations, cities, villages, and families, and perpetuating a rampant strife which but for this profound schism might well have been moderated and settled far short of the point of utter exhaustion. The call to unlimited war echoes in Martin Luther's appeal to his friend Spalatin: "I implore you, if you rightly understand the gospel, do not imagine that its cause can be furthered without tumult, distress, and uproar. . . . The word of God is a sword, is warfare, is destruction, is wrath, is spoiling, is an adder's tongue, and as Amos says, like the lion on the foot-path and the bear in the forest."[4]

The extremities of the Religious Wars were sometimes the direct re-sult of religious fanaticism, as in the case of the massacre of Calvinists on Saint Bartholomew's Day. But, for the greater part, they were a by-product of religious animosities and the direct consequence of the con-tinual roving of an undisciplined soldiery and camp followers forced to feed and clothe themselves at the expense of the local inhabitants. The resulting butchery and plunder and the general disruption of society were most devastating in the Germanies.[5] For years on end noncombatants were regularly tortured and massacred, their property looted and burned. Crops were laid waste. Cities were besieged. Some towns lost half their population; some villages were completely annihilated. Large numbers of peasants were forced to migrate. That these wars did not produce still greater havoc can be attributed to purely technological limitations and to economic deficiencies (the shortage and high price of metals; the diffi-culty of raising money; the simple, largely subsistence economy of the countryside). One can well imagine their vast scale if the religious zealots and ambitious kings had had access to the weapons, the communications and transportation facilities, and the capital and industrial resources of the late nineteenth century. Yet, one can infer from the extent of devasta-tion wrought by the relatively limited military means available that the dimensions and impact of warfare are as much a product of will as of matter. All in all, the Religious Wars were a somber illustration of a re-current phenomenon. Ideological differences, when submitted to the judgment of the sword, tend to produce unlimited violence; unlimited ends lead to unlimited force.

The wars of the French Revolution and Napoleon, like the Religious Wars, manifested a distinct dynamism, springing from radical moral and emotional issues that militated against the careful political limitation of warfare. It was no accident that the French Revolution brought Europe's greatest period of limited war to a close; for in shattering the old regime the Revolution also shattered many of the old restraints upon war by injecting both nationalistic and universal moral goals into the relations among states. The democratization of society destroyed the social and political system in which a homogeneous ruling group conducted war and politics merely for the limited, prosaic objectives that could be justified by "reasons of state." By giving the masses a share of control in the affairs of state and erecting the popular will as the touchstone of state policy, democracy enabled the common people to identify their personal welfare with the welfare of their country. Henceforth, it became difficult for even the most autocratic governments to ignore the opinions and sentiments of the people; and this fact was bound to inhibit the flexible accommodation of power among nations on the basis of pure expediency, by which the old regime had mitigated and adjusted conflicting interests among states. Moreover, once it was demonstrated that popular sentiment could be recruited for state purposes, governments came to realize that they possessed a vast untapped source of military power that could be mobilized by stirring appeals to national pride and universal moral principles. The democratization of war reached its culmination in the huge conscripted armies at the close of the century, which placed warfare on a scale that had been inconceivable before the Revolution. Despite their novel scale and intensity, the wars of France between 1792 and 1815 were still restrained by eighteenth-century technology; but in their popular identification of national self-interest with a quasi-religious ideology, they were true precursors of the total wars of our own century.

The dynamism of these wars reflected the emergence of a national crusade. It is doubtful whether the French armies that fought the Revolutionary Wars undertook them, initially, for the sake of extending the blessings of Liberty, Equality, and Fraternity to the rest of Europe; yet in the pressure of war Frenchmen did come to conceive of their country as the exclusive embodiment of these principles, and France's external affairs tended to assume the same passionate ideological overtones that characterized the domestic upheaval. As the mass of the populace mobilized for the war effort and the French armies first tasted victory, the simple objective of national self-defense was supplanted by more ambitious goals—first the "natural frontiers" and, under Napoleon's leadership, hegemony in Europe—while patriotic enthusiasm was joined with a missionary zeal to spread the blessings of the Revolution to other lands. And so it was only a short step from the Constituent Assembly's solemn declaration of May 22, 1790, renouncing all wars of conquest and swearing that French forces would never be used against the liberties of any people, to the Convention's decree of November 17, 1792, pledging *fraternité et secours* to all peoples who wished to regain their natural liberties.

The First Coalition, which fought France, had no intention of undertaking an armed counterrevolution; and even when the Declaration of Pillnitz provoked France to rise up in arms, France's adversaries anticipated a brief, orthodox contest that would end in an equitable division of the spoils. Instead, they ran headlong into a mass crusade that eventually swept across all Europe. The crusading spirit, combined with the military necessity of countering the quality of Allied troops with the quantity of Revolutionary armies, led the French government to take a momentous step that was to transform the scale and intensity of war in succeeding generations: It instituted universal military conscription and raised a huge citizen army, proclaiming the principle of the "nation in arms." But the government did not stop there. It added to military conscription the conscription of workmen for the armories. Through a concerted propaganda campaign it encouraged voluntary co-operation to match official decrees. It persuaded scientists to contribute their skills to industry; it urged ordinary citizens to save and collect all kinds of goods for the common effort. In their massive mobilization for war Frenchmen found, if not the elusive Equality of the Revolutionary slogan, a mystic equality of sacrifice for *la patrie*. This spirit of sacrifice is embodied in the famous proclamation of the *levée en masse*, which the Committee of Public Safety announced during a desperate stage of the war in August, 1793: "Young men will go forth to battle; married men will forge weapons and transport munitions; women will make tents and clothing and serve in hospitals; children will make lint from old linen; and old men will be brought to the public squares to arouse the courage of the soldiers, while preaching the unity of the Republic and hatred of kings."

Thus the radical motives and goals of this French crusade, by making war a mass effort instead of the sport of kings and nobles, the business of mercenaries, and the last resort of social outcasts, ended by revolutionizing the organization of war. Moreover, by inspiring citizen armies with a ferocity and initiative that shocked the practitioners of eighteenth-century warfare, they made possible and necessary the tactics of camouflage, mobility, and destructive pursuit that overwhelmed opposing armies drilled for the older kind of war. Napoleon took the new mass enthusiasm, the huge conscripted army, and the novel tactics developed by Carnot and added to them the genius of a bold field commander and the inordinate ambition of a military conqueror. In the end his reckless military adventures brought his defeat at the hands of a coalition united by fear that no European state could be secure until the menace of France had been extirpated from Europe and the balance of power restored. But Napoleon left an indelible mark on warfare. He had given his victims and eventual conquerors an example of the great military utility of those radical sources of military power unleashed by the Revolution, and he had aroused in them something of the same spirit of nationalism that sustained his own armies.

In the period of limited war that followed the defeat of Napoleon one can again trace the interaction between the means and ends of war. As the limitation of ends facilitates the restriction of war's physical dimensions and its political and social consequences, the increase of the means available, coupled with the influence of the Napoleonic heritage, sets the stage for unlimited war.

During the restoration of the European political system and the long period of peace among the major powers from 1815 to 1854 the example of Napoleon's military power was largely ignored. Military thinking seemed to revert to the pre-Revolutionary era, while statesmen once more became absorbed in operating the balance-of-power system. Only in one state did the democratization of war exert an immediate impact. Ironically, this was Prussia, the most militaristic state in Europe, where a group of patriots, stung by Prussia's defeats at Jena and Auerstädt and impressed by the power of popular enthusiasm, undertook basic social and political as well as military reforms in order to harness to Prussia's national ambitions the military energy exploited so successfully by Napoleon. "The chief idea," as Stein explained, "was to arouse a moral, religious and patriotic spirit in the nation, to instil into it again courage, confidence, readiness for every sacrifice in behalf of independence from foreigners and for the national honor, and to seize the first favorable opportunity to begin the bloody and hazardous struggle."[6]

In the period of reaction after 1819 the hopes for constitutional reform were largely frustrated, but one major military reform remained in force: the system of universal military service, which Prussia had adopted in 1814. Of all the measures in their entire program, the Prussian reformers attached the greatest value to this one; for, as Stein wrote, "Through this it will be possible to inculcate a proud warlike national character, to wage wearying distant wars of conquest and to withstand an overwhelming enemy attack with a national war."[7] When Prussia won quick and overwhelming victories in her wars with Austria in 1866 and with France in

1870–71, other European statesmen reached the same conclusion as Stein; and soon Austria (in 1868), France (in 1872), Russia (in 1874), and Italy (in 1875) had imitated Prussia's system.

Nevertheless, despite the organization of military potential on a much larger scale, warfare remained limited throughout the nineteenth century. Again, a large part of the explanation lies in the nature of the objectives for which states fought, especially the objectives of Bismarck, who directed the course of the most powerful state on the Continent. Whatever one may think of Bismarck's ethics, one must concede that he was shrewd, cautious, and moderate in international politics and the conduct of war. He played the game of war and politics in the spirit of the aristocratic school of diplomacy—the school of Metternich, Castlereagh, Talleyrand, and the eighteenth-century statesmen before them—which regarded diplomacy as the science of adjusting calculable magnitudes of power for the self-sufficient purposes of state interest. If he lacked their sense of a transcendent European community united by common moral premises, he nevertheless displayed something of their prudence and circumspection, which was born of a recognition of the interdependence of politics and force. Thus he repeatedly rejected the military advice of his general staff when that advice would have pressed war beyond the limits of political expediency, and he repeatedly insisted upon the necessity of quick and moderate settlements. Referring to Prussia's triumph over Austria in 1866, Bismarck wrote, "In positions such as ours was then, it is a political maxim after a victory not to inquire how much you can squeeze out of your opponent, but only to consider what is politically necessary."[8]

Bismarck's sense of the political limits of force was perhaps the major contribution to the limitation of warfare in his time. Yet his conduct of the Franco-Prussian War made unlimited war more likely in the future. The Franco-Prussian War revealed that subtle interaction between the military means and the motives and objectives of war which had been undermining the eighteenth-century restraints. It revealed two factors, in particular, that were making the limitation of war increasingly difficult: the psychological impact of mass sentiment responding to moral and nationalistic issues, and the physical impact of modern military organization and tactics.

Bismarck's objective in the Franco-Prussian War was to complete the unification of Germany and acquire a limited amount of new territory. He had no desire to annihilate France or to destroy the balance-of-power system. According to standards of *Realpolitik* common to the eighteenth century, he decided to annex Alsace against the will of the populace and to accede to Moltke's demand for the French-speaking parts of Lorraine. His chief purpose was the simple one of denying France a gateway for attacking the south German districts beyond the Rhine. But his mistake was in not appreciating the intensity of modern French nationalism. Whereas a strategic adjustment of this kind would probably have caused little disturbance to the political system in the eighteenth century, in 1871 it had tremendous repercussions throughout Europe. Bismarck had ridden roughshod over the national sensibilities of all Frenchmen. The loss of Alsace and Lorraine, added to the humiliation of defeat, made *revanche* a national slogan that was to remain a rankling source of tension in international relations until the cry was answered in the Treaty of Versailles in 1919.

The Franco-Prussian War and the Peace of Frankfurt that followed held no more legitimacy outside France than within. After all, Prussia had unilaterally violated the Franco-German frontier, one of the cornerstones of the political system which the European powers had established at the Congress of Vienna. Moreover, the very effectiveness of Prussia's military campaign, overwhelming the paramount power on the Continent in little more than a month, struck the statesmen of Europe as an alarming threat to the whole balance-of-power system. The new scale of armed force cast doubts upon the validity of a system of limited political objectives which purported to establish mutual restraints upon the exercise of national power.

In England Disraeli sensed the magnitude of the threat to the balance of power. Vigorously criticizing Gladstone's failure to intervene in order to preserve the European balance, he warned:

It is no common war. . . . This war represents the German Revolution, a greater political event than the French Revolution of the last century. . . . Not a single principle in the management of our foreign affairs, accepted by all statesmen for guidance up to six months ago, any longer exists. There is not a diplomatic tradition which has not been swept away. You have a new world, new influences at work, new and unknown objects and dangers with which to cope. . . . We used to have discussions about the balance of power . . . ; but what has really come to pass in Europe? The balance of power has been entirely destroyed, and the country which suffers the most is England.[9]

As Disraeli suggested, with some hyperbole, the Franco-Prussian War not only struck a blow at the balance of power; it forebode a fundamental change in the whole conception of war and politics. It recalled to the leaders of Europe a lesson they had almost forgotten since the defeat of Napoleon: that military power, organized on a mass basis and supported by the whole resources of the nation, not only could gain small pieces of territory as a basis for negotiation but could win a lightning-like victory and impose a decisive peace upon an enemy whose power of resistance had been destroyed.

No nation could feel secure knowing that other nations might accomplish what Prussia accomplished and much more. Therefore, every great nation on the Continent set out to secure Prussia's kind of military potential by the same means that Prussia had secured hers: universal military service. And when nations adopted universal military service, they also adopted the Napoleonic conception of warfare, the conception of war as a romantic adventure of entire nations rather than as a chess game among professionals.

One who was especially impressed by the lesson of the Franco-Prussian War was General Ferdinand Foch of France, who in 1918 became the commander of the Allied armies in the first war to fulfil the awful potentialities of the nation-in-arms system. In his lectures at the French War College at the turn of the century Foch pointed to Prussia's adoption of compulsory military service and declared, "It is because we failed to recognize this total change in our neighbors and the consequences it must bring that we who had created national warfare became its victims. . . . It is because all of Europe has returned to this theory of armed nations that we must again take up today the absolute conception of war as it exists today."[10] In the same vein, Foch opened his book *The Conduct of War* (1903) with this proclamation:

> The old systems of war, seeking to spare the armed forces, tried to achieve their objectives by stratagems, threat, negotiation, maneuver, partial actions, occupation of hostile territory and the capture of fortified places. Since Napoleon, war is conducted without regard to wastage; it recognizes only one argument: force. Not until the enemy has been crushed in battle and annihilated by pursuit is there any question of parley with him.[11]

In short, Foch was urging nothing less than the abandonment of limited warfare and a return to the "absolute" wars that Napoleon had exemplified and Clausewitz had described. In this kind of war popular sentiment and ideology would supply the driving force, not the meticulous political designs of the professionals. For victory, Foch asserted, is pre-eminently a product of the will to victory, of the "moral superiority of the victors" and the "moral depression of the vanquished"; and since the moral factor is decisive, it follows that soldiers must fight because they are inspired, because they feel the whole spirit of the nation in their hearts. Therefore, France must prepare to fight wars that "absorb into the struggle all the resources of the nation" and that are "aimed not at dynastic interests, not at the conquest or possession of a province, but at the defense or spread of philosophical ideas first, of principles of independence, unity, immaterial advantages of various kinds afterwards."[12]

One reads in Foch's words the antithesis of limited warfare—indeed, of the very idea of war as a rational instrument of national policy—for they exemplify an irrational fascination with the sheer destructive potentialities of war as an instrument of ideology. In Foch's conception of war one sees the fatal reciprocity between extreme means and extreme ends that was to drive war beyond the bounds of rational control and prediction in the period of total war that opened in 1914.

Already, by the time Foch advocated the return to the Napoleonic conception of war, the physical potentialities of armed force had reached such extremities that it was no longer sufficient to limit the objectives of war in order to confine war to dimensions compatible with the rational and effective control of force. By this time another condition of limitation, much less important before the Industrial Revolution, had become almost essential for major powers to observe. This condition was that belligerents deliberately forego the use of certain military means within their capacity, in a calculated effort to limit the scale and intensity of destruction. Yet if it was no longer *sufficient* for the limitation of war that major powers limit the objectives of war, it had become *necessary* in proportion as the military potential of nations had weakened or destroyed all other restraints upon war.

The Environment of War

Theoretically, the observance of these two prerequisites of limitation has always been a matter of free choice for the belligerents. However, in practice, their observance has been greatly helped or hindered by the existence or absence of certain non-material characteristics of the international environment.

The limitation of the means and ends of war implies that the belligerents recognize elementary rules of mutual self-restraint. In the absence of such rules, the bounds of national egoism must be uncertain and the conduct of states unpredictable; and, consequently, states will be afraid to jeopardize their vital interests by practicing self-restraint unilaterally unless they enjoy an overwhelming preponderance of power. However, rules of mutual self-restraint cannot be established merely by an effort of will, as one might determine the rules for a game of sport. Where mutual restraints have operated between belligerents, they have evolved from the practice of war and politics in a congenial political, social, and moral environment. In general, this environment has been characterized by three primary conditions, aside from the inherent physical limits of the military means available: (a) a political system based upon the mutual self-interest of all nations in limiting their pursuit of power; (b) the existence of habitual personal and group loyalties transcending state boundaries; and (c) general agreement among states as to the rational and moral validity, that is, the legitimacy, of the rules by which they regulate their conduct in politics and war. The existence of these three conditions has enhanced the effectiveness of legal restraints upon war; but in the absence of political, social, and moral restraints, legal restraints have been ineffective.

Politically, the environment of limited war has been characterized by a mobile, flexible balance-of-power system operated by a continual, discreet, sensitive diplomacy. This system has worked most effectively when it has included a number of states of roughly comparable strength, when political relations have been free of rigid attachments and "permanent" coalitions, when there have been strong neutrals to play the role of balancers, and when major powers could exchange colonial and overseas areas without upsetting the balance at home. Insofar as the limitation of war depended upon supranational loyalties, these loyalties have been rooted in bonds of class, family, and culture among the governing and fighting elite. As for the moral environment, mutual restraints upon war have been most effective when they have arisen from a genuine moral consensus among the elite, based upon a shared body of philosophical principles and intellectual concepts conferring an aura of legitimacy upon the prevailing political system and the conventions of war. In the eighteenth century all these political, social, and moral conditions combined to sustain an elementary system of self-restraint in war and politics, which all states conceived to be in their interests to preserve. But this system was steadily undermined under the influence of democracy, nationalism, and the Industrial Revolution during the nineteenth century.

The limited objectives of eighteenth-century warfare sprang directly from the prevailing international political system, the balance of power. In accordance with this system a dozen or so major states of roughly equal power continually combined, separated, and combined again in ever-shifting alliances and alignments in order to prevent any single power or coalition from gaining preponderance and thereby threatening the common interest of all powers in maintaining a stable international order. The system expressed a consensus among sovereigns that the maintenance of the international order, like the orderly processes of nature, which so intrigued that age, depended upon an equilibrium of its parts, which might be upset by any inordinate ambitions or erratic movements among states. Its central purpose was the establishment of certain rules of the game by which all states might pursue their ends without jeopardizing the political independence of any state.

The management of this system was far from being the precise, almost mathematically exact science implied in the mechanistic images by which its contemporary adherents customarily described the balance of power. But the important thing is that the system put a premium upon rationality, circumspection, and moderation. These prudent qualities are admirably expressed in Lord Bolingbroke's common-sense prescription for the balancing process:

The scales of the balance of power will never be exactly poised, nor in the precise point of equality either discernible or necessary to be discerned. It is sufficient in this, as in other human affairs, that the deviation be not too great. Some there will always be. A constant attention to these deviations is therefore necessary. When they are little, their increase may be easily prevented by early care and the precautions that good policy suggests. But when they become great for want of this care and these precautions, or by the force of unforeseen events, more vigor is to be exerted, and greater efforts to be made. But even in such cases, much reflection is necessary on all the circumstances that form the conjuncture; lest, by attacking with ill success, the deviation be confirmed, and the power that is deemed already exorbitant become more so; and lest, by attacking with good success, whilst one scale is pillaged, too much weight of power be thrown into the other. In such cases, he who has considered, in the histories of former ages, the strange revolutions that time produces, and the perpetual flux and reflux of public as well as private fortunes, of kingdoms and states as well as of those who govern or are governed in them, will incline to think, that if the scales can be brought back by a war, nearly, though not exactly, to the point they were at before this great deviation from it, the rest may be left to accidents, and to the use that good policy is able to make of them.[13]

The balance-of-power system did not prevent war. It would have been miraculous if three hundred or more sovereign states, large and small, had been able to adjust their interests within a delicate equilibrium by peaceful means alone. However, it did moderate the nature of the issues that led to war and hence the objectives for which wars were fought. For in the eighteenth century, war was truly a continuation of political intercourse. The objectives for which states fought were substantially the same as the ones for which they resorted to war in the first place, and diplomacy kept the political aspects of the struggle foremost throughout hostilities. Thus even in the midst of war, states remained alert to their interest in preserving the balance of power. If they pushed war too far, they would be checked by a counteralliance. If they upset the balance of power entirely, they might lose the protection that it could afford them in some future war. If they destroyed the balance-wheel of the struggle for power, they might precipitate the kind of unrestrained dynastic conflict that had afflicted the Thirty Years' War.

The limited wars of the eighteenth century were also a reflection of the social composition of the armies, which, in turn, reflected the structure of society at large. The officers of dynastic armies were the hereditary nobility and, with the increasing sale of offices, the well-to-do from the growing middle class, who emulated the nobility's standards of conduct. These officers, like the monarchs and diplomats of the age, felt a corporate identity that transcended their allegiance to particular states. In fact, a commanding general might with impunity change his allegiance as different sovereigns competed for his services. For officers were not expected to fight from passionate loyalties to a regime, a nation, or an ideology. They fought because it was their profession, and they fought for the sake of their personal honor and prestige. Consequently, they were free of the collective hatred of the enemy, which had animated the leaders of the Religious Wars and which was to characterize the national and ideological wars in the twentieth century. On the contrary, they were generally on good terms with the officers of opposing armies, whom they sometimes joined in feasts and entertainment, even in the midst of sieges. The social habits and preferences of the officer class imposed limitations upon war in more direct fashion. These gentlemen were conscious of some ordinary personal comforts to be gained by not pushing warfare to extremes. They liked their heroism leavened with a little luxury. And this entailed, among other things, huge, cumbersome baggage trains that were patently incompatible with mobility of operations or with stratagems of surprise.

As for the mass of the soldiery, it was composed of the dregs of society, the non-productive elements—the unemployed, the criminals, the debtors, and the vagrants—so as not to interfere with agricultural and industrial production. For mercantilist statesmen were anxious to have the maximum number of skilled artisans to meet the demands of an expanding economy, and they believed that the state could not afford to squander the better elements of society in purely destructive enterprises. The resulting social composition of the armies acted as an important restraint upon the tactics, the scale of battles, and the impact of war upon society. Soldiers were recruited with considerable difficulty and, commonly, by force and trickery. They were a heterogeneous lot, hired from many states and principalities other than the one for which they happened to be fighting. They fought because they needed the money or because they were forced to fight, not because they wanted to fight or because they loved their country. Naturally, under these conditions, the morale and reliability of eighteenth-century armies were abysmally low. Large portions of armies commonly deserted. Soldiers passed from one army to another with a facility that became inconceivable after the French Revolution. Therefore, in order to minimize desertions, as well as to spare civilians from plunder and enable them to tend to productive enterprises, armies were discouraged from roving the countryside. Instead of being forced to live off the land, they were supplied by a system of state magazines.

Moreover, since armies were small, expensive, and unreliable, generals did not dare permit them to engage in destructive pursuit of the enemy, in night battles, forest skirmishes, and other maneuvers that would facilitate escape. In order to retain the troops and to get them to fight, military leaders were compelled to substitute rigorous discipline for a lack of fighting spirit. Consistent with Frederick the Great's maxim that the common soldier should "be more afraid of his own officers than of the dangers to which he is exposed," eighteenth-century battle formations commonly included lines of officers who were prepared to shoot recalcitrants. For social reasons as well as military, individual initiative was discouraged. Armies were trained to fire volleys in unison, like a machine, at the command of their officers. Through years of meticulous drill, in accordance with the system introduced by Jean Martinet under the regime of Louis XIV, they were trained to perform on the battlefield the maneuvers they had rehearsed on the parade ground—and with no more concession to concealment. Since these military techniques were unsuited for anything more daring than highly stylized wars of position, tactics were, in effect, tailored to fit the social and political conditions of the time. Limited war was the natural by-product.

The moral environment of the eighteenth century was a more subtle and intangible, but no less important, influence upon warfare. It contributed to the limitation of war in two ways: it permitted the dissociation of the objectives of war from universal moral issues, and it sustained positive ethical and legal restraints upon war.

The eighteenth century was weary with ideological strife. Statesmen were more interested in expanding commerce and industry than in extending the true faith. They were content to pursue limited objectives that could be justified by "reason of state," as if by tacit agreement they had recognized that their mutual self-interest lay in eschewing more ambitious goals. But for a certain indifference to universal moral issues in the conduct of war and politics, it is hard to imagine the successful management of such a highly flexible system of *Realpolitik* as the balance of power. International relations—or, more accurately, interstate relations—were, indeed, pitched on a low moral plane. The fine mechanism of the balance was copiously oiled with intrigue, deceit, and double-dealing. In the constant reshuffling of alliances and the unceasing scramble for territorial aggrandizement treaties were lightly broken. Thus in the War of the Austrian Succession the powers who had promised, in return for considerable concessions, to respect the Pragmatic Sanction, by which Charles VI had conferred the Hapsburg dominions upon Maria Theresa, quickly violated their promises after Charles's death in order to join in a compact of spoliation. Moreover, although the balance of power gave the major powers a remarkable sense of security, it proved to be much less protection for weak states, when the stronger states could divide up the spoils equitably or compensate each other at the expense of other states. The partition of Poland in 1772, 1793, and 1795 was a striking demonstration of this fact.

However, it is easy to exaggerate the immorality of eighteenth-century politics. Actually, the partition of Poland was an exception, not the rule. It profoundly shocked the Western world precisely because it showed that the balance of power, which was designed to protect the political independence of all states, could not prevent the destruction of even a large state. Moreover, the moral significance of such predatory behavior was not so serious as it seems from our contemporary perspective. For the relations among states were largely the concern of the ruling class. The vast majority of the people were unaffected. They went on living about the same way regardless of changes of regime and shifts of alliance. Since they lacked that intense personal identification with their state that developed in the nineteenth century, they were not morally or emotionally involved in the diplomatic fortunes of their rulers.

In the cosmopolitan atmosphere in which the aristocracy circulated, patriotic feeling was so slight an influence upon external affairs that it was not unusual or unacceptable for diplomats, like generals, to transfer their state allegiance in response to more favorable opportunities of employment. Bribery of diplomats was taken for granted; governments set aside special funds for the purpose. In a sense, it was the very sordidness of diplomacy that enabled the balance of power, with its accompanying restraints, to operate as smoothly as it did. Despite the unedifying moral tone of eighteenth-century diplomacy, it at least had the virtue of militating against the passionate extremities of war that have plagued our own era, when nations are so jealous of universal moral pretensions and so fiercely proud of their uniqueness.

However, we should not stretch the irony of history too far by concluding that the limitation of war resulted from an exclusive preoccupation with narrow, selfish state concerns. These selfish concerns were not self-limiting. They might well have become unlimited had they not been subject to certain positive moral restraints among the ruling class. Except within the framework of a moral consensus it is hard to conceive of the statesmen of that age sustaining the emotional and intellectual discipline that kept the intricate balance of power in operation.

For convenience, this consensus can be summed up as the Enlightenment. The term covers a considerable diversity of philosophical principles and presuppositions about the nature of man and society; but, without belaboring its intellectual content, one can perhaps convey the essence of the Enlightenment by noting certain characteristic qualities of mind it encouraged: a desire for order, method, and rationality in human relations; a humanitarian distaste for cruelty and suffering, coupled with a benevolent impulse to improve man's condition of living; a confidence in man's ability to achieve happiness on earth through the application of science to his material and social environment; tolerance, not unmixed with skepticism, toward divergent moral and religious convictions; a belief in the coincidence of reason and morality, in a harmony of interests; and a steadfast dedication to moderation in all things.

The moderating influence of the Enlightenment shines most splendidly in two works that enjoyed widespread popularity in the eighteenth century.

The Dutch jurist Hugo Grotius' *De Jure Belli et Pacis*, written at the height of the Religious Wars and first published in 1625, and the Swiss diplomat Emeric Vattel's *Droit des Gens*, published in 1758, both formulated rules of conduct intended to render warfare moderate and humane. Significantly, the authors based these rules not on divine law but on natural law or the dictates of right reason, the validity of which was independent of religious sanction. They appealed for the observance of these rules on grounds of the enlightened self-interest of states, repeatedly arguing that humanity, discretion, justice, leniency, and moderation toward the enemy would be repaid by the enemy's display of these same qualities toward one's own state and, incidentally, by great benefits to commerce and the economy. Thus they were careful to preserve the function of universal moral principles as a restraint upon violence and to guard against warfare becoming an instrument of ideology.

Underlying their conception of limited war there was an assumption, common to the Age of Enlightenment, that all men and all states have an equal interest in preserving a larger community, which is the political embodiment of a moral consensus and which transcends the particular political fragments that compose it. The English historian Edward Gibbon expressed this view when he wrote, with that blend of optimism and self-satisfaction so typical of the eighteenth-century gentleman:

> It is the duty of a patriot to prefer and promote the exclusive interest and glory of his native country; but a philosopher may be permitted to enlarge his views and to consider Europe as one great Republic whose various inhabitants have attained almost the same level of politeness and cultivation. The balance of power will continue to fluctuate, and the prosperity of our own or the neighboring kingdoms may be alternately exalted or depressed; but these partial events cannot essentially injure our general state of happiness, the system of arts and laws

and manners, which so advantageously distinguish, above the rest of mankind, the Europeans and their colonies.[14]

One should not suppose that the ideals of the Enlightenment coincided perfectly with the actual practice of politics and war among states. Not infrequently, the balance of power served as a handy rationalization for the most shameless acquisitive instincts. The image of a European Republic was scarcely an accurate description of the predatory political rivalries or of the great religious, social, and economic conflicts that actually divided Europe. Nevertheless, if one judges the efficacy of principles reasonably rather than by the standards of perfection, it seems fair to conclude that the ideals of the Enlightenment constituted a moral consensus without which the conflicts among states would have been more acute and the wars less moderate. At the very least, they reinforced among princes, generals, and diplomats a consciousness of kind, rooted in the close personal and family ties of the aristocracy—a sense of corporate identity apart from national identity, which enabled them to conduct the affairs of state somewhat in the spirit of members of the same sporting club.

These characteristics of the international environment help to explain the fact that warfare was, on the whole, a rational instrument in the hands of the cosmopolitan, autocratic, circumspect, and somewhat cynical monarchs of the century before the French Revolution. But if this fact must be explained so largely in terms of the political, social, and moral, not to mention the material, environment of the age, one must wonder what bearing the limited warfare of the eighteenth century has upon warfare in our own time.

Before the nineteenth century had passed, the democratization of society, so greatly accelerated by the French Revolution, had destroyed the social system that permitted the conduct of politics and war with substantial indifference to mass sentiment. By dissolving the bonds of culture, family, and class which had sustained the cosmopolitan restraints of the eighteenth century, it created a powerful source of dissension among states. For in the absence of these genuine bonds among the citizens of different states, each nation was inclined to interpret the dictates of morality and sentiment in any given conflict of interests in quite contradictory terms, while vehemently claiming exclusive virtue for itself.

Democracy and nationalism worked hand in hand undermining the restraints of the old regime. The Industrial Revolution uprooted the common man from his familiar patterns of existence; the spread of democracy dissolved his traditional loyalties and taught him that he was the master of his fate. Having been liberated from the old regime, the people recovered a sense of purpose and belonging by identifying themselves with a national entity, believed to possess distinct characteristics of exclusive virtue, and by projecting upon this vicarious personality the same emotions of pride, hatred, fear, and authority that individuals might feel in their personal relations—except that these collective passions were not restrained by the same humility or sense of responsibility. This psychological transformation, which is not without its precedents even in the fourteenth century, was tremendously accelerated by the surge of democracy that followed the French Revolution. In the course of the nineteenth century it proved profoundly corrosive of the moral consensus and the sense of a larger community, which had mitigated the struggle for power in the eighteenth.

Needless to say, this psychological transformation did not take place overnight. Even on the eve of World War I statesmen of nations about to become bitter antagonists could feel that they belonged to a moral and cultural community which, in some sense, transcended national loyalties. Moreover, the prevailing social and political ideologies of the age still clearly reflected their common heritage in the Enlightenment. It remained for the aftermath of that war to witness the burgeoning of Fascist and Communist ideologies that directly repudiated the Enlightenment. Yet even before the first total war unleashed the fury of nationalism and ideological fervor, the fragile restraints of a genuine moral consensus had for all practical purposes disappeared from the international environment of war.

To the extent that the non-material characteristics of the international environment of the nineteenth century contributed toward the limitation of war, one must ascribe that effect chiefly to the political system within which war and politics were conducted. Yet this system, too, was in a state of rapid deterioration by the eve of World War I. For a decade or two after the defeat of Napoleon the Quadruple Alliance succeeded in restoring something of the old international order. The chief instrument of this restoration was the Concert of Europe. The Concert—composed of Austria, Prussia, Russia, France, and Great Britain—acted jointly to maintain international "tranquillity" through the balance of power and internal "stability" through monarchical rule. It was auspiciously launched by a peace of reconciliation with France, designed to bring that country back into the society of nations, which the Revolution had disrupted. The Concert represented an attempt to expunge from international society the radical forces that had thrown all Europe into a cycle of insecurity, fear, and violence and to restore legitimacy to the exercise of state power. It was an attempt to make international politics predictable and controllable once more by reviving the traditional rules of the game.

However, as an attempt to halt and reverse the social and political processes released by the Revolution, the Concert was a distinct failure. Moreover, concerted political action broke down when it conflicted with the separate national interests of the Allies. The political system which the architects of the Congress of Vienna had envisioned turned out to be a stopgap device. It was not sufficiently in harmony with the social and cultural environment or sufficiently rooted in a moral consensus to survive. It ran counter to the most powerful moral and political forces of the age. The democratic revolutions of 1830 and 1848 and the German and Italian wars of unification in the second half of the century showed that, henceforth, no international order incompatible with basic democratic and nationalistic aspirations could be more than a holding action. Increasingly, the very governments pledged to preserve the legitimacy of monarchical rule found it expedient to support their external policies with appeals to popular sentiment, while they evoked stirring images of the national mission. In short, the world witnessed again the breakdown of a moral consensus and the emergence of new and conflicting allegiances. In the ensuing political and social turmoil international politics became more uncertain, nations grew more insecure, and statesmen became less willing to trust their affairs to prudence and mutual self-restraint. Even before the eruption of the armaments race at the turn of the century Europe was ripe for unlimited war.

And yet, despite the failure of the Concert of Europe, the Congress of Vienna did partly restore a balance-of-power system among the major powers, which succeeded in restraining any one of them or any combination from pushing war too far or aiming for too much in peace, for fear that the others would combine against it. And this was no idle fear. In the Crimean War and in the Congress of Berlin (1878) following the

Russo-Turkish War, a concert of powers openly enforced limitations upon the political spoils of war, to the disadvantage of Russia.

Until international politics crystallized into the pattern of the Triple Entente and the Triple Alliance after the turn of the century, there was sufficient "play" in the European system of alliances and alignments to enable it to operate with something of the flexibility of the eighteenth century. However, that the system operated as effectively as it did must be attributed less to the Congress of Vienna than to the diplomatic skill of Bismarck and the British statesmen. The British, with England in a position of unchallengeable security and power, played the role of balancer with moderation and wisdom. Bismarck, having transformed Germany into a powerful unified state through three wars in eight years, devoted the remaining twenty years of his tenure to shoring up the balance with such an intricate system of alliances that any radical alteration of it became too risky to make the effort worthwhile.

Yet before the nineteenth century had passed, there were growing signs that diplomacy, no matter how shrewd and circumspect, could not by itself preserve a stable international order in the absence of a broader system of social and moral restraints. Too much depended upon the chance configurations of power and the wit of statesmen, too little upon a common conception of mutual interest. The political system itself underwent changes that seriously weakened whatever restraints it had imposed upon national ambitions and the struggle for power.

The successful operation of the balance-of-power system in Europe during the last quarter of the nineteenth century had depended, in part, upon the distractions of empire-building outside Europe. Great Britain looked toward India and Africa and the development of her world trade; Russia looked toward central Asia and the Far East; France and Italy looked toward North Africa; and, eventually, Germany sought imperial prizes in Africa and the Far East. By diverting acquisitive instincts from Europe and providing a field for expansion and territorial compensations, nineteenth-century imperialism helped moderate the struggles for power within the European system. But by the end of the century most of the opportunities for colonial acquisition had been exploited, and conflicts outside Europe were threatening to ignite a general European war.

Even more disruptive of the European balance-of-power system was the rise of the great new industrial powers—Germany, the United States, and Japan; for this foretold the end of Britain's role as the balancer of the international political system. Furthermore, after Kaiser Wilhelm dropped Bismarck, in 1890, it soon became evident that Bismarck's system of alliances was too complicated for his successors to manage, even if they had had the inclination. His moderate policies were supplanted by rash ambitions of national aggrandizement. Increasingly, the Prussian General Staff became the arbiter of foreign policy. Whereas Bismarck's cardinal aim had been to keep France and Russia separate by diplomatic means, German policy under the influence of the general staff was subordinated to an inflexible military plan—the famous Schlieffen Plan—which was designed to fight an "inevitable" two-front war against France and Russia.

By the turn of the century the system of transitory alliances and alignments that Bismarck and the British had managed so skilfully was giving way to the more rigid system of "permanent" alliances dominated by two coalitions. Only men of extraordinary wisdom and moderation could have kept this concentration of power from exploding. European statesmen were not equal to the task. Many matched Bismarck's cynicism, but few possessed his shrewdness or his self-restraint. Lacking Bismarck's facility for coldly calculating the course of power within the real limits of political expediency, they were inclined to pitch their policies to the whims of popular sentiment. But popular sentiment had little patience with the careful weighing of power against commitments, the balancing of military means and political ends. Ironically, it was Bismarck's own inability to gauge the new force of popular sentiment that helped provoke the international tensions symbolized in the French slogan of *revanche*. By inciting France to war, Bismarck had unwittingly started a chain of events which, propelled by the patriotic fervor of Frenchmen, ended by inflicting one of the most serious blows to the balance of power in the entire period of limited war from 1815 to 1914.

And so it came about that, with the deterioration of all those political, social, and moral restraints that had previously facilitated the limitation of the ends and means of war, the twentieth century opened with an increasingly intense competition for military might, which rendered the limitation of war more and more dependent upon the scrupulous restriction of military means at a time when nations were less and less inclined to practice forbearance.

Chapter Five

THE ADVENT OF TOTAL WAR

The Eve of World War I

Despite the tremendous potentialities for unlimited war inherent in the international situation on the eve of World War I, the ominous developments of the preceding century had stirred no widespread apprehensions. On the contrary, there was a common assumption that wars were growing less frequent and more moderate. After all, there had been no general war for a century; and no nation, however bellicose, sought such a war; no nation, however ambitious, had unlimited aims. Besides, military leaders assumed that, if wars should occur, the nature of modern military organization and techniques would make them short, local armed conflicts, like Prussia's wars in 1864, 1866, and 1871.

In the whole century preceding World War I only the American Civil War had revealed the devastating effects of a war of attrition, fought for the largest political stakes and supported by great resources of men and material, the latest developments in transportation, and the newest weapons. In the Civil War at least 600,000 soldiers were lost out of a population of little over 31,000,000. The combat ranged over vast stretches of territory and cost astronomical sums of money by European standards. It was fought with an intensity and yet for a duration far surpassing anything that European powers had experienced since the Napoleonic Wars. The Civil War was truly a preview of World War I. However, its significance was lost upon Europeans. They drew from it no lessons applicable to their own situation, with the exception of the few who recognized its demonstration of the military importance of armored ships, railroads, and other technological innovations. Rather, they drew their lessons from the short, decisive Franco-Prussian War.

And so the prevailing mood on the eve of World War I was not apprehension but confidence—confidence in the progressive improvement of the conditions of international society, as in the advancement of material and social welfare throughout civilization. Men were conscious of great obstacles to progress, but they were sure that they could surmount them. To those who lived in this period and looked back on it in the perspective of two world wars, it seemed like an era of unexampled hope. Decades later, in the dawn of the cold war, the British scholar Gilbert Murray recalled the incredible atmosphere of those happier days.

> Before August, 1914, the civilized world took peace for granted. . . . We travelled where we liked without passports. . . . We were happier too. . . . We were still living in the Century of Hope. Everything seemed to be getting better. We took progress for granted. The nineteenth century had been the great age of emancipation for all oppressed classes. . . . The advance of science had been so constant and rapid that it was taken as a matter of course. The emotions of humanity, of hatred of cruelty, were given new life. It was also a notable age in art; in poetry and literature—a very great age indeed. No wonder men who were young when I was young were full of pride in the past and almost boundless hope for the future.[1]

His reminiscence echoes a lingering sense of a European moral and cultural community in the years preceding World War I. Indeed, the growing middle class throughout Europe seemed to share far more in the way of moral values, manners, and taste than mere differences of national origin could nullify. The deep ideological cleavages arising from antithetical governmental systems had not yet appeared. It seemed as though all modern nations were evolving toward some form of parliamentary government. And there was a widespread belief that in proportion as commerce and industry advanced, the interests of all nations were drawing closer and war becoming less likely. The young Englishman Norman Angell won world-wide fame by writing a book, *The Great Illusion* (1910), in which he argued that if only nations would realize that war does not pay in economic terms, there would be no more wars.

Never since the emergence of the modern state system has the conscience of the civilized world been so strongly opposed to war and to all forms of violence and cruelty as in the decade preceding World War I. These years were conspicuous for the growing number of efforts to abolish war, to limit armaments, to make war more humane by international law. And many important people were becoming persuaded that, with the growth of the peace movement and the progressive sensitivity of the conscience of mankind, the balance of power and all the other trappings of the old diplomacy had become outmoded and were in the process of yielding to a universal society of nations above power politics.

This view found its most eloquent and influential exponent in President Woodrow Wilson.

Nor was there more than a hint of catastrophe in the diplomatic prelude to World War I. Over and above the seething nationalism, the feverish military preparation, and the solidification of two hostile coalitions, the fine mechanism of diplomacy continued to effect delicate rectifications of power and prestige which concealed the disturbance beneath. For months governments negotiated the most sensitive matters on the brink of war, and yet war never came. In *The World Crisis* Winston Churchill wrote a brilliant description of the diplomatic atmosphere that existed in the very month in which the modern era of unlimited warfare began.

> The world on the verge of its catastrophe was very brilliant. Nations and Empires crowned with princes and potentates rose majestically on every side, lapped in the accumulated treasures of the long peace. All were fitted and fastened—it seemed securely—into an immense cantilever. The two mighty European systems faced each other glittering and clanking in their panoply, but with a tranquil gaze. A polite, discreet, pacific, and on the whole sincere diplomacy spread its web of connections over both. A sentence in a dispatch, an observation by an ambassador, a cryptic phrase in a Parliament seemed sufficient to adjust from day to day the balance of prodigious structure. Words counted, and even whispers. A nod could be made to tell. Were we after all to achieve world security and universal peace by a marvelous system of combinations in equipoise and of armaments in equation, of checks and counter-checks on violent action ever more complex and more delicate? Would Europe thus marshalled, thus grouped, thus related, unite into one universal and glorious organism capable of receiving and enjoying in undreamed of abundance the bounty which nature and science stood hand in hand to give? The old world in its sunset was fair to see.[2]

In his definitive analysis of the origins of World War I Sidney Fay summed up the immediate reasons for the outbreak of war in these words: "Because in each country political and military leaders did certain things, which led to mobilizations and declarations of war, or failed to do certain things which might have prevented them."[3] In other words, war came not by deliberate design but because of miscalculation, because of a "diplomatic failure." In retrospect, as we reconstruct from the documents the crystallization of European politics into rigid alliances and alignments, it is not surprising, despite the prevailing confidence in peace, that some slight disturbance in the intricate configurations of power and interest should have eventually touched off a war. Such a result was encouraged by Europe's very complacency about the prospects of peace and the dangers of war. But why did that war become unlimited? Even when the long-postponed rupture came, little on the surface of events indicated the extent and duration of the violence that followed. Certainly, the war did not become unlimited because any of the belligerents had inordinate objectives at the outset.

Why World War I Was Unlimited

In the most general way, the explanation of the extreme scale and intensity of World War I lies in the fact that the various restraints that had limited warfare in the eighteenth century had vanished since the French Revolution, while new circumstances conducive to unlimited war had arisen in their wake. Yet for a century other wars had remained limited despite the mounting potentialities for unlimited war. The decisive difference of 1914 lay in the fact that war reached physical dimensions beyond the bounds of political control or limitation. Thus World War I assumed something of the characteristics Tolstoy attributed to Napoleon's invasion of Russia; it was as though war had a logic of its own, with unfathomable consequences, determined by imponderable vicissitudes of the human spirit.

The uncontrollable dimensions of World War I were partly the result of the very absence of design. When governments design war, war is likely to have direction and control; but when war comes in spite of their designs, it is more likely to determine its own course. The governments of 1914 drifted into war with no clear and well-defined reasons for fighting. All the great powers had specific political aims, which were the object of the complicated prewar struggle for power; but none of them intended to attain these aims by force. When war nevertheless broke out, none of them was content to undertake the great sacrifices the war entailed merely for the sake of these limited aims. Consequently, the great powers entered World War I with no more definite and limited aims than the defeat of the enemy. They talked in general terms of national security, national honor, and national prestige. But when is a nation secure? When is its honor satisfied? When is its prestige established? The universal answer that emerged from the holocaust of 1914–18 was, "Only when the enemy has been crushed!" In the absence of effective political limitations, the sheer massiveness and intensity of the war drove men, out of fear and hatred, to become preoccupied with the simple objective of destroying the enemy. Their entire energy was absorbed in staving off defeat and pursuing military victory.

Therefore, we might sum up the chain of consequences leading to unlimited war in this way: Because "political and military leaders did certain things" and did not do other things, war broke out. Because the complex web of secret alliances so entangled the commitments of nations with one another that the involvement of one member of a coalition in war made it impossible for the other members to maintain their security except by joining the belligerent in battle, the war became a general European war. Because governments failed to subject war to the discipline of precise political objectives and because the sheer weight of military force reached such extreme dimensions, warfare became virtually an end in itself. When the war attained these dimensions, all the latent conditions underlying the decline of limited war—democratization, messianic nationalism, dissolution of moral consensus, deterioration of the balance-of-power system—became the actual sources of unlimited war.

The sheer physical dimensions of the violence induced nations to seek in nebulous inspirational goals, which were antithetical to compromise and negotiation, some moral compensation for war's awful sacrifices. By sublimating the war into a crusade for the sanguine aspirations which they had entertained on the eve of war, the peoples of Europe reconciled their sensitive consciences and their high expectations of peace and progress with the havoc and slaughter around them, and each nation was able to imagine itself the truest exponent of virtue. The Allies were particularly fortunate in this respect, for the stirring slogans of Woodrow Wilson supplied them with war aims commensurate with the scale of suffering. By elevating the struggle, which the United States itself had entered solely to protect its neutral rights, into a "war to end war," a war for the liberation of oppressed nationalities and for a democratic world order, Wilson enabled those with the tenderest consciences to become the most ardent warriors.

Amid the drama of a crusade, the prosaic and confused political conflicts that had originally provoked the war faded into insignificance. What mattered were the highly charged issues that emerged from the war itself. An explosive fusion of national particularism and moral universalism drove war toward its utmost material limits. For by its very nature, a war of principle was not subject to compromise. Only when the adversary had lost its capacity to fight could one be sure that one's principles prevailed.

Perhaps if the accidents of war had occurred somewhat differently—if, say, the Germans had won the Battle of the Marne or the Allies had succeeded in forcing an early peace—World War I might have followed the pattern of the Franco-Prussian War as the military experts had anticipated. Instead, defensive power balanced offensive power, more in the pattern of the American Civil War; and before the end of 1914 the struggle had turned into a stalemate—a war of trenches and blockade, of attrition and exhaustion. In this contest of endurance the resources of manpower and industry became as much a part of warfare as the military operations that devoured them; and once the entire resources of nations were mobilized, it developed that the gigantic machines of war could not be halted until they had run their course.

If there was any opportunity to limit the war by decisive military action or by diplomatic action, that opportunity had passed by the spring of 1916; for by then all nations found themselves so deeply committed to salvaging victory from the massive sacrifices of battle that none could honorably settle for less. Although President Wilson had sought to end the war by mediation in order to prevent the United States from being dragged into the conflict in defense of its neutral rights, his efforts proved unavailing as long as both England and Germany had hopes of achieving a military victory. "Thereafter," as Churchill described the deadlock that set in during 1916, "events passed very largely outside the scope of conscious choice. Governments and individuals conformed to the rhythm of the tragedy, and swayed and staggered forward in helpless violence, slaughtering and squandering on ever-increasing scales, till injuries were wrought to the structure of human society which a century will not efface, and which may conceivably prove fatal to the present civilization."[4]

The Aftermath of Total War

It was, above all, the unprecedented scale and intensity of the hostilities that marked World War I as an unlimited war. It was the massive mobilization of men and material that marked it as the first truly total war. The unconscionable number of soldiers killed and disabled was the most obvious index of the dimensions of violence. Although France emerged from the war as a nominal victor, 1,400,000 of her soldiers had been killed, and an additional 4,500,000 had been wounded out of a population of some 40,000,000. Even the British, who had traditionally harbored their manpower by shoring up the continental balance of power with small professional armies to fight limited wars in support of allies, found it necessary to adopt universal conscription and send a huge citizen army to fill the trenches of France.

A no less significant index of the intensity of the war was the extent to which it exceeded the bounds of ethics to which men had grown accustomed. German submarine warfare outmoded all standards of international law and morality by sinking ships without warning and leaving the passengers to their fate. The British blockade amounted to an instrument of deliberate mass starvation. The use of poison gas and aerial bombing revealed new possibilities of mass killing. And, although wartime propaganda exaggerated the atrocities, the civilian population of Europe had not suffered so much at the hands of armies since the Religious Wars.

A war as extreme in all respects as World War I was bound to leave the world substantially altered in many unpredictable ways. One can measure the consequences of the war in the staggering statistics of human casualties and economic and material devastation, but these statistics give no indication of the disruption of institutions, habits, and beliefs that made a far deeper and more lasting impression upon civilization.[5] Nor do they tell of the disintegration of the European political system.

In the mood of postwar disillusionment, many attributed the international turmoil of the interwar period to the deficiencies of the peace settlement. But in this view they failed to grasp a fundamental characteristic of unlimited war: the nature of the peace following such a war is largely determined by the vicissitudes of the war itself rather than by the conscious designs of statesmen. In retrospect we can see to what extent the injuries to society wrought by the first total war sowed the seeds of a second. In Germany the economic dislocations and the social and political disruption created by war, added to the war-bred rancor and humiliation, prepared the ground for fascism. In Russia military collapse ushered in revolution and paved the way for the Bolsheviks' seizure of power. The very presence in Russia of Lenin, who organized the seizure, was the result of a military expedient, since the Germans had permitted him to cross through their territory in the expectation that he would obstruct Tsarist Russia's military effort. Thus in Germany and Russia the war was a major factor in establishing two revolutionary movements that were to exert an impact upon international society no less momentous than the French Revolution.

Similarly, it was the circumstances of the war more than the designs of the peacemakers that upset the whole political system of the nineteenth

century. By demolishing the power of Russia and Germany and dis-
membering the Austro-Hungarian Empire, the war removed from that
great region between the Rhine and the Urals the distribution of national
power that had been the basis of stability and a rough equilibrium for a
century. In its place it created a host of small, weak, inexperienced, nationalistic political units that seemed made to order for international instability and dissension. The nineteenth-century balance-of-power
system was destroyed beyond restoration. Neither Britain nor France had
the power to reconstruct order in the center of Europe. Neither was in a
position to bring Germany into a European political system as England
and Austria had brought France back into the balance-of-power system
in 1815. Exhausted and decimated by the war, they were not deeply
concerned with reconstructing a viable political system; but they were
intensely concerned with their special national purposes. Keenly sensitive to the temper of a populace who had suffered so much, they were
bent upon retribution, not reconciliation.

The prelude to World War II is the story of the failure of the great
powers to establish a political system capable of meeting the threat of
aggression before it attained dimensions that could be countered only by
total war. This failure was, in many ways, a result of the psychological
impact of World War I upon the victors as well as the vanquished; but it
was, equally, a result of the almost complete absence of that element of
consensus and legitimacy that had sustained rudimentary rules of self-
restraint in the Age of Enlightenment.

Like the settlement at Vienna in 1815, the viability of the settlement
at Versailles in 1919 depended upon the willingness of the nations involved to support it with their power; and this willingness implied their
mutual acceptance of the legitimacy of a working political system. In the
full flush of Allied victory it seemed possible that democracy and the
principles of the Fourteen Points, however vague and contradictory some
of them might be, would constitute this basis of legitimacy, sanctioning
and stabilizing the political system established by the Treaty of Versailles and the League Covenant, just as the principles of monarchical
rule and the balance of power had provided the inner discipline of the
Concert of Europe. This was President Wilson's expectation, and it was
the hope of anonymous millions throughout the world, for whom he
spoke so eloquently. Democracy had never seemed so much like the wave
of the future as in its moment of triumph in 1919. The Fourteen Points

had played a major role in bringing about the surrender of Germany. Especially among the smaller European nations, they were hailed as the basis of a new world order.

However, the situation of 1919 was far less favorable for the restoration of international stability than the situation of 1815 had been. The makers of the Treaty of Versailles were not bound together by class interests transcending national differences. Their common acceptance of the general principles of democracy did not moderate their responsiveness to the concrete influence of democracy in the form of nationalistic pressures. The impression of an international moral consensus—conveyed by the surge of libertarian sentiments throughout Europe—proved to be illusory in that these sentiments, when translated into concrete political terms, became little more than rationalizations of particular national ambitions and interests. Divorced from consciousness of a community of interests, the common faith in the democratic principle of national self-determination divided nations more than it united them.

If the political system established at Versailles lacked a basis of legitimacy among the victors, it seemed positively illegitimate to the vanquished. In 1919 there was no Talleyrand to guide a defeated power back into the community of nations as an equal partner, equally committed to preserving the political system. And there was no Metternich and Castlereagh among the victors to facilitate such a political restoration by arranging a peace of reconciliation. The victors and the vanquished did not meet in the privacy of their exclusive aristocratic society. Nor did they meet in the knowledge that all governments had an interest in preserving a political system that took precedence over the special interests of any particular government. Instead, they met in an atmosphere of popular passion, of nationalistic and ideological antagonism, in which the victorious populations demanded retribution from the defeated enemy and the statesmen dared not reward their sacrifices meagerly by conceding a "peace without victory."

Under these circumstances it is not surprising that the peace of 1919 was more nearly dictated than negotiated. Despite the vindictive War Guilt clause and the reparations agreements, the Versailles settlement was by no means so harsh and unreasonable as its critics maintained; but the circumstances surrounding it were, nevertheless, designed to humiliate rather than to conciliate Germany. If the humiliation of Germany in 1919 was more intense than even the humiliation of France in 1871, it was because World War I, far more than the Franco-Prussian War, had been a war of peoples rather than of governments.

Woodrow Wilson was aware of the need for a peace of reconciliation. He undoubtedly exercised a moderating influence upon the Versailles settlement. However, he placed his ultimate faith in a new world order—not upon the concrete terms of the settlement, but upon the League of Nations—for he believed that the League would be the institutional means of adjusting inequities and reconciling differences within a universal society of nations. It would be the means of enforcing the collective will against the separate wills of its members. The trouble with this expectation was that, unlike the balance-of-power system which the conquerors of Napoleon had restored in 1815, the League that Wilson envisioned was not the kind of political system with which nations were prepared to identify their security. The kind of League Wilson aspired to was not the kind of League that could have accomplished the political purpose he intended.

If the League were to have really served the purpose Wilson intended, it would have had to rest upon a configuration of national power and interests capable of supporting the legal provisions for collective security. But Wilson envisioned the League as a "community of power," in which all members would pledge themselves in advance to resist aggression regardless of their particular interests; and no nation, including his own, was willing to do that. Wilson proclaimed the end of the balance-of-power system, and in doing so he was pronouncing an accurate historical judgment insofar as the traditional eighteenth-century system was concerned. But he was dangerously mistaken in thinking that an international order could be maintained without the vigilant support of a coalition prepared to restrain military threats to the configurations of power upon which it rested. In the postwar era the logical nucleus of any such coalition would have been an Anglo-American partnership capable of guaranteeing French security, since the war had demonstrated that the British and French could no longer prevent the domination of the Continent without American aid. Yet this was precisely the kind of bilateral arrangement of power that Wilson expected the League to supplant.

Furthermore, the political basis of a successful League would have had to rest not just upon the potential power of its adherents, but upon available military power, which nations were ready and willing to use for the purposes of collective security. Wilson found this notion repugnant and envisioned the real deterrent to aggression as world opinion, supplemented if necessary by economic boycott and blockade. Although the Allies were not ready to pool their strength in any such "community of power" as Wilson envisioned, they might have been willing to concert their power for specific political purposes, such as a guarantee of western European frontiers, providing that the United States had taken an active part in such agreements. But Wilson had no enthusiasm for this kind of intervention, and it is doubtful whether even vigorous presidential leadership could have persuaded Congress and the American public to support it anyway.

The United States did not join the League, and it did not take an active part in a coalition designed to preserve a postwar political system. Instead, it lapsed back into isolation, more determined than ever to avoid the adversities of world politics. Thus the single most important potential bulwark of a political system capable of moderating power conflicts and keeping warfare limited was withheld from the world. The lack of a viable political system proved disastrous to the democracies in the interwar period. It led directly to a second total war within a quarter of a century.

Actually, the twenty years between 1919 and 1939 were a period of limited war, when one considers the small scale of the Japanese war in Manchuria, the Italian war against Ethiopia, and the Spanish Civil War. But the war in Spain was limited primarily because Germany, Italy, and the Soviet Union regarded it more as a military testing ground than as an area in which they had important political interests, and the other two wars were limited by default, because the democracies failed to oppose the aggressors. In the perspective of the sequence of events leading from the first to the second world war, the wars in the intervening period are merely skirmishes during an uneasy armistice in the midst of one great upheaval.

This is not to say that the period of totalitarian aggression leading to World War II was inevitable. With a modicum of foresight and courage the democratic nations might have combined to check the Fascist military threat; and then, conceivably, World War I would now look like an isolated, accidental eruption instead of the initial outbreak in a period of unlimited war. If France and Great Britain alone had been willing to take the risk of fighting limited wars at an early date—for example, in 1936, when Hitler's troops reoccupied the Rhineland—they might have avoided the terrible choice between acquiescence and total war later. Instead, they met the initial challenges to their security with numb fear and bewilderment.

On the other hand, this fear and bewilderment was itself a product of unlimited war. In large part, the paralysis of the victorious powers during the interwar period can be attributed to the traumatic impact of their experience in World War I. When the war-weary democratic peoples counted the cost of war and compared its somber results with the exhilarating hopes they had entertained during the war, they were overcome with disillusionment. Since war could only be justified by exalted goals, and since this war had failed to achieve exalted goals, it seemed to follow that all war was useless. And if all war was useless, so were policies that entailed the risk of war, and so was armed preparation for war. From their disillusionment with this particular war many concluded that war in general was the supreme, the absolute evil, to be avoided at all costs, and that man's only salvation lay in renouncing war and abolishing armaments. Of course, it was generally conceded that war might have to be fought in self-defense. But, in that event, defense was conceived in the narrowest terms possible, as merely the physical protection of the national boundaries from invasion; for this was the conception of security that demanded the least sacrifice and effort of the nation. The Maginot Line mentality was not confined to France. Thus one unlimited war not only created the social, economic, and political conditions for a second one but also sapped the will of the democracies to resist its perpetrators.

Hitler's Conception of War

In its principal features the international environment in the interwar period registered an intensification of all those material, economic, social, political, and moral factors that had steadily undermined the restraints upon war since the French Revolution. This development is too familiar to require elaboration, but we may single out one factor for its crucial significance: the hastening dissolution of a moral consensus among nations and the intensification of ideological hostilities.

The liberal and humane principles were less effective in moderating the conduct of states in the nineteenth century, when they became associated with democracy and nationalism, than in the eighteenth century, when they represented a consensus among a homogeneous ruling class. But at least they were taken for granted in the Western world as the foundation of a common conscience. Perhaps, in the absence of other restraints upon war, these principles sometimes exacerbated war more conspicuously than they civilized it. Nevertheless, they kept alive the fragmentary outline of a moral system to which all civilized nations were in some measure bound. But in the twentieth century the Fascist and Communist movements flagrantly repudiated the most fundamental tenets of Western idealism. Henceforth, international relations were to assume the characteristics of an ideological struggle of such intensity and profundity as to make the propaganda-fed contest between Autocracy and Democracy in World War I seem petty and artificial by comparison. This raised the prospect that future wars among the major powers would be not only national wars but, in a deeper sense, civil wars, like the wars of the sixteenth and seventeenth centuries, in which states became the political agents for combating heresy and establishing the true faith throughout the world.

Among the liberal tenets that the totalitarian movements rejected was the moral disapproval of war itself. In the Communist view war was simply a violent form of an inexorable class struggle, and its validity was only a function of its service to the power of the Party. But in the Fascist view war had a positive moral value, as the ultimate expression of the distorted human values it idealized. Mussolini declared, "War alone brings all human energies to their highest tension and sets a seal of nobility on the peoples who have the virtue to face it." But the romantic exaltation of war reached its zenith in Hitler's ranting militarism. Because the Communist approach to violence is rational, the political limitation of war with Communist powers is possible despite ideological antipathies; but, in the light of the Fascist glorification of war, it seems almost inevitable that a war with Hitler's Germany should have become unlimited, once he gained the military capacity to wage such a war and once the Western powers offered resistance.

It was the irrepressible dynamism of Hitler's will-to-power, not a cautious calculation of limited political ends, that impelled Germany to undertake its successive aggressions. Strategically, as well as tactically, Hitler knew how to advance but not how to retreat. One conquest became the prelude to another one, as each objective attained added to the illusion of omnipotence. Hitler was shrewd, not wise. With diabolical cunning he capitalized upon his victims' timidity and confusion; but he lacked the cold rationality and the sense of moderation that had enabled

Bismarck to employ warfare within a feasible plan of limited political objectives.

The appeasers, who sought to prevent the outbreak of war by political accommodation, made the mistake of supposing that Hitler's aims were really limited, as he said they were. But once the democracies met Nazi aggression with war, there was no longer any question about the unlimited nature of his aims. The chances of a war of limited liability, such as Liddell-Hart and others had advocated in their revulsion from the mass slaughter of World War I, dissolved in the German invasion of France in 1940.

And yet, in spite of his fanaticism, Hitler in some respects, like his more circumspect totalitarian counterpart in the Soviet Union, understood the primacy of politics better than his adversaries. Above all, he realized that modern war is a war of peoples and that, ultimately, it is the human will that determines the outcome of struggles for power. Accordingly—at least at the outset of his career of conquest—he regarded the use of armed force by itself as an ineffective method for promoting German hegemony. He comprehended war in its full variety—not just in its most overt form—as a combination of economic, psychological, and political methods for shaping the will of nations.

Hitler exploited these methods with terrifying effectiveness, both in his mobilization of the German people for war and in his fostering of disunity, panic, and defeatism among the democratic peoples. It is significant that his greatest triumphs were in the realm of psychological and political warfare, such as his bloodless conquest of Czechoslovakia, when he reserved armed force as an implicit threat in support of some diplomatic maneuver or used it only as a *coup de grâce* after the victim had been isolated and subverted. The victorious powers of World War I were not prepared for these unorthodox tactics. As Edward Mead Earle wrote in 1943,

> Under modern conditions military questions are so interwoven with economic, political, social, and technological phenomena that it is doubtful if one can speak of a purely military strategy. Much of Hitler's success up to the invasion of Russia in 1941 was due to the remarkable understanding of this fundamental fact. His opponents in the field and in the chancelleries of Europe were still thinking, until the fall of France, in terms of the seventeenth century, when politics and war, strategy and tactics, could in some measure be put into separate categories. But in our day politics and strategy have become inseparable.[6]

However, Hitler's great and fatal disadvantage was, as Stalin once remarked, that he did not know when to stop. As one historian has speculated, "If Hitler had been satisfied with the annexation of Austria and Sudetenland, he could have gained ever increasing control over southeastern Europe through peaceful economic and political penetration."[7] If he had been satisfied with his conquest of Poland, Denmark, Norway, or even France, he might have achieved hegemony in Europe. But the fact is that he was temperamentally incapable of being satisfied with limited gains. His inner compulsions drove him inexorably toward a preoccupation with military conquest as an end in itself. In a way, this is fortunate for us, for it proved his undoing.

The very extent of Germany's conquests brought an end to Hitler's ability to isolate and to paralyze his victims by diplomatic, psychological, and political means. His political ends were too ambitious, his haste in achieving them too reckless. In his obsession with conquest he tried to apply to military operations the uncanny intuition that had brought him diplomatic victories, but his intuition failed him. His compulsion to realize Germany's mission of conquest, combined with his unquestioning faith in his own omniscience, infused his conduct of warfare with an inflexible irrationality that eventually assured Germany's defeat.

But even if Hitler had gained complete military success, it is unlikely that he could have secured a viable Eurasian empire. The methods by which he gained his conquests could not have consolidated those conquests, for they were purely destructive in their intent and their effect. The strategy of terror and the cultivation of confusion and defeatism could never have gained a shred of legitimacy for a German empire. They left the power of the conqueror exposed for what it was: naked coercion in the service of the Master Race, devoid of any moral or intellectual claims upon the minds of the conquered. One must conclude from Hitler's military and political failure that an obsession with power is as poor a ground for bringing force and policy into effective balance as an aversion to power.

World War II

When one belligerent is as ambitious and as reckless as Hitler, there can be little chance of limiting a modern war between evenly matched powers. Therefore, it is not surprising that World War II became a general war extending to virtually every part of the earth and absorbing the resources of nations on a scale surpassing even World War I. Fifth columns, guerilla warfare, the deportation of civilians, death camps, the area bombing of cities, and finally the unleashing of death by nuclear explosion and radiation—all these methods and the perfection of violence in hundreds of other ways reflected the totality of war.

A war of these dimensions was bound to leave the world substantially altered. Who could tell what the results might be? No belligerent could know the political consequences of victory, but all might expect a national disaster as the result of defeat. This very uncertainty put a premium upon victory. Consequently, the nature of the peace that followed victory was bound to be determined less by the calculated designs of statesmen than by war's own momentum.

The sheer momentum of war decimated the strength of two of the five great industrial powers in the world, Germany and Japan. It placed Russian troops in central Europe, Manchuria, and northern Korea, thereby greatly increasing the material foundations of Soviet power while giving the Kremlin control of an important portion of the resources necessary to any full restoration of German and Japanese power. At the same time, it seriously weakened Great Britain and France and suddenly left the United States as the only nation capable of restoring countervailing power to vital areas in Europe, the Middle East, and the Far East, which had become America's first line of defense. Finally, it vastly complicated the whole problem of establishing order, by accelerating an anticolonial, anti-Western revolution throughout the underdeveloped areas of the world. Thus, through no design of the participants, World War II ended by leaving the United States and Russia with a preponderance of power in the world, confronting each other with hostile aims and interests all along the whole vast periphery of Eurasia.

It is important to understand now how largely these momentous developments were beyond control or prediction, because with the dissolution of the Grand Alliance and the frustration of original hopes for the United Nations, many have come to view the adversities of the cold war as the result of mistakes committed during the war. Accordingly, they attribute the Soviet advantage or the West's disadvantage in one or another segment of the world to this policy or to that particular act or decision. Others have pointed to the incongruity of the United States trying after the war to reconstruct the very nations it was determined to destroy during the war, and they have attributed this situation to a lack of foresight on the part of democratic strategists. Such critical appraisals of the political consequences of the conduct of World War II are indispensable if we are to learn anything at all from recent history; but it would be well to make them tentatively and with qualification, lest the implication that it was in the power of strategists precisely to control and predict the political outcome of such gigantic military operations conceal the central lesson that total war is an exceedingly blunt instrument of national policy.

In large measure, the determining political conditions of the cold war are a result of the distribution of power created by the military operations during World War II. The economic and political weaknesses among European allies and the tempting political vacuums in the lands of former enemies are, largely, the product of the exigencies of war. Russia's expanded spheres of influence in Asia and Europe are the direct consequence of the Red Army's sphere of military operations during the war. Once the Red Army occupied an area, whether in eastern Europe or Manchuria, it is certainly unrealistic to suppose that America could have determined the fate of that area by diplomatic conversations at Yalta or anywhere else. Therefore, those who contend that America's political position would be more favorable if this or that decision in the conduct of the war had or had not been made must demonstrate that another course would have improved the political outcome, especially by diminishing the area of Russian occupation, while assuring the democratic powers of victory. This is very difficult to demonstrate.

Nevertheless, the difficulty of demonstrating such a proposition should not conceal another central lesson of World War II: that it is possible to maintain the primacy of politics to some extent even in a total war and absolutely essential to make every effort in that direction. On this score there can be no doubt that the United States was woefully negligent. By the nature of things it is not possible to prove that history would have been altered in certain ways if men had acted differently, but one may discern in the existing historical record of World War II both the limits of political control and the failure of the United States to capitalize upon the opportunities within those limits.

Since the distribution of power underlying the cold war is so largely the result of the vicissitudes of combat, in order to test the limits of political control we must ask, What political or military measures could have altered the conduct of the war so as to produce a more favorable postwar distribution of power?

In Europe we might simply have permitted Germany and Russia to bleed each other to death. However, this would have meant incurring the grave risk, at a time when the survival of the Western world hung in the balance, that the Nazis would entrench themselves on the Continent or that Germany and Russia would arrange a joint division of Eurasia, either of which eventualities might have prolonged the war indefinitely and left us in a far less advantageous position than we actually obtained.

We might have negotiated a settlement with Germany earlier in the war so that she might have served as a buffer against Soviet power. However, from what we know of internal developments in Germany, there is little evidence that the Allies could have reached a satisfactory agreement with German leaders early enough to have made any great difference in the postwar distribution of power. Reaching a satisfactory negotiated settlement with Germany depended upon the replacement of Hitler by a politically reliable regime, which would have purged the army and the government of Nazi influence, and which would have had sufficient internal political power to carry through the terms of settlement. This result could only have come about—and even then, by no means, would it have been certain—if the Beck-Goerdeler conspiracy had succeeded in assassinating Hitler and seizing control of the government. But John Wheeler-Bennett's thorough study of that conspiracy shows that, while the revolting generals might have been willing to make a deal of some sort if Hitler had not been in control, when it came to the point of eliminating Hitler, they held back, despite their complete loss of faith in his conduct of the war, because of their rigid fealty to the supreme commander. Wheeler-Bennett reaches the conclusion that the formula of "unconditional surrender" played no part in their hesitancy.[8] (Of course, the fact that the formula of unconditional surrender had no discernible influence upon the actions of the revolting generals does not prove that a deliberate policy of negotiated peace would have been ineffectual.)

Furthermore, both President Roosevelt and Prime Minister Churchill were conscious of the divisive effect upon the Grand Alliance which any attempt to determine the exact terms of a negotiated settlement would have had. Could they have afforded the risk of breaking up the alliance when the very survival of their countries was at stake? We know enough of Russia's territorial aims and demands even while she was hard-pressed in battle to infer that she would have placed formidable obstacles in the way of any settlement the Western Allies might have proposed, assuming that they could have agreed among themselves. This might have given a German regime a splendid opportunity to play one part of the alliance against the other. The fear of a separate Russo-German peace always loomed large in the minds of Roosevelt and Churchill. There is no documentary evidence that their fear was actually warranted under the existing circumstances, but could they have wisely risked the contingency by bargaining with the Russians in the midst of war or by undertaking separate negotiations with Germany when the success of such negotiations was so uncertain?

Perhaps, despite these difficulties, the Western powers could have made a spheres-of-influence agreement with the Russians that would have kept them from advancing so far into Europe. Without any support from the United States, Churchill undertook something like this in October, 1944, when he sat down with Stalin in Moscow and agreed upon a rough percentage division of influence in the Balkans between Russia and the West.[9] However, this ambiguous informal agreement—which, it should be noted, was based upon an estimate of relative military positions—provides no grounds for believing that the Western powers could have gained through a bargain any more favorable sphere of influence than the one which they actually held at the end of hostilities. To have obtained a better distribution of power would probably have required driving a hard bargain when the Russians were in the most precarious military position, but this was precisely when the West needed the Russians most and when the Russians would have been least willing to make such a bargain. The exasperating failure of Hitler and Ribbentrop to induce Stalin and Molotov to divide up the world in November, 1940, shows just how hard a bargain the Russians could drive, as well as the magnitude of their territorial ambitions. In any case, the actual postwar positions of Russian and Western troops would have been determined by the vicissitudes of war rather than by advance agreements. Stalin would never have permitted free elections or any other arrangement that would have jeopardized Soviet control of territory won with the blood of the Red Army.

Therefore, aside from diplomatic measures for achieving a more favorable distribution of power, we must ask, How might the Western allies have conducted military operations so as to have obtained a more advantageous position in Europe at the end of the war? They might, for example, have concentrated their military effort upon invading Europe through the Balkans in 1943 instead of saving their strength for the assault of western Europe in 1944. But considering the speed and strength of the Russian drive into eastern Europe, it is quite unlikely that American and British troops could have occupied much, if any, of the Balkans before the Russians; and what success they attained in this venture would probably have been won only at the tremendous cost of permitting the Russians to overrun western Europe. A more feasible plan would have been to follow Churchill's advice by trying to strike up through the Ljubljana gap in the summer of 1944 in order to get to Vienna before the Red Army instead of diverting troops from the Mediterranean theater for the invasion of southern France. However, even if this effort had succeeded, it might have had to be made at the sacrifice of the West's advance into Germany; and if so, this would have been a far more serious blow to our postwar position than Russian occupation of Vienna. Competent military authorities argue both sides of the question even now. One cannot reasonably expect the military and political leaders at the time to have reached an indisputably correct decision on the basis of a strategic foresight surpassing our own hindsight.

On the other hand, there can be little doubt that Western troops could have reached Berlin and Prague before the Russians without suffering great military disadvantages elsewhere, if they had been willing to pay the cost in casualties to achieve this political gain. This would have meant incurring Russian displeasure and the risk of incidents as a result of the juncture of two huge armies at a more easterly point than the agreed lines of demarcation, but this inconvenience would certainly have been outweighed by the political advantage of occupying two key points in Europe. It is true that the British zone of occupation in Germany, established long before Western troops entered the Reich, ran some 100 miles to the west of Berlin; but the Anglo-American forces might wisely have retained their line of advance until political differences with Russia in eastern Europe had been settled, as Churchill repeatedly proposed. If these differences had remained unsettled, as seems likely, then our position in Germany would still have deprived Russia of a thorn in our European flank and would have considerably weakened a Soviet instrument of political leverage which has plagued us ever since.

Nevertheless, we will do well to bear in mind that even the question of occupying Berlin raised an important military problem of a kind that democratic powers locked in large-scale war cannot readily ignore. The decision as to whether to direct the main Anglo-American drive toward Berlin or toward the "National Redoubt" in central Germany fell to General Eisenhower. To the best of his knowledge, the latter course promised relatively cheap and quick military returns; whereas the former course, he was advised, would cost 100,000 casualties. Would the drive toward Berlin, for the sake of some incalculable "prestige" value, be worth the sacrifice of 100,000 casualties and the prolongation of the war? Under the circumstances Eisenhower chose what he believed to be the quicker and less costly way of ending the war.[10] Especially where such huge numbers of troops are involved, commanders of democratic armies will always share this bias.

If we examine the war in the Far East, the bounds within which the West could conceivably have controlled it advantageously for political purposes by alternative military and diplomatic measures seem a bit broader than in Europe. In the Far East our troubles in the cold war stem, in large part, from the Communist occupation of northern Korea and the mainland of China. The division of Korea was a direct result of Russian intervention in the war against Japan. The ascendance of the Chinese Communists owes a very great deal—though certainly not everything— to the Japanese withdrawal from Manchuria and the Russian invasion of Manchuria, both of which events made possible the consolidation of Communist power in the north. If the American government had made peace with Japan before the Russians had entered the Far Eastern war, leaving the Japanese army intact in Manchuria and, perhaps, establishing Japanese power there as a buffer against Russian expansion; if it had discouraged rather than besought Russian intervention, we might now enjoy a far more favorable distribution of power in the Far East.

Of course, as long as we insisted upon unconditional surrender, it was reasonable to aim for the defeat of the Kwantung Army in Manchuria. And under this condition it is understandable that we should have made concessions to the Soviet Union at Yalta as the price of Russian intervention; for the prevailing military advice, with the exception of some naval opinion, indicated that unconditional surrender could not be obtained without a huge and deadly invasion of the home islands unless Russian troops engaged the Kwantung Army. Although we now know that this military calculation greatly overestimated Japanese strength and Japanese will to resist, we did not know it then. But if, on the other hand, the American government had not insisted upon the formula of unconditional surrender—which it modified anyway when it finally agreed to preserve the status of the Emperor—and if it had kept open the channels of negotiation with the Japanese moderates, the United States might well have secured peace on its own terms before Russia intervened and perhaps even before the Yalta agreement. From what we know now of internal developments in Japan, it appears likely that the Japanese peace leaders could have managed at the time of Germany's surrender to agree to the same settlement they eventually accepted in August, 1945, despite the reluctance of the militarists to surrender the army, if the United States had actively pursued a negotiated settlement.[11] The establishment of a Japanese buffer against Russia in Manchuria would have made a settlement almost irresistible. At the very least, Japan's desperate attempts to secure Russian mediation from May to July, 1945, suggest that the United States could have obtained Japanese surrender several months earlier than August; and in that event there would have been no reason to drop the atomic bombs.

It may be true, as some believed at the time and many have maintained since, that Russia was determined to intervene in the Far Eastern theater with or without the invitation of the United States. But she would not have had the opportunity to intervene if Japan had conceded defeat on or before the day the war ended in Europe, and at any time the United States would have been in a stronger diplomatic and moral position if Russian intervention had come in spite of American wishes rather than because of them.

Still, there is a consideration of a different nature here, which cannot be dismissed. Would the American public have tolerated a deal with the enemy who struck at Pearl Harbor? After all the sacrifice of total war and all the passions that the war inevitably engendered, could the American government have seemingly reversed the whole direction of the war by compromising with the enemy at the expense of America's Chinese ally in order to contain America's Russian ally? To posit such a maneuver implies that a democratic nation will dedicate its whole substance to the ends of pure *Realpolitik* without regard for the most elementary scruples and passions of war.

Even if Roosevelt and Churchill had not been guided by such scruples and passions themselves, they would have hesitated to risk national disunity and the integrity of their own political regimes by bargaining for the kind of settlement that pure expediency might have dictated. If they had nevertheless sought such a settlement with Germany or Japan before either power had, beyond a doubt, conceded defeat, they would probably have been impelled to seek much harsher terms than were eventually arranged. In fact, Churchill has written that this was his chief consideration in supporting the formula of unconditional surrender.

> My principal reason for opposing, as I always did, an alternative statement on peace terms, which was so often urged, was that a statement of the actual conditions on which the three great Allies would have insisted and would have been forced by public opinion to insist, would have been far more repulsive to any German peace movement than the general expression "unconditional surrender."[12]

Democratic governments can conceivably display leniency toward an enemy who has made retribution by conceding defeat, but it is hard to conceive of them foregoing such retribution for the sake of the balance of power.

These are some of the considerations, then, that indicate the serious practical limits upon the political manipulation of large-scale war. At the same time, they also suggest that even in total war there is a margin of political control that governments must be ready to exploit. One cannot know exactly what, if any, political advantages might have accrued if the American government had fully exploited this margin of control in World War II; but it is evident that the government was prevented from making even a minimum effort toward this end by its preoccupation with the purely military objective of total victory.

From this standpoint the significant thing about the Allies' formula of unconditional surrender during World War II is that the United States simply took the ambiguous phrase for granted, with scarcely a hint of critical appraisal.[13] Although it represented a policy—the policy of eschewing peace on the basis of compromise or negotiation (which had crucial political implications)—to the overwhelming majority of Americans it was simply a fighting slogan. It embodied the nation's unquestioning conviction that the overriding purpose of the war was to achieve such a complete military victory over the aggressor nations that they would never forget the terrible penalties of breaching the peace of the law-abiding world. Despite Roosevelt's and Churchill's disavowals of any intention to destroy the Axis nations, "unconditional surrender" was a symbol of the punitive conception of war, and Roosevelt often said as much.[14]

No one can prove now that the slogan and the assumptions behind it affected the political outcome of the war adversely or that a wiser settlement could have been reached by a different course of action. Nevertheless, the Allied refusal to negotiate with the enemy short of complete surrender—a policy, it should be noted, eventually abandoned in the case of Italy and Japan—was indefensible on the grounds of general principle. Yet it was primarily on grounds of general principle that the American people and the American government adhered to the policy. One can adduce some rational reasons for adhering to the unconditional surrender formula. Among these, President Roosevelt seems to have been most impressed by the following: to maintain domestic and Allied harmony by avoiding disputes over the terms of surrender, to reassure the suspicious Russians that their allies would continue a vigorous war against Germany, to encourage occupied peoples and resistance movements, and to deprive the Germans of the post–World War I alibi that they had not been defeated but only tricked into surrendering. However, these reasons were certainly secondary to the President's simple desire to prosecute the war under a fighting slogan expressing the popular determination to crush enemy resistance in the quickest, most efficient way and his obvious reluctance to encumber the pursuit of victory with the problems of postwar political commitments. To Americans engaged in a global struggle it seemed self-evident that war was war and that there was no other legitimate purpose of war except the total defeat of the enemy. Roosevelt understood this sentiment, and he shared it.

The American sentiment for unconditional surrender is thoroughly understandable. Yet uncritical adherence to this formula automatically excluded a whole range of alternative ways of conducting the war, which deserved long and careful consideration on the most elementary grounds of political primacy. Thus the inflexible determination to gain unconditional victory in the shortest time possible led logically to the decision to invade the industrial heart of Japan,[15] which in turn led to the decision to seek Russian intervention in Manchuria and finally to the decision to drop atomic bombs on Japanese cities. At the same time, this chain of decisions precluded serious consideration of alternative methods of ending the war so as to achieve limited, well-defined political objectives, bearing some rational relation to America's postwar position. In describing how he reached the agonizing decision to employ the atomic bomb, Secretary of War Stimson later wrote, "My chief purpose was to end the war in victory with the least possible cost in the lives of the men in the armies which I had helped to raise." With this purpose in mind he weighed the "terrible responsibility" of dropping the bomb on heavily populated cities against the cost of an invasion of Japan, which he was advised would result in one million American casualties and would prolong the war until the latter part of 1946. He decided that using the bomb was the "least abhorrent choice," but in doing so he recognized that he was "implicitly confessing that there could be no significant limits to the horror of modern war."[16] Stimson's dilemma was real, and his resolution was logical, providing that the sole objective of the war was to gain an unconditional surrender as quickly and cheaply as possible. On the other hand, if the government had actively exploited the possibilities of ending the war short of unconditional surrender, there would probably have been no need for either atomic bombs or the invasion of Japan. But the farthest any official would go in this direction was to propose in the final months of the war that the government give assurances against the abolition of the Emperor. Even this measure would probably have been sufficient to secure Japan's immediate surrender, but the proposal was rejected as "appeasement."[17]

The same political blindness embodied in the formula of "unconditional surrender" appeared in the actual conduct of military operations. One cannot be sure that America's postwar political position would have been greatly improved if, for example, the democratic powers had occupied Prague and Berlin. Nevertheless, the complete exclusion of such political considerations from military plans, the failure even to discuss them seriously, is indefensible—especially at a time when the decisive phase of military operations had passed. In this latter phase of the war Churchill and the British Chiefs of Staff were alert to the possibilities of conducting operations so as to place the West in the best possible power position with respect to the Soviet Union, but the Americans repeatedly excluded political considerations from their own calculations and regarded the British approach as simply a guise for the pursuit of special spheres of influence.[18]

Thus at the beginning of April, 1945, Churchill, in urging the move toward Berlin, wrote that he deemed it "highly important that we should shake hands with the Russians as far to the east as possible." But the

United States Chiefs of Staff stated, "Such psychological and political advantages as would result from the possible capture of Berlin ahead of the Russians should not override the imperative military consideration, which in our opinion is the destruction and dismemberment of the German armed forces."[19] General Bradley has written of these events, "I could see no political advantage accruing from the capture of Berlin, that would offset the need for quick destruction of the German Army on our front." He added, "As soldiers we looked naïvely on the British inclination to complicate the war with political foresight and nonmilitary objectives."[20]

At the end of April, 1945, when the war in Europe was virtually over, the British Chiefs of Staff proposed that the Supreme Commander of the Western forces utilize any improvement in his logistical situation in order to gain the great political advantage of liberating Prague and as much of the rest of Czechoslovakia as possible. But General Marshall, in relaying this proposal to General Eisenhower for his comments, simply noted, "Personally and aside from all logistic, tactical or strategical implications I would be loath to hazard American lives for purely political purposes."[21]

The same depreciation of political considerations characterizes the Allied strategic bombing campaign against Germany. The best information on the conduct of this vital part of the war in Europe is contained in the able and voluminous *United States Strategic Bombing Survey*. The documents in this study confirm its conclusion that Allied air power was decisive in defeating Germany,[22] but they also show that the whole conduct of the strategic bombing campaign, from over-all planning to target selection, was governed by purely military considerations. In effect, the sole criterion for the success of the campaign was the maximum destruction of the enemy's capacity to fight. Some American officials objected to what they regarded as indiscriminate "terror" raids; but they did so primarily on humanitarian grounds rather than because they attributed any political significance to the raids.[23] Virtually everyone supported the frequent "area bombing" of large German cities; but they did so on the sole ground of military necessity, without regard for the possible effect of the bombing on the postwar balance of power. As for the psychological impact of such bombing on the German populace, the prevailing view was expressed in the conclusion of the *Survey*, which notes approvingly, "It brought home to the German people the full impact of modern war with all its horror and suffering. Its imprint on the German nation will be lasting."[24] It may be that the postwar political implications of alternative forms of bombing were debated within British and American air staffs; but if so, such considerations were always subordinated in in the end to the purely military objective of crushing German resistance as quickly and thoroughly as possible. Even after Allied forces had broken the back of German resistance, the air arm continued to direct its utmost effort against industrial and transportation facilities, thereby vastly complicating the postwar problems of reconstructing Europe and filling the dangerous vacuum at its center.[25]

No one can say with any assurance in what ways, if any, the Western allies might have altered their bombing campaign in order to improve their postwar political position; but there is no logical justification for having failed to give more serious attention to these possibilities at the time. The historical explanation, however, is clear enough: As was true of all aspects of American war strategy, the principal source of political blindness was the weight of American tradition, combined with the inability of the top leadership to foresee that the United States would become irrevocably involved in a bipolar struggle for power with the Soviet Union after the Axis had been defeated.

Indeed, it was President Roosevelt's deliberate policy to avoid defining concrete postwar political objectives in Europe of the kind that could have guided the conduct of bombing missions or any other military operations. He hoped thereby to avoid the embarrassment and furor that had been caused by the secret treaties at Versailles in 1919. Moreover, he assumed that when the war ended, the United States would withdraw its troops from Germany as quickly as possible and participate in European politics only insofar as this might be necessary to mediate between the British and the Russians. To the extent that the American government was concerned at all with the political objectives, its overriding concern was to avoid "spheres of influence" and to concentrate, instead, upon securing Big Three support for the establishment of an international organization that would end the old balance-of-power system.

It goes without saying that the responsibility for the political blindness of American military strategy in World War II lies more heavily upon the nation's civilian leaders than upon its military leaders. It was primarily the task of the highest civilian officials of the nation to formulate guiding political objectives that could be translated into specific operational directives. They failed to do this. As a matter of fact, military leaders were somewhat more aware of the need for political guidance than their civilian superiors; but, in the absence of political directives, they were obliged to fulfil their military missions in the most effective manner possible. Thus in a memorandum to the Combined Chiefs of Staff, dated April 7, 1945, General Eisenhower gave the following explanation of his strategy of making the central thrust toward Leipzig instead of Berlin.

I regard it as militarily unsound at this stage of the proceedings to make Berlin a major objective, particularly in view of the fact that it is only 35 miles from the Russian lines. I am the first to admit that a war is waged in pursuance of political aims, and if the Combined Chiefs of Staff should decide that the Allied effort to take Berlin outweighs purely military considerations in this theater, I would cheerfully readjust my plans and my thinking so as to carry out such an operation.

But there is no evidence that the Combined Chiefs of Staff ever considered the question Eisenhower raised.[26]

Actually, America's non-political approach to the war was so entirely consistent with the approach of the nation as a whole that it was completely above question at the time. The responsible political authorities failed to formulate specific political objectives because they simply took it for granted that the determining purpose of war was military victory and because they looked to peace as the end rather than the continuation of power politics. It was inconceivable at the time that the government should have conducted the war with a mind to containing the Soviet Union or to exerting pressure upon her by means of lend-lease, if only because the overwhelming body of Americans believed that the United States had no reason to fear its Russian ally but absolutely needed her co-operation to establish a lasting peace. Even those few in the government who had grown suspicious of Soviet intentions since her violations of the Yalta agreement were reluctant to antagonize the Russians in any way until postwar collaboration had a trial run.

It is doubtful that even the most skilful and forceful presidential leadership could have modified the prevailing American approach to the war and led the nation into the paths of long-run political interest that critics have since suggested. But, in any case, the fact is that President Roosevelt directed all his great energy and political talent toward the orthodox goal of overwhelming the enemy in the quickest time with the least cost in men. Roosevelt was a controversial figure in his country on many other grounds; but there are no grounds for doubting that his conduct of the war was, by the nation's own standards, a magnificent achievement. In his preoccupation with the purely military requirements for winning the war as rapidly as possible, he was the ideal proponent of the American way in war; and America might not have won that war so readily if he had not been. Nevertheless, the United States can never again afford to follow his example of pursuing victory in a political vacuum.

The Relevance of the Past to the Present

The history of total war amply confirms the general proposition that the sheer physical magnitude of warfare conducted with modern military means defeats the conduct of war as a continuation of political intercourse and a rational instrument of national policy. It indicates that there are narrow but significant bounds within which even a total war can be directed toward limited, concrete objectives, and that it is all the more imperative to exploit this narrow margin of political control to the maximum when warfare tends to reach such extreme dimensions. But regardless of the designs of statesmen, the political consequences which shape the peace that follows such a war will be more the product of military exigencies than of conscious political choice. Therefore, consistent with the theory of war and policy outlined in chapter i, it follows that the United States has a vital interest in keeping warfare limited and, above all, in avoiding that modern form of military irrationality, total war. Given the present vast military potential of nations, it is essential but no longer sufficient to limit the political objectives of war. Now it is absolutely imperative to limit the use of the military means available. Yet it is evident that such limitation of military means can only be made in terms of an overriding political decision.

What, then, does the history of war, as we have surveyed it, tell us about the possibilities of limiting war under present circumstances? Clearly, it is not encouraging, for almost none of the conditions that have permitted limited wars between major powers in past centuries exist today, whereas almost all of the circumstances that have led to unlimited war do exist and, indeed, have grown more intense.

Among the principal adversaries in the present struggle for power, there are none of the bonds of culture, morality, custom, sentiment, class, or family which injected an element of self-restraint, reliability, and legitimacy into the conduct of states in the eighteenth century. We can never recover, and would not want to recover, all those social, political, and cultural conditions that made war the affair of kings and governments rather than of peoples. We cannot regard war coldly and professionally as a game without deep moral and emotional significance. We cannot wish away the profound ideological conflicts that divide the world. We cannot shed our own profound national loyalty, even if that were desirable; much less can we check the flood of nationalism and racialism surging through Asia, Africa, and the Middle East.

The present bipolar concentration of power deprives international politics of even the modicum of flexibility which the multilateral balance-of-power system held at the beginning of the century. Instead of the ever-shifting alignments, alliances, and counteralliances of an earlier period, the struggle for power now takes predominantly the form of a race for armed strength and a contest for the allegiance of uncommitted peoples between two hostile powers. The increased rigidity of the political system has been accompanied and aggravated by a declining circumspection and finesse in diplomacy.

At the same time, the most obvious obstacle to the limitation of war, the physical potentialities for unlimited war, has grown immensely more formidable throughout the whole realm of industry and finance, transportation and communication, and military technology; and the world has long since mastered and perfected the techniques of recruitment and mobilization for bringing the whole weight of the nation-in-arms to bear upon the enemy. It is inconceivable that, having gained access to such tremendous military potential, nations will voluntarily abandon it. Moreover, the whole history of "disarmament" shows that no effort to limit arms can succeed without a resolution of the political conflicts which cause states to arm in the first place; and no such resolution of the present struggle for power seems possible in the foreseeable future.

If it is inconceivable that nations will voluntarily abandon their military potential, history also suggests that it is improbable, to say the least, that they will refrain from using it if they can gain a military advantage by doing so. Although nations have sometimes refrained from waging wars to the utmost of their physical capacity with the weapons and other military resources they possessed, there are few wars in which they have refrained from using all the available weapons and resources in some measure. Where nations have refrained from using certain means of destruction, such as gas in World War II, it has been not because of ethical prohibitions but because of military inexpediency. Although civilization has repeatedly been shocked by the invention of more destructive weapons and has repeatedly predicted that they were too horrible to be used, horror in itself has never prevented nations from using any device that "military necessity" required. This grim axiom is not confined to tyrannies, as examples from America's recent experience illustrate.

In World War I the American people were deeply shocked at the brutality of German submarine warfare. Contrary to existing laws of war and standards of humanity, this unorthodox weapon sank passenger vessels without warning and left the innocent to drown. It was German unrestricted submarine warfare that finally drove the United States into the war. Yet in World War II the United States adopted unrestricted submarine warfare as a matter of course on the same grounds of military necessity that it had condemned twenty-five years earlier.

In 1938 Japan's aerial bombing of Chinese civilians aroused tremendous moral indignation in the United States. Secretary of State Hull publicly condemned this barbarous practice. The Department of State notified manufacturers and exporters that the United States strongly opposed the sale of airplanes and aeronautical equipment to countries that bombed civilians—a "moral embargo" resulting in the suspension of the export of these items to Japan. In December, 1939, President Roosevelt declared a similar moral embargo against the Soviet Union as a protest against its bombing of Finnish civilians. Yet in World War II the German bombing of Warsaw and Rotterdam set a pattern of indiscriminate "area bombing" that became the principal feature of Allied operations against the Continent with the enthusiastic support of the citizenry. Accordingly, the American people applauded when massive formations of American and British bombers dropped "block-busters" and ignited "fire storms" with incendiaries in the cities of Germany and Japan. And, finally, the nation that envisioned itself as the world's champion of humane warfare decided that military necessity required it to devastate Hiroshima and Nagasaki with the most destructive weapons that man has invented.

Therefore, if one were to base one's judgment solely on the history of warfare in modern Western civilization, one would have to conclude that the likelihood of unlimited war is immense and the chances of limited war exceedingly small. Yet the past is only a guide to the future; it establishes no fatal inevitabilities. Men and nations are not the passive creatures of disembodied trends and factors. The areas of conscious choice among alternative courses of action are too large to be subject to scientific determination. War is certainly one of the most unpredictable social phenomena, not only because of man's inability to control the complex elements that compose it, but also, paradoxically, because of the large opportunities it affords for the ingenuity of the autonomous human will.

The history of war itself shows that men have always had a significant area of choice in the conduct of war, despite their physical capacity to annihilate each other. The limited warfare of the eighteenth century was, in large measure, a deliberate reaction to the unlimited war that preceded it. The limitation of war in the nineteenth century was, pre-eminently, a product of diplomatic skill. Who can say that a little more statesmanship in 1914 might not have prevented a war or at least limited it, or that a little more fortitude and foresight in the postwar period might not have halted the sequence of events that produced another total war? At all times political, social, and cultural factors, in addition to material conditions, have set bounds upon the alternative courses of action available, and they have determined the probable consequences; but the most fundamental condition determining the scale and scope of warfare—the nature of the ends for which men fight—has never been absolutely prescribed or foreclosed by factors beyond the control of human intelligence. The selection and restriction of military means is not automatically excluded by the mere physical capability of waging unlimited war.

In any case, historical events have none of the regularity and uniformity that permit scientific prediction, if only because of the role that chance and accidents play. We should avoid the illusion that nothing that has happened could have happened differently, simply because we can see, in retrospect, so many reasons for things having happened as they did. A study of past regularities and uniformities in the history of warfare points to certain future probabilities, but one must always add the qualification "providing conditions remain the same." In an era of rapid social, political, and technological change conditions never remain the same for long, even though man's basic predispositions may be constant. New and unpredictable conditions are always emerging, and men are continually presented with new alternatives they could not have foreseen.

Therefore, in the light of the vicissitudes of chance and the human will, we must be cognizant of the history of warfare for the potentialities and probabilities that it discloses; but, at the same time, we should judge the relevance of the past to the present in full awareness of the unique opportunities that each historical moment unfolds.

Part III | *AMERICAN STRATEGY*

Chapter Six

THE PRESENT PERIOD OF WAR

Contemporary Limited War

After explaining the ways in which wars differ according to the nature of their objectives and circumstances, Clausewitz stated that the "greatest and most decisive act of the judgment which a statesman and commander performs is that of correctly recognizing . . . the kind of war he is undertaking, of not taking it for, or wishing to make it, something which by the nature of the circumstances it cannot be. This is, therefore, the first and most comprehensive of all strategic questions."[1] Translated into the terms of this study of national strategy, Clausewitz' statement means that America's over-all strategy must be shaped so as to prepare the nation to fight the kind of wars most likely to occur. Because the crucial test of any strategy must be its success in deterring or resisting the kind of military contingencies that threaten the nation's interests, we must try to form an accurate idea of the nature of warfare in the foreseeable future in order to understand the basic requirements of American strategy.

The history of war indicates with frightful clarity that the world is ripe for unlimited war. Yet in view of the elements of free will and uniqueness in history, we cannot say that unlimited war is inevitable or that we may not actually be on the threshold of a new era of limited war. In judging the present prospect of limited war the most obvious relevant fact is that, in spite of the vast potentialities of unlimited war, the period since World War II has actually been a period of limited war. The Greek civil war (1947–49), the Berlin blockade and air lift (1948–49), the Korean War (1950–53), and the long war in Indochina (ending in 1954) all testify to this fact. All of these struggles involved the Communist and the Western blocs and, directly or indirectly, the Soviet Union and the United States. Yet in each struggle both sides observed definite self-imposed limits upon their objectives and upon the means by which they sought to attain them.

In keeping warfare limited, the adversaries have implicitly observed a kind of economy of force, sustained by their recognition that total war could not serve their interests. Because they have foreseen that an exercise of force on too large a scale or for too ambitious objectives would lead to unlimited war, they have deliberately avoided employing military measures that would carry a risk of total war incommensurate with the importance of the political objectives at stake; and for the same reason they have refrained from pursuing by military means political objectives that could not be attained without provoking the adversary to extreme measures.

On the basis of this sort of calculation the Communists have refrained from armed aggression in western Europe, where the magnitude of the threat to the NATO powers and to American security would carry a grave risk of provoking massive retaliation and total war; but they have not hesitated to employ armed aggression in the Far East, where they have calculated correctly that the United States did not regard the immediate threat to its interests and prestige as serious enough to warrant more than local resistance by limited means. The United States, for its part, has been willing to combat Communist aggression by local armed resistance when it could do so effectively by means commensurate with the limited objectives at stake; but it has refrained from employing measures of resistance disproportionate to the importance of the objectives at stake, which might threaten Communist interests and prestige to the extent of provoking counter-retaliation leading to total war. Whether the United States would have dropped atomic bombs on Moscow if Russia or the satellites had resorted to armed aggression in vital strategic areas like western Europe is uncertain. Whether Communist leaders would have taken large risks of total war in secondary strategic areas if the United States had not imposed particular limits upon the form of its retaliation, as in Korea, cannot be known. But regardless of the likelihood of these hypothetical eventualities, it appears that both sides considered the risk of their occurrence disproportionate to the possible advantages to be gained by testing the adversary's reactions to more extreme measures.

In frustration over self-imposed restraints upon a struggle with an enemy who is pledged, ultimately, to destroy their political system,

Americans may overlook the fact that the enemy has also operated under certain self-imposed restraints in order to keep warfare limited. In the Greek civil war the West refrained from attacking the Communist-led guerillas' sanctuary and source of supplies in Yugoslavia and Bulgaria, but the Communists refrained from committing Bulgarian and Yugoslavian troops to Greece. During the blockade of Berlin both the United States and Russia might easily have taken more drastic measures, but both powers limited their efforts to measures short of an armed clash— to air lift and blockade, respectively—in the belief that stronger measures in this sensitive area would have entailed a greater risk of precipitating total war than the objective warranted. In the Korean War, for both military and political reasons, the UN command conceded Communist forces a "privileged sanctuary" north of the Yalu and refrained from bombing Chinese mainland targets; but, for military and political reasons of their own, the Chinese Communists and their Soviet ally virtually conceded air superiority to the UN forces over Korea, refrained from bombing American ports of supply in Korea and American air bases in Okinawa and Japan, and withheld air and submarine attacks against American carriers and tankers in Korean waters.

In other words, what we seem to have been witnessing in this postwar period of limited war is the operation of a kind of rudimentary system of self-restraint, based on mutual understanding of a rough economy of force and sustained largely by fear of the awful potentialities of total war. This rudimentary system is not supported by a sense of community and a moral consensus or by a refined diplomacy regulating an intricate balance-of-power mechanism. However, it does have a substantial foundation in mutual self-interest. Whether the major antagonists have calculated the requirements of limited war as advantageously as possible from the standpoint of advancing their interests is debatable, but it is self-evident that they have, at least, calculated the requirements correctly from the standpoint of avoiding total war.

"Nuclear Stalemate"

The fact that wars have been limited since World War II does not indicate that they will remain limited. In order to examine the prospect of limited war more closely we must answer two questions: What basic conditions account for the present period of limited war? Are these conditions likely to continue to limit war?

As we observed in the Introduction, two basic, historically unique conditions encourage limited war but militate against total war: a deep conflict of aims and interests—known as the cold war—between the two nations that hold a preponderance of world power; a terrifying capability of the two antagonists to destroy each other. The second condition makes unlimited war resulting from either massive aggression or massive retaliation less likely, because both the Soviet Union and the United States know that they would suffer prohibitive penalties; but the two conditions operating together increase the prospect of limited war resulting from a struggle for lesser stakes, because Communist leaders know that the United States, like the Soviet Union itself, will be restrained from turning a small war into a big one when no government would rationally regard the stakes as worth the risk of all-out nuclear destruction. Churchill was thinking of the second condition when he envisioned a "balance of terror" in his notable address to the House of Commons on March 1, 1955: "It may well be that we shall by a process of sublime irony have reached a stage in this story where safety will be the sturdy child of terror, and survival the twin brother of annihilation."[2] He was describing what we commonly call the "nuclear stalemate," which is a calculus of risks that leads the nuclear powers from rationally and intentionally precipitating total war.

The "balance of terror" may have reduced the likelihood of the United States or the Soviet Union precipitating total war, but it would be a serious mistake to assume that it has made total war impossible. That is the very assumption that could break the nuclear stalemate by leading us to neglect the vigilance and the measures of military preparedness that are necessary to preserve it. Actually, the basic conditions that underlie the present period of limited war also create new dangers of unlimited war. In order to judge the prospect of limited war more soberly, we must be fully aware of the various ways in which total war may come about. There are four ways that deserve special attention:

1. The Soviet government might undertake major aggression or the American government might undertake major retaliation on the basis of a deliberate and rational calculation that total war would probably result.

2. The Soviet or the American government might either deliberately or accidentally provoke total war because of an irrational indifference to the consequences of their actions.

3. The Soviet or the American government might unintentionally precipitate total war by miscalculating the consequences of their actions

4. Total war might result from circumstances beyond the control of the United States and the Soviet Union, especially the actions of other nations.

Only in the narrow sense of avoiding the first contingency can we properly speak of preserving the nuclear stalemate. Therefore, let us first consider the possibilities of total war coming about as the result of a deliberate and rational calculation. There are two important factors operating against this contingency: first, total war is bound to be fought with strategic nuclear weapons; second, the Soviet Union and the United States both realize that with the unlimited use of these weapons they could not help suffering such terrible devastation as to outweigh any conceivable advantages they might gain. Therefore, as long as both nations can decimate each other with nuclear weapons and neither can prevent such decimation, it is probable that the resulting balance of terror will impede either power from deliberately taking the measures that would almost certainly provoke all-out nuclear war. No one can be sure of the exact measures that might precipitate such a war, but presumably they include, as a minimum, direct aggression or retaliation on the homeland of either country, massive aggression or retaliation on major strategic areas essential to the security of either country, and, perhaps, the employment of thermonuclear "city-busters" under any circumstances.

The terror of total nuclear war is a unique kind of terror in the history of warfare. Heretofore, fear of particular weapons has been offset by the prospect that the enemy would bear the chief brunt of their destruction and that, even in the case of effective enemy retaliation, only a small part of a nation's homeland and citizenry would suffer the direct impact of war. But this condition no longer exists if both of the potential belligerents believe that they will, in effect, automatically inflict disaster upon themselves when they inflict it upon the enemy. There is good evidence that they do believe this. Since the United States and the Soviet Union succeeded in exploding hydrogen weapons (in November, 1952, and August, 1953, respectively), both governments have apparently concluded that a war fought with these weapons cannot possibly serve any rational purpose, except as a measure of desperation. Thus President Truman in his final address to Congress declared that a thermonuclear war "is not a possible policy for rational men";[3] and President Eisenhower is understood to have expressed the same view when he said, "There is no longer any alternative to peace if the world is to be happy and well."[4]

On numerous occasions the heads of all the major Western powers have pointed to the futility of all-out nuclear war, but until Stalin's death Communist leaders followed his position of depreciating the importance of the atomic bomb and claiming that only capitalist society would be destroyed in an atomic war. This prompted President Truman, in his final official address, to deliver a significant admonition to Stalin:

> You claim belief in Lenin's prophecy that one stage in the development of Communist society would be war between your world and ours. But Lenin was a pre-atomic man, who viewed society and history with pre-atomic eyes. Something profound has happened since he wrote. War has changed its shape and its dimension. It cannot now be a "stage" in the development of anything save ruin for your regime and your homeland.[5]

Since the Geneva Conference of July, 1955, the successors of Stalin have publicly adopted the position that Truman in corporated in his warning. Khrushchev and Bulganin, announcing a doctrinal departure first voiced by Malenkov, have proclaimed the inadmissibility of thermonuclear war on the grounds that it would bring disaster to all mankind and not just to capitalist society; and Khrushchev, in his notable address before the Twentieth Soviet Communist Party Congress on February 14, 1956, explicitly rejected Lenin's thesis of the inevitability of war.[6]

As the terrible effects of thermonuclear war continue to impress themselves upon the consciousness of the whole world, the deliberate and rational undertaking of such a war by the Soviet Union or the United States becomes less likely. This applies to retaliation as well as to aggression. The American government has never considered aggression or "preventive war" as a possible course of action, but until Russia's explosion of an atomic bomb in 1949 and a thermonuclear device in 1953 it could at least envision undertaking with relative impunity a one-sided war in retaliation against Soviet aggression. But now the nation knows that nuclear retaliation upon the Soviet Union can be countered by Soviet nuclear retaliation on the United States. As realization of this fact spreads and "sinks in," the President and his advisers are bound to grow increasingly reluctant to employ America's nuclear deterrent. As they become increasingly conscious of the nation's mounting fear of counter-retaliation, they may even hesitate to employ full-scale nuclear retaliation against attacks on major strategic areas. Whatever effect this development may have on America's military and diplomatic position, it undoubtedly reduces the likelihood of intentional total war, unless we anticipate the United States reaching a state of desperation as the result of piecemeal reverses.

However, we must wonder whether this nuclear stalemate is a condition upon which we can base firm strategic plans or whether it is merely a temporary state of equilibrium. Let us consider the chances of the stalemate coming to an end. It might end in at least two ways: (*a*) either the United States or the Soviet Union might gain a decisive superiority in defensive or offensive capabilities; (*b*) both powers might gain defensive capabilities greatly superior to each other's offensive capabilities.

In the first case, either power might reduce its relative vulnerability to nuclear attack or increase its relative offensive nuclear capability to such an extent that it would be willing to undertake total war in anticipation of the adversary's inability to retaliate effectively enough to outweigh the benefits of the initiative. It is not difficult to imagine such a development as a theoretical possibility. It might take place, for example, as the result of sudden and substantial alterations in relative offensive and defensive capabilities. These alterations might result from technological advances, from internal political and economic developments within the United States or Russia, from the acquisition, neutralization, or defection of allies, or from internal developments within allied nations.

Even if such alterations occurred, however, total war would still be worthwhile to a nation with defensive or offensive superiority only under special conditions. It might be worthwhile if the nation undertaking total war could prevent or neutralize nuclear retaliation, if the war ended so quickly that the attacking nation escaped serious damage, or if the attacking nation foresaw that total war was the only chance of avoiding an even more desperate situation. However, aside from these conditions, any relative defensive or offensive advantages the United States or the Soviet Union may acquire will decrease in significance, since even a power with substantial inferiority in both defensive and offensive capabilities could devastate the homeland of the superior power. In fact, the United States and Russia may already have reached the point of "saturation," where, although one power may become stronger in the instruments of total war than the other, both will be capable of inflicting crippling injuries.

For the same reason, it is quite unlikely that the superiority of both powers' defensive capabilities can ever be sufficient to vitiate the nuclear stalemate. Even supposing that both powers could destroy 95 of every 100 thermonuclear missiles launched, the 5 that burst would kill and destroy whole populations and cities. Thus neither power would be likely to gain anything that would be worth its losses—again excepting the contingencies of a quick war or a war of desperation.

Moreover, the difficulties of calculating relative defensive and offensive capabilities or the length of a war would be so great and the consequences of miscalculation would be so disastrous that it is hard to imagine either power rationally taking great risks of unlimited war unless it were so hard-pressed that even a slight chance of saving or improving its position seemed worth the risk of total destruction. For one thing, the tremendous acceleration of military invention and the enormous magnification of military potential in the last century have rendered the estimation of relative military capabilities in advance of war exceedingly difficult. The technological advances since World War II are so momentous and the actual military implications of these advances are so uncertain as virtually to preclude either power from rationally undertaking total war on the basis of an estimate that its armament had overcome the conditions of stalemate and saturation. The possibility of "technological breakthroughs," including temporary superiority in chemical and biological weapons, during war itself makes such an estimate still more tenuous.

Finally, even if the balance of terror did not deter war, it would be difficult to conceive of either the United States or Russia precipitating total war as long as they could maintain their security otherwise; for the very destructiveness of all-out nuclear war seems incompatible with most political objectives that one can imagine, short of the mere opportunity to survive as a nation. For example, a full-scale nuclear war in Europe would certainly wreck industry, transportation, and communication so thoroughly and so lastingly as to render victory useless and probably an unconscionable burden.

Therefore, as long as the Soviet and American governments act rationally, and the balance of military power between them undergoes no radical and sudden alteration, neither will deliberately precipitate total war by aggression or retaliation except under certain special contingencies. One cannot exclude from these contingencies the possibility that the United States, lacking means of countering Communist aggression locally and by limited war and suffering a disastrous chain of piecemeal military and political reverses, will finally risk nuclear devastation rather than accept passive defeat.

The Possibility of Irrationality

In the foregoing hypothetical situations we have assumed that both the American and the Soviet governments act rationally; that is, that they both eschew rash and impulsive moves and base their actions upon objective calculations of the best means for achieving their national self-interest, weighing gains against costs, advantages against disadvantages, and always exhibiting a scrupulous regard for the consequences of their actions. But, considering the importance of this assumption, we must wonder whether it is a valid one. Fortunately, both powers so far have been sufficiently rational to fight cold war or limited war only, even though this has entailed decisions and actions that were unpalatable. But the real test of rationality is the long-run test. What will be the effect of prolonged political tension and continually mounting nuclear capabilities upon American and Soviet conduct? These circumstances might drive the American and Soviet governments to take rash and capricious actions, but they might also prove an inducement to caution and deliberation.

In appraising the chances of the American and Russian governments remaining rational, we must first recognize that no state has ever been content to pursue its self-interest purely on the basis of a cold-blooded calculation of material advantages and disadvantages. All states are in some measure sensitive to considerations of honor, prestige, and principle, which are not susceptible to a rigid cost accounting. Therefore, even though they might follow the rational imperatives of power in other respects, American and Russian leaders might be driven to precipitate total war for the sake of these intangible values, regardless of the consequences. For example, on the basis of an objective comparison of gains and losses it might not pay the United States to retaliate against a Communist seizure of Berlin or Iran at the cost of a total war resulting in the obliteration of New York, Detroit, and Chicago. Yet it may be that no government that placidly acquiesced in such a blow without retaliating against the center of aggression could survive the wrath of public opinion, even though such a measure were ineffective in regaining the territory. Presumably, the Soviet government is more amenable to accepting reverses and to compromising principles; but undoubtedly it, too, has limits beyond which it will not tolerate humiliation for the sake of material advantage.

The limitation of war is made more uncertain when governments must take account of considerations beyond a strictly objective calculation of military and political gains and losses. But even if such considerations were excluded, the chances of Soviet and American leaders remaining sufficiently rational to avoid total war would be quite incalculable, simply because it is difficult to predict the incidence of such qualities as patience, self-control, circumspection, and foresight. One can only speculate about Russian and American rationality on the basis of their fundamental approaches to war.

Nothing in Communist doctrine or Soviet practice is incompatible with the rational restraint of war. The Soviet approach to war and politics differs profoundly from the fanatical compulsions of Hitler. It condemns rash and impulsive moves. It not only sanctions but positively prescribes a great flexibility of tactics. The qualities of flexibility, patience, and circumspection, exalted in revolutionary doctrine and experience, are reinforced by Russia's long pre-Bolshevik experience in diplomacy. Consequently, Soviet leaders are emotionally and intellectually predisposed to manipulate power cautiously in order to attain specific political objectives—one calculated step at a time and, if necessary, one step backward in order to take two steps forward. They will not shrink from employing armed force in a large-scale war like World War II if they have to, or in a limited war, as in Finland and Korea, when there seems to be little risk involved; but, being well versed in revolutionary techniques as well as in the theories of Clausewitz, and possessing a metaphysical confidence in the eventual triumph of their cause, they much prefer the more stealthy, indirect methods of diplomacy, economic pressure, propaganda, subversion, infiltration, and insurrection, in which the political aspects of warfare are accentuated. Moreover, they are willing to halt or retreat in the face of superior power. They have retreated in Iran and Berlin; they have accepted defeat in Greece and stalemate in Korea; and, politically, they have made tactical retreats in Yugoslavia and Austria. Therefore, as long as Russian security and prestige are not seriously threatened, Soviet statesmen are not likely to run extreme risks of war in order to attain their ends when they have so many less risky methods available to them. Of course, one cannot be sure that the rulers of Russia will remain cautious, calculating realists forever. Under the pressure of either the internal or the external struggle for power they might submit to the unreasoning and desperate ambition that has seized so many despots. Perhaps there are psychological processes accompanying the possession of totalitarian power that will inexorably undermine circumspection. Yet, in the absence of any evidence of such a development, we must operate on the assumptions that practice leads us to make about Soviet conduct.

Speculations about American rationality must begin by recognizing that in the nature of things a democratic power has more difficulty in conducting a flexible, circumspect, and patient strategy than a power that is not dependent upon the winds of public sentiment. Public sentiment in a democracy is likely to be both more volatile and more rigid in its approach toward foreign relations. It is subject to sudden, erratic shifts of direction that run contrary to the continuity of international politics; yet it is also slow to adopt a new direction and reluctant to abandon an old one in response to changing circumstances.

The United States is by its predispositions and experience especially ill prepared to conduct a patient, circumspect struggle for power over an indefinite period of time with no conclusive outcome in sight. Americans are not accustomed to the irritating restraints imposed by limited, morally unappealing objectives. They prefer to pursue their national objectives in bold, massive thrusts, not by circuitous routes or by alternate retreats and advances. They are not attuned to the stolid waiting upon events, the deviousness, the bargaining, the maneuvering for position, which the Russians take for granted.

And yet, considering these facts, it is remarkable to what extent the American people have time and again acted contrary to their basic predispositions in order to meet overriding demands of national security. They have continued to talk and sometimes to think in terms of the simpler principles and purposes of an earlier day; but when the practical alternatives have been clear, they have somehow managed to meet concrete situations with a measure of pragmatic wisdom that has characterized American conduct in other spheres of activity. In this encouraging fact there is no cause for complacency. America's *ad hoc* adjustment to a series of crises gives no assurance that we shall develop the maturity and poise that are indispensable for the "long haul." Still, throughout the nation's whole history the American people have shown an encouraging facility for learning from experience. For example, compare the way in which they entered and fought the Spanish-American War, World War I, and World War II, and you must certainly discern a steadily sobering approach to war. Or compare the national reaction to the sinking of the "Maine," the torpedoing of the "Lusitania," the strafing of the "Panay" in 1937, and the more recent Chinese Communist attacks on American planes and the imprisonment of American aviators. Some will discern in the decreasing emotional response to these successive incidents a progressive deterioration of moral fibers; but they might better regard this phenomenon as a rough gauge of the extent to which the nation has supplanted an impulsive and somewhat romantic approach to international conflict with a more mature approach, largely because it has learned to reckon with the increasingly serious consequences of its actions.

It takes two, as a minimum, to play the postwar game of cold war rationally; but considering the major antagonists' compelling incentives for moving cautiously and keeping their wits about them, unlimited war would seem more likely to result from miscalculation or from events beyond the control of the United States and the Soviet Union than from design or an abandonment of reason.

The Possibility of Miscalculation

We have examined the circumstances in which the United States or the Soviet Union might destroy the nuclear stalemate by rationally and deliberately precipitating total war and have concluded that this eventuality is unlikely except under certain special conditions. But there is an element of unreality in this examination, for it assumes that governments know the consequences of their actions in advance of the event, whereas, actually, they must act on the basis of estimates of probabilities and risks. This makes a substantial difference, for a government might quite rationally take a course of action on the basis of a *calculation* of the risk of total war which it would not take if it had *positive knowledge* that such a course would result in total war. At the same time, the difficulty of calculating risks accurately is immense. The factors of relative power, political gains and losses, the importance of objectives, and the anticipated reaction of the adversary, all of which would presumably enter into a rational decision to undertake a particular military measure, are not scientifically determinate; nor are the magnitude and impact of the military elements that would enter into the equation of war readily discernible. Moreover, the difficulties of calculating the adversary's reactions to various measures are compounded by subjective factors such as honor, prestige, principle, and sheer impulse.

In the eighteenth century, when the means of war were inherently limited and the ends of war were confined to dynastic, trade, or territorial objectives of limited scope, war and politics approached a science of adjusting calculable magnitudes of power; but the material and non-material conditions that made this possible have long since vanished. Moreover, insofar as the limitation of war is a matter of intellectual skill, it is discouraging to observe that even the most masterful diplomats of the eighteenth century repeatedly miscalculated what a nation would fight for and what it would forego, what a nation could get by bargaining and what it could get by fighting. The balancing of armed power and diplomacy, the application of force to political ends, is an art, not a science. In the practice of that art the shrewdest intellects are fallible. On the other hand, the statesmen of the eighteenth century took much greater risks of miscalculating than any rational statesman would take today, simply because the penalties of miscalculation were relatively small. If they had known that every commitment, every threat of force, and every clash of arms might grow into a total war approaching mutual destruction, one must suppose that they would have calculated and acted upon their calculations with much greater caution.

The necessity of acting cautiously in apprehension of the great opportunities for miscalculation may minimize the chances of total war resulting directly and immediately from some American or Soviet move, but the danger of unintentional total war lies not only in such direct provocation but also in the possibility of a limited war gradually growing out of control. Thus a limited war in which the United States or Russia were involved might become so unfavorable to one of them that this power would feel compelled to extend the war, despite the increased risk of total war, rather than acquiesce in defeat. The opposing power might then be provoked to retaliate by means that threatened the beleaguered adversary still further. And so, step by step, through no original intention of either power, a limited war might grow beyond control.

The likelihood of such a development would be increased by one adversary's belief that the other would not dare to precipitate total war. For example, let us imagine that the Soviet Union or Communist China conducted a series of successful limited military actions or threats of military action that the United States failed to counter for fear of precipitating total war. Eventually, this might encourage Communist leaders to underestimate the bounds of American acquiescence and undertake a military venture which the United States, in desperation, would be compelled to meet by measures incompatible with limited war.

The chances of limited war becoming unlimited as a result of miscalculation are made greater by the fact that the United States and Russia possess tactical nuclear weapons—that is, a variety of relatively small atomic shells and bombs with an exposive force in the range of 1 kiloton (equivalent to 1,000 tons of T.N.T.) to 40 kilotons (twice the power of the Hiroshima bomb), suitable for use on military targets directly related to the battle—in addition to thermonuclear bombs as large as 20 megatons (equivalent to 20,000,000 tons of T.N.T.), designed to obliterate entire cities. It would be a great mistake to assume that the use of tactical nuclear weapons must necessarily lead to the use of strategic city-busters and total war; it might actually provide the best chance of keeping warfare limited when a power would otherwise have to choose between defeat and strategic retaliation. Nevertheless, the fact remains that the actual military and political effect of these powerful new weapons, untested under actual war conditions, is more unpredictable than the effect of conventional weapons. It is not difficult to see why.

In the first place, any weapon with such tremendous destructive power and with such a wide range of uses will have to be employed with great restraint and foresight in order to be militarily effective and yet not so destructive as to provoke measures of retaliation that will lead to a general war involving the major ports and cities of the belligerents. For example, the chances of keeping a tactical atomic war limited and localized may depend, in large measure, upon the ability of the belligerents to distinguish between tactical and strategic targets, between military installations in the zone of battle and centers of population and industry outside the zone of battle. But the specific restraints incumbent upon the belligerents in order to make such a distinction effective, especially in highly integrated industrial areas, are quite speculative, even if we assume a mutual desire to observe the distinction.

In the second place, the psychological reaction of civilian populations to the use of these weapons cannot be foreseen. If people become convinced by fear of the unknown and by the alarms of publicists that any nuclear destruction is so horrible that it is exclusively an instrument of total war, then military situations involving tactical nuclear weapons which might otherwise be compatible with limited war may, nevertheless, become the provocation for total war. If, for example, a city adjacent to an airfield in the zone of battle becomes the incidental victim of an atomic bomb, public pressure might force retaliation upon enemy bases and cities outside the combat zone, and soon all distinctions between tactical and strategic targets would disappear. Such a result is by no means inevitable, but the point here is that it is highly unpredictable and, to that extent, conducive to miscalculation.

Possibilities beyond Russian and American Control

So far we have considered the chances of unlimited war resulting from the actions of the United States and the Soviet Union, but now we must take account of the fact that these two powers do not have exclusive control over either the outbreak or the waging of warfare. Actually, the increasing power and independence of their allies and the mounting ferment among uncommitted nations and peoples are progressively reducing the ability of both powers to shape the course of politics and war according to their own designs. As the bipolarization of world power breaks down, we may expect the cold war to become increasingly a war of active political maneuvering rather than a war of position and political stalemate between two controlling powers.

The greater the number of states that become significant weights in the world balance of power, the more opportunities there will be for all states to miscalculate the consequences of their acts. This situation, by creating a more flexible political system, might conceivably moderate the conduct of states and enforce greater caution upon the major antagonists. But, more likely, it will be the source of unprecedented tension by encouraging rash acts on the part of nations just becoming aware of their power to assert new ambitions and redress old grievances.

Already it is apparent that some of the junior members of the two coalitions may not be under the same compulsions to avoid war and to limit war as the heads of the coalitions. South Korea and Nationalist China continually tug at the American leash. Red China, despite the general patience and circumspection of her leaders, probably has less reason for caution than Russia: Red China's external interests are not so well satisfied, and at the same time the states on her border are more vulnerable to aggrandizement. Through continual probing of each other's political and military positions, the United States and the Soviet Union show signs of a prudent relationship, born of their estimates of the limits beyond which they cannot safely press one another; but some of their allies, who have experienced these limits only indirectly through the frustration imposed upon their special interests by the major antagonists, may regard this prudence as something to be overcome. Moreover, in view of their relatively undeveloped economies and their secondary strategic importance to the chief antagonists, they are likely to see more to gain and less to lose from a total war than the highly industrialized nations that are in the direct line of fire, so to speak.

As allies may sometimes increase the difficulties of preventing or limiting warfare by a lack of restraint, at other times they may just as surely exert the same effect by an excess of caution. Thus America's European allies, acutely conscious of their vulnerability in a total war, may fail to assume the necessary risks of a strong diplomatic and military posture outside the sphere of their immediate interests or fail to combine the proper proportion of daring with self-restraint in order to induce moderation in a potential aggressor. The mere knowledge of Soviet nuclear capabilities could induce a paralysis of decision among allies that would prevent the free world from checking Communist incursions until the stakes became so high that it was too late to do so by limited means.

Certainly, the chances of the United States and Russia avoiding unlimited war will not be improved if a number of other nations gain the capability of waging nuclear war, a capability which Great Britain has already acquired in significant measure. And it seems likely that they *will* gain this capability, perhaps in the next decade or two, through the acquisition of weapons or fissionable material from the major atomic powers. This development will probably increase the chances of the United States and the Soviet Union becoming involved in a small war begun by other powers; and it will increase the chances of smaller powers, out of desperation or compelling subjective impulses, employing nuclear measures that will involve the major powers in warfare on terms they will find difficult to control. The interests of third powers will not necessarily coincide with the interests of the United States or the Soviet Union with respect to the form and the scale of warfare. For example, a war that is limited and peripheral from the standpoint of these two giants may be virtually unlimited in the eyes of a small power whose very survival is at stake in the contest. Under this condition the smaller power will not be under the same compulsion to avoid expanding the war by foregoing the employment of its nuclear weapons as the major powers, whose homelands are not directly involved. In fact, it may feel compelled to take exactly the opposite course.

There is another danger stemming from the dispersion of nuclear capabilities among many nations. It will raise the possibility of anonymous nuclear attack by making it extremely difficult to determine the source of an attack. The possibility of anonymous attack might tempt small powers to use their nuclear capabilities rashly. It might tempt larger powers to use small powers for proxy attacks. It will put a premium upon preventive action. It is bound to create an atmosphere of tension and uncertainty conducive to miscalculation and impetuosity.

The Future Contingencies of War

One may guess that the cold war of the foreseeable future will be characterized by a diminished danger of war coming as the result of deliberate actions of the Soviet Union or the United States and by increasing danger of war resulting from the actions of third powers and from Soviet and American miscalculation—especially the kind of miscalculation that would permit limited war to expand beyond control. Minor Communist aggressions in the vulnerable rimlands of Eurasia and limited Communist intervention in the wars of third powers in vital strategic areas such as the Middle East will probably be the most serious strategic problem facing the United States.

In this period of nuclear stalemate between the great powers and o increasing military and political activity among lesser states, we may expect the Communists to pursue their aims with flexibility and resourcefulness. When the opportunities for political and economic penetration are promising, the Soviet Union will prefer to reserve military power as an implicit threat and an instrument of blackmail. But when the opportunities for direct military gains are more promising, Russia or China or both may choose overt military action, ranging from guerilla warfare to direct or indirect support of large-scale attacks on limited territorial positions. One method of aggrandizement will not exclude the other; but always in the background there will be the Communist military threat under a variety of conditions that will properly preclude resistance except by means short of total war, and this threat of limited aggression will be reinforced by the growing Communist capacity for total war.

Of course, in assessing future military contingencies we must recognize that the dangers of unlimited war and the prospects of limited war do not exist independently of the conscious direction of American strategy. As one of the two most powerful nations in the world the

United States can exert a significant marginal influence upon the incidence and the form of warfare. If total war were either impossible or inevitable, it might be to American advantage to confront Communist aggression with a strategy that was indifferent to the risks of precipitating an all-out nuclear struggle; and this sort of strategy might even be more compatible with the traditional image of America's role in the world. But we cannot know whether total war is impossible or inevitable; we can only estimate probabilities. On the other hand, this much is clear: If we act on the assumption that a continuing limitation of war is possible, then there is some hope that war will remain limited; but if we act on the assumption that total war is either impossible or inevitable, then we shall forfeit this hope. Between these two courses there is only one rational choice: to act on the assumption that wars, though they are not entirely avoidable, may at least be limited; to bend every effort to develop a strategy designed to maintain American security by methods that maximize the prospects of limited war while minimizing the dangers of unlimited war.

Chapter Seven

CONTAINMENT BEFORE KOREA

The Conflict between Reality and Predispositions

The history of American strategy since World War II shows that American security has become increasingly dependent upon a national capacity and will to contain Communist aggression by means compatible with limited war. It also shows that the traditional American approach to war has seriously impeded the development of the requisite capacity and will. One cannot but marvel at the general common sense and maturity with which the nation has adjusted to a revolution in American foreign policy in the face of extraordinary military and political developments. Yet there is no assurance that the adjustment will be commensurate with the bewildering pace of events.

As a nation we have been preoccupied in this postwar period with the threat of another total war, but we have given only grudging and sporadic attention to the problem of limited wars under the pressure of crises. In practice we have been unwilling to assume large risks of total war in order to contain local Communist aggression; but, at the same time, we have not reconciled ourselves to supporting military policies and a national strategy capable of meeting such aggression by means short of total war. We have almost instinctively pursued limited political ends and limited military means in response to specific threats; but we have been disposed to talk—and in large measure to think—in terms of policies free from such frustrating limitations. These contradictions in our foreign policy are partly a product of the discrepancy between concrete imperatives of power and our traditional image of America's role in the world, and they are partly the product of our ambivalent approach to war—the juxtaposition of pacific and pugnacious predispositions. Fundamentally, they spring from a deep aversion to the material, emotional, and spiritual demands of this unprecedented period of cold and limited war.

During the past decade the nation has been forced by the circumstances of the cold war to conduct its foreign relations in accordance with a strategy that is contrary to its basic predispositions, a strategy of limited ends and limited means, an expensive, frustrating, and morally ambiguous strategy. Our reluctance to acknowledge this strategy candidly, our failure to implement it adequately, and our attempt to escape from its concrete implications are the measure of our difficulty in adopting military and political policies capable of meeting the threat of limited war.

In the most general way, American strategy can be described as containment. The overriding objective of containment is to keep the Soviet sphere of control from expanding beyond its postwar boundaries by building local situations of strength and by demonstrating a capacity to meet force with counterforce. This strategy received its definitive exposition in the famous article by "Mr. X" on "The Sources of Soviet Conduct," which appeared in the July, 1947, issue of the magazine *Foreign Affairs*. As Washington correspondents immediately surmised, the article was written by George F. Kennan, then the director of the State Department's Policy Planning Staff. It was an outgrowth of a memorandum he had written more than a year before as chargé d'affaires in Moscow.[1] However, the strategy of containment did not spring full-grown from Kennan's fertile mind; it developed out of the concrete conditions of the postwar struggle for power. Containment was forced upon the American government by the menace of Soviet incursions in the Middle East and the Mediterranean area. It emerged from a gradual and reluctant recognition of three crucial facts: that the Soviet Union was bent upon extending its control, cautiously but persistently, to every adjacent area in which a military and political vacuum permitted; that American security absolutely depended upon keeping Communist power out of vital strategic areas threatened by Soviet expansion; and that the United States was the only nation that had the power to check Soviet expansion into these areas.

America's assumption of an active role in power politics on the basis of its recognition of these three grim facts was bound to be a painful process, because it directly contravened the nation's prevailing postwar expectation that the old spheres-of-influence game would be replaced by a system of collective security, based upon continuing Big Three collaboration within the framework of the UN Charter. Nevertheless, the American government proved to be less reluctant to adopt the strategy of containment than it was to acknowledge it or to recognize its true implications. Kennan wrote that "the main element of any United States policy toward the Soviet Union must be that of a long-term, patient but firm and vigilant containment";[2] and the whole world has since described American strategy as "containment." Yet, significantly enough, the initiators of containment never accepted this description. Obviously embarrassed by its "negative," purely defensive connotations, they studiously avoided the term, except on several occasions when they felt compelled to counteract partisan criticism. In fact, they did not speak in terms of strategy at all. They preferred to dress America's military and political policies in the more elegant vocabulary of "collective security," which, by conveying the impression that the exercise of American power is governed solely by an impartial concern for maintaining a universal system of international law and order, concealed the fact that the United States is actually forced to pick and choose the exercise of its power according to the impact of the surrounding configurations of national power upon its special security interests.[3]

Spokesmen of the Eisenhower administration, feeling no pride of authorship, were not satisfied merely to ignore containment; they ostensibly repudiated the whole conception as unworthy of traditional American boldness and initiative in foreign affairs. In its place they proclaimed a new and "positive" strategy, which they promulgated in terms of "liberation," "massive retaliation," and other stirring phrases.

Nevertheless, in practice neither postwar administration departed from the strategic objective which Kennan had described. Both merely pursued it by somewhat different methods. On a number of occasions since 1947 the American government has had the opportunity of choosing an alternative strategy by making certain concrete political and military decisions, but it has consistently rejected the alternative. Yet, just as consistently, the government has described its policies and actions in words that avoided the slightest suggestion of containment. This is not simply a matter of semantics. It is a sign of the nation's profound distaste for the whole idea of containment.

Just how repugnant containment is becomes manifest when one considers its logical implications. Containment is directly and immediately concerned with achieving a particular configuration of power, not with punishing aggression or vindicating universal principles of justice and law. Its determining objective is the limited one of keeping the Communist sphere of control within its postwar boundaries, not the more ambitious goal of rolling back Communist power and liberating peoples enslaved by Communist control. It accepts coexistence between non-Communist and Communist powers and aims merely to improve the terms of coexistence. It aims, not to eliminate communism or Communist nations, but merely to reach a more advantageous basis for mutual survival.

The limited—some would say "negative"—objectives of containment are a reflection of the logic of the cold war, which forces the United States to concentrate upon preserving the status quo against an imperialist power. We are seeking security, not aggrandizement; stability, not instability. Therefore, we cannot escape an essentially defensive role, and we cannot prevent the Communists from seizing a large measure of the initiative as long as they have the ambition and the ability to make trouble. This is not to say that containment precludes the pursuit of many desirable "positive" goals beyond its defensive objective; but if we speak of a strategy—a plan for employing a nation's resources so as to achieve feasible objectives—as opposed to general aspirations, then it is clear that the only strategic objectives which are consistent with containment and which have had concrete operational significance for the day-to-day conduct of America's foreign relations are the limited ones described in the preceding paragraph. And it is these objectives which have, in fact, determined our employment of national power in the past decade, no matter what ultimate purpose we may have sought.

Furthermore, containment promises no clear and conclusive end to the struggle for power but only an indefinite period of tension and sacrifice. Containment must continue as long as the cold war continues. Spokesmen of both the Truman and Eisenhower administrations have repeatedly stated that it may last for generations. As compensation for this somber prospect, the tacit practitioners of containment have been able to present nothing more than the meager hope that, in the end, if we persist, the Communist system will either crumble from within or else abandon its aggressive aims and settle down to truly civilized coexistence. The Truman administration added to these faint hopes the prospect that a time would come when the United States could negotiate from "situations of strength," when negotiation would be the normal way of settling disputes. But since it could not envision the termination of the cold war by negotiation until the Communists, in effect, ceased being Communists, this prospect scarcely brightened the outlook for containment.[4] The truth of the matter is that if the cold war cannot be ended by diplomacy or by the disintegration or mellowing of Communist power, then containment may well be, as its critics charge, a strategy of indefinite stalemate.

Thus it is plain to see that containment involves the acceptance of limitations and restraints that directly contravene America's traditional image of itself as a bold and forthright nation which stands above power politics and conducts foreign relations according to universal moral and legal standards but which, once forced to enter the fray, marshals its full strength, seizes the initiative of battle in the name of self-determination, collective security, or some other supranational principle, overwhelms the enemy in a crushing offensive, and finally secures a definitive peace on the basis of unconditional surrender.

If the intangible spiritual demands of containment stir a deep-rooted moral and emotional repugnance in the American soul, its concrete material demands strike directly at the "pocket-book nerve." It is inevitable that a strategy that requires meeting a wide range of military contingencies by means suitable to the nature of the contest and proportionate to the objectives at stake will cost far more in men and money than a strategy designed merely to meet the single drastic contingency of a major attack initiating a total war. But preparation for the multifarious contingencies of limited war is implicit in the effort to contain Communist expansion by the measured application of counterforce to a ceaseless, resourceful pressure upon shifting points of Western power. This effort demands the maintenance of a flexible and diversified military establishment in constant readiness over an indefinite period of time. Although the resulting economic costs to the taxpayer and consumer would be insignificant in a total war, they press hard upon the bounds of sacrifice that a materialistic and individualistic democratic society is willing to support in a period of cold and limited war.

The real wonder is that a nation, compelled to follow a course so contrary to its predispositions, has adjusted to the imperatives of limited war as well as it has. Nevertheless, America's adjustment to reality has been more of an *ad hoc* response to unanticipated crises than a product of strategic foresight and planning. We have planned our policies for fighting and deterring a total war, but we have only improvised our policies toward limited war as each crisis has arisen. One important reason for this is that we have scarcely dared admit to ourselves that we are pursuing a strategy that makes the problem of limited war inescapable, for concerted strategic planning implies an emotional and intellectual adjustment to realities which Americans have never completely achieved. The real strategic question facing the nation has never been whether or not to adhere to containment, for we have consistently rejected every alternative, but rather by what methods to implement containment so as to be able to avoid total wars, to keep wars limited, and to fight limited wars successfully. Unfortunately, this problem has always been obscured by our profound distaste for the very notion of containment and limited war.

The Genesis of Containment

Kennan concluded from his analysis of the sources of Soviet conduct that "Soviet pressure is something that can be contained by the adroit and vigilant application of counterforce at a series of constantly shifting geographical and political points, corresponding to the shifts and maneuvers of Soviet policy"; and so he advocated "a policy of firm containment, designed to confront the Russians with unalterable counterforce at every point where they show signs of encroaching upon the interests of a peaceful and stable world."[5] But could the United States meet every conceivable Communist incursion with unalterable counterforce everywhere along the whole periphery of Soviet power? If it succeeded in containing the Communists at one point, would they not merely burst out at some other point? Would this not mean draining American resources in a series of futile peripheral contests, fought on the Communists' initiative and on the Communists' terms?

The genesis of containment is commonly dated from the announcement of the Truman Doctrine and the Greek-Turkish Aid Program in March, 1947. From the outset, at the time of America's intervention in the Greek civil war, our active effort to contain the Communist sphere of control raised the perplexing problem of limited war implicitly posed in Kennan's analysis. And yet there was scarcely any evidence of the conscious initiation of a well-conceived national strategy in the American decision to give economic and military aid to Greece and Turkey. There was no sign of official or public recognition of the nature and scope of the problem of limited war at the time this decision was made. In fact, the problem was largely concealed by the way in which the government appealed for public support of its program. It appealed not in terms of containment but in terms of a contest between free peoples and totalitarianism.

The origins of the Truman Doctrine and the Greek-Turkish Aid Program lie in the Russian-American struggle for power centering upon the Middle Eastern and Mediterranean area. For at least eighteen months preceding the sudden and dramatic announcement of America's decision to take an active part in this struggle, Soviet intentions in Iran, Turkey, and Greece had been a matter of serious official concern. In March, 1946, the United States had taken the lead in securing the withdrawal of Russian troops from Iran by pressure exerted through the UN Security Council. However, until the British government informed Washington at the end of February, 1947, that it could no longer bear the economic burden of resistance in the area and would have to withdraw entirely from Greece, the American government did not face up to the full extent of its involvement in this sphere of historic British supremacy.

The decision to ask Congress for a huge appropriation to render assistance to Greece and Turkey, of which well over half was directed toward military aid, was a direct response to urgent strategic considerations. It was a direct reflection of a general view in the government that the whole Middle Eastern and Mediterranean area was a strategic unity, no part of which could be allowed to fall to Russian imperialism if the United States were to preserve the geopolitical bases of its security. Yet it was not in these terms that the decision was presented to Congress and the general public.

In his famous address before a joint session of Congress on March 12, 1947, President Truman began his appeal for aid to Greece and Turkey by describing the tragic economic and political unrest in Greece. He said that "democratic Greece" needed American aid in order to survive as a nation. He added that Turkey needed aid too; for, as he explained in the latter part of his address, the fall of Greece and Turkey might spread confusion and disorder throughout the whole Middle East and even to other parts of the world. But these observations were secondary to the main burden of the President's message. American security, he declared, depends upon the preservation of an international order in which "free peoples" can "maintain their free institutions and their national integrity against aggressive movements that seek to impose upon them totalitarian regimes." He portrayed a current struggle between two ways of life—the way of freedom and the way of oppression. And then he proclaimed the sentence that soon became known throughout the world as the Truman Doctrine: "I believe that it must be the policy of the United

States to support free peoples who are resisting attempted subjugation by armed minorities or by outside pressures."[6]

Clearly, the core of President Truman's address was an attempt to dramatize a straightforward power-political move in phrases that evoked quite different images of America's traditional conception of its role in the world. The key sentence was, in fact, lifted almost word for word from a paper entitled "Public Information Program on United States Aid to Greece," which was drafted by a State Department subcommittee charged with presenting the government's decision in a manner that would secure public support. As one of the participants in the drafting has accurately observed, this paper "was policy expression of so wide and sweeping a nature that it became far-reaching policy determination."[7]

President Truman's bold but abrupt departure in American foreign policy won remarkably instantaneous and comprehensive support in Congress and the nation at large, and it might not have elicited such a gratifying response if it had not been pitched to a crusading tone. Nevertheless, the manner of its presentation left its implications for American strategy excessively ambiguous. One indication of this ambiguity appeared almost immediately when questions concerning the scope of the Truman Doctrine arose in Congress and the press. Did it mean that the United States was committing itself to resist "aggressive movements" threatening "free peoples" anywhere in the world, regardless of America's immediate national interest? Taken at face value, that was the logical implication of President Truman's words. If so, the Doctrine might be laudable from the standpoint of the ideal of collective security; but from the standpoint of a strategy designed to promote American security, it would be a formula for disaster. For a strategy deals with the effective employment of limited national power, and it must of necessity keep power and commitments in balance by selecting the circumstances of intervention according to their effect upon the nation's security position, not simply according to universal standards of international welfare.

For this very reason no one was more disturbed by the implications of Truman's message than the purported author of containment, George Kennan. Kennan objected to the size of the military aid slated for Greece and to aid of any kind to Turkey, because he believed that this entailed too great a risk of provoking a general war. But what really alarmed him was the ideological content of the message, with its implied blanket commitment to aid free peoples resisting totalitarian aggression everywhere.[8]

Shortly after the purported author of containment objected so strenuous-ly to its first major enunciation and application, Walter Lippmann began criticizing Kennan's idea of confronting the Russians with counterforce "at every point" as involving the nation in military commitments far beyond its material power and its psychological ability to sustain.[9]

What alarmed Kennan and Lippmann also aroused some members of Congress, chiefly "isolationist" Republicans and "left-wing" Democrats. They pointedly asked whether the United States was adopting a policy of resisting totalitarian threats to free institutions all over the world, and they charged that such a policy would bankrupt the nation and involve it in an endless attempt to prop up decadent regimes with military force. Congressman Judd wanted to know why the Truman Doctrine was not being applied in China.

It fell to Under-Secretary of State Acheson to clarify these points. In his testimony before the Senate and House committees that were con-sidering the program, he explained, in effect, that the United States would aid free peoples if the circumstances warranted it from the standpoint of American interests; and he contended, with obvious reluctance to go into the matter, that the circumstances in China were different.[10] This anti-climactic elucidation of the Truman Doctrine at least established the limited scope of the government's intentions, but it did little to illuminate the real nature of the strategy that the United States had presumably launched. James Reston, reporting upon the passage of the aid bill, ob-served that "there has not been in recent history a bill that won such compelling majorities and at the same time produced so many disagree-ments and so much mental confusion."[11] Perhaps the principal reason for this was, as Walter Lippmann charged, that administration spokesmen had oversold and overgeneralized a simple strategic move. "They be-lieved," he wrote, "that the American people are not adult enough to support a strategic action designed to make effective a diplomatic policy, and that the right decision had therefore first to be spiced up to attract their attention and then watered down and sugared over to meet their doubts."[12]

Only one thing was clear: that the government had undertaken a new course of active intervention in the cold war. But by what sort of plan, if any, would it govern its course of intervention? Under what circum-stances and by what methods did it intend to meet force with counter-force? Such questions were destined to be answered only by pragmatic responses to unanticipated events. There is no evidence that the principal policy-makers were consciously unfolding a farsighted strategic plan at this time, even though events had forced them to execute the first major measure of containment; and it is certain that they had not grasped the problem of limited war which a strategy of containment would entail. Nevertheless, the Greek-Turkish Aid Program led directly to America's intervention in the Greek civil war, which lasted until the fall of 1949. It was, above all, America's dispatch of military advisers, its reorganization of the Greek army, its donation of enormous military supplies, its granting of economic aid, and even its intervention in internal political affairs that kept this key position on the southern flank of Europe out of Russian control.

Preoccupation with Total War

The unfolding of events, more than the conscious cerebrations of American policy-makers, has revealed the nature and scope of containment since it was almost unwittingly launched with the Greek-Turkish Aid Program. These events reveal that the government has sought to contain the Communist sphere of power by three principal methods: (a) deterring aggression with America's capacity to retaliate against the center of aggression by the means of total war; (b) meeting force with counterforce in a local, limited action; and (c) building situations of strength through economic, technical, and military aid.

The United States applied all three methods in Europe. In the Greek civil war and during the Berlin blockade it successfully employed local, limited action. While deliberately assuming certain risks of total war in these actions, it sought to keep the risks commensurate with the objectives at stake by limiting and localizing countermeasures and, in the case of the Berlin blockade, by agreeing to a limited settlement. In the European Recovery Program (known as the Marshall Plan) the United States undertook its major effort to build situations of strength and its single most successful measure of the cold war. Through a co-operative program of American aid the European countries were able to restore their economies, and western Europe was probably saved from becoming a power vacuum from which it would have been extremely difficult to exclude Soviet political or military penetration. Throughout the world, however, the United States relied primarily on the deterrent of nuclear retaliation to contain the Communist sphere. Consequently, although limited war was implicit in the conception of containment, American military policies were designed almost exclusively to meet the contingency of total war. To bridge the gap between these military policies and America's general strategic objective, the government relied on improvisation and luck.

Under President Truman the government's overwhelming reliance on nuclear retaliation as the military means of containing communism sprang from two principal and closely related views of the military and political situation. In the first place, the administration was preoccupied with the threat of a third world war, resulting from a Soviet invasion of Europe or from a sudden attack on the United States itself. In the second place, it was fascinated by the vast and strange power of the atomic bomb; in the absence of other military means with which to contain Communist expansion, it placed an almost superstitious faith in its monopoly of this weapon as a guarantee of American security.

It should be noted that the government's approach was in perfect accord with the attitude of the nation as a whole. The statements of congressmen, publicists, and journalists before the Korean War indicated that the informed American public, insofar as it was concerned about the external Communist threat to American security, was keenly interested in the problem of meeting a major Soviet assault on Europe or the United States, but it was almost totally ignorant or apathetic about lesser aggressions, especially by Communist powers in secondary strategic areas.

The national preoccupation with total war was reflected concretely in Congress' generosity with appropriations for the Air Force, in marked contrast to its imposition of "economies" on the other two services, especially the Army. Thus in 1948 Congress cut deeply into the government's recommendations for the Army but went beyond the recommendations for a forty-eight-group Air Force by authorizing, almost unanimously, appropriations designed to create seventy groups. Again, in 1949, Congress—this time in spite of strong Senate support of the administration program—appropriated more than the President requested for the Air Force; and the President, although he signed the appropriation bill, felt impelled to direct the Secretary of Defense to place the extra money in reserve. In the congressional debates and reports on these two appropriation bills the reasoning behind the prevailing view ran about as follows: The Communist seizure of Czechoslovakia and the

Soviet imposition of the Berlin blockade indicate Russia's expansionist inclinations and reveal the danger that the United States may become the victim of another Pearl Harbor if it is not prepared to counter Soviet aggression. But in order to deter Russian expansion and prevent World War III the United States cannot hope to match the land power of the Soviet Union; it must rely upon its ability to retaliate swiftly by striking at the heart of aggression with land-based bombers and atomic bombs. For this is the only means of reaching Russia directly, and it is the means that provides America with the most security for its money.

Internal struggles and compromises within the high echelons of the defense establishment helped to inhibit the Truman administration from allocating expenditures quite so freely to the Air Force in proportion to the Army and Navy as Congress seemed willing to do. Nevertheless, the congressional view of military strategy which underlay the increases in the Air Force budget over the administration's protest was, in fact, shared by the administration's own Secretary of Defense, Louis Johnson, who was brought in to replace the tireless advocate of "balanced forces," James Forrestal, in 1949. Johnson was only expressing a view that the great majority of Congress and most informed citizens took for granted when he told an audience in December, 1949, "There is only one nation in the world that might seek to give us trouble, and it is my job to see that America is strong enough to deter it and to win the war if trouble starts."[13] He was only stirring memories that held sway over all Americans who had felt the shock of Pearl Harbor when, on the eighth anniversary of that catastrophe, he declared, "We shall make sure that no four o'clock in the morning attack will leave us prostrate at five."[14] From his preoccupation with the threat of a third world war it was logical that Johnson, like the nation at large, should envision the whole purpose of America's military strategy as countering Russia's great land power with superiority in air-atomic power. "Our strategy," he said in another address, "must be to strike back where it is likely to weaken the land power's long lines of communication and transportation, his production facilities, and to defend ourselves against the strategy he is likely to concentrate—a blitz ground attack against the nations friendly to us, atomic raids upon our industrial centers."[15]

Not all American strategists shared Secretary Johnson's confidence in the efficacy of air-atomic retaliation, but they all shared his preoccupation with preventing a third world war. A long-brewing controversy between the Navy and the Air Force over strategy and weapons boiled to a head in the summer and again in the fall of 1949 in the hearings on the B-36 bomber program and the unification of the services.[16] In these hearings all the major military leaders in the nation aired their views on military strategy. They said a great deal about the kind of war the United States should be prepared to fight. Yet the published statements are notable for their exclusive concern with the best way to fight a third world war with the Soviet Union. The opponents of the B-36 program, led by Admiral Radford, claimed that it symbolized a strategy of indiscriminate air attacks on enemy cities which would be militarily ineffective, morally wrong, and politically disastrous; and they argued for the efficacy of the Navy's carrier-based tactical air force, designed for precision bombing. The supporters of the B-36 program retorted that strategic bombing was the cheapest, most effective method of defeating the enemy, denied that they depreciated the utility of the other branches of the armed service or of tactical air power, and charged that the Navy's emphasis on "supercarriers" was based on the obsolete World War II conception of island-hopping, whereas the real enemy was a land power deep in the heart of Eurasia. But the common assumption running through all these arguments was that the sole test of America's military strategy and weapons system was her ability to fight a total war against Russia. This is the more remarkable because the best case the Navy could have made for its tactical air power against the "superbombers" of the Strategic Air Command was the utility of carrier-based planes in limited wars on the rimlands of Eurasia. This case was neglected, not because of any failure to exploit every known argument, but because of the fact that the proponents of the naval view were in complete agreement with Air Force and Army spokesmen that the one war for which the United States needed to prepare was a total war with Russia. As Admiral Radford put it, "I do feel that at this time there is certainly only one potential enemy of the United States in the world, and we do have to largely make our plans to cover an eventuality of aggression by that power."[17]

Preoccupation with total war was also both a consequence and a cause of the overwhelming reliance upon America's monopoly of the atomic bomb in the absence of sufficient ground forces capable of containing aggression locally. A total war was the only kind of war the United States was prepared to fight, if indeed it was prepared for that. Therefore, an inflexible military capacity tended to reinforce a single-minded strategic outlook.

By 1947 America's ground forces had dwindled to 670,000 men in the rush of demobilization, and only a small portion of this force could be considered ready for combat. Economic and military retrenchment was the watchword in Congress. Contrary to the stated wishes of the President and his military advisers, the Eightieth Congress during 1946–48 insisted on still further reductions in the defense budget and armed strength; and it turned down repeated requests for the enactment of a peacetime universal military training program. In the spring of 1948 General Albert C. Wedemeyer, director of Plans and Operations, called the manpower situation "critical" and urged "drastic action." He declared that the existing ground complement of 540,000 troops ranked the United States Army sixth among nations and provided less than 50,000 men or "two and one-third under-strength divisions" that "could be deployed quickly to meet an emergency involving the security of our country."[18] Momentary increases in the armed forces followed the Berlin crisis and the Communist seizure of Czechoslovakia in 1948; but in 1949 President Truman and Secretary of Defense Johnson, aided and abetted by the new Under-Secretary of State, James Webb (former director of the Budget Bureau), joined the economy group in paring defense expenditures still more. Until the Korean War upset all calculations, the military establishment was the creature of rigid budgetary restrictions reflecting the general optimism about peace and the President's desire to promote Fair Deal welfare programs. Given the prevailing estimate of the Communist military threat, budgetary restrictions led logically to a growing reliance on air-atomic retaliation. By 1948 defense expenditures had fallen to $11 billion from the 1946 level of $45 billion. By the spring of 1950, on the eve of the Korean War, the Army stood at ten divisions, of which only two were at full strength. Even the Air Force had a scant forty-eight wings, only three of which were composed of heavy bombers.

While the United States was returning its soldiers to civilian life as fast as possible, the Soviet Union retained an army of almost four million men and three times as many reserves, and it continued to conscript more than 800,000 men a year for extensive training.[19] By the time American forces had reached their postwar low, the Soviet Union, with an estimated 175 divisions ready for combat, possessed by far the largest ground force in the world and the largest air force as well.

The military imbalance between Soviet and American ground forces was somewhat redressed by the formation in the spring of 1949 of the North Atlantic Treaty Organization, in which the United States joined twelve other nations pledged to regard an attack upon one as an attack upon themselves, and by America's subsequent program of military assistance to its allies. These measures were a direct result of the intensification of the cold war, brought about by a series of Russian moves to counter the progress of the European Recovery Program, moves including the formation of the Cominform, a campaign of strikes and violence in Italy and France, the seizure of Czechoslovakia, and the Berlin blockade. From America's standpoint NATO served two major purposes: to deter the Russians from attacking the United States' first line of defense in Europe, and to provide the European allies with an atmosphere of security conducive to economic progress. For the government realized that from the European point of view security depended on the hope of preventing Russian occupation, not upon the prospect of eventual liberation.

Thus NATO and the military-assistance program reflected a growing belief that America's capacity for atomic retaliation, despite an atomic monopoly, was not by itself a sufficient deterrent to contain communism even in the primary strategic region of Europe. However, these measures did not reflect any change in the prevailing preoccupation with total war; rather they were a response to a heightened fear of a third world war that would be precipitated by a Russian attack on Europe. Probably neither American nor European strategists believed that western Europe's small ground-defense forces could prevent the Red Army from rolling to the Atlantic if it wanted to. They merely hoped that it would prevent a sudden Soviet coup. In accordance with the "plate-glass" theory of defense, they viewed the NATO army as a thin line of protection that would set off the burglar alarm and send America's atomic retaliatory force winging from NATO bases toward the strategic centers of Russian military strength. Secretary of State Acheson said about as much for the military efficacy of NATO as could reasonably be claimed when he told the House Committee on Foreign Affairs:

We do not believe that to discourage military aggression it is necessary to create Western European defensive forces which are by virtue of their size capable of successfully resisting an all-out attack. What is required is rather sufficient strength to make it impossible for an aggressor to achieve a quick and easy victory. The dictators of recent times have become involved in war when, in their belief, their intended victims would fall easy prey without substantial risk to themselves. The strengthening of the defenses of Western Europe is designed to prevent a repetition of the tragic consequences of such dangerous self-deception.[20]

For all practical purposes, then, the United States continued to place overwhelming reliance upon its air-atomic capacity as the military means of containment. It is doubtful whether even American air power was adequate for a total war.[21] However, it was evidently sufficient to deter the kind of aggression it was designed to counter; and perhaps it was not only sufficient but, as Churchill implied, indispensable, although we cannot know in what way, if any, Russia would have acted differently in the absence of America's atomic monopoly. In any case, the fact that Russia did not launch a major attack upon Europe confirmed the American government's confidence in the adequacy of its military policies. For since the government was concerned almost exclusively with the kind of military attack that would lead to total war, and since no such attack occurred, it naturally assumed that its policies were a success; and it concluded that as long as the United States maintained its existing military posture, the Communists would not resort to force but would be content to pursue their aims by subversion.

The Greek civil war was regarded as a unique event, as an exceptional incident, rather than as a prototype of wars to come. Besides, Europe was now protected by NATO. Having seemingly received confirmation of the magical powers of its atomic monopoly, the government continued to stress the bomb's awesome qualities as an instrument of American security. As it did so, it scarcely realized that it was not only deterring the potential enemy from starting a third world war but was also deterring itself from employing a weapon of such terrifying destructiveness, except in the most desperate circumstances, which might never occur.

It took the argument of events to reveal the serious liability that a single-minded military system was bound to suffer in the unceasing competition with an opponent reared in the flexible and resourceful management of power. Three major developments exposed the inadequacy of America's early postwar military system for supporting the strategy of containment: (a) Russia's detonation of an atomic bomb at the end of August, 1949, (b) the shift of the main thrust of Communist power to the peripheral areas of Asia, and (c) the Communist invasion of South Korea on June 25, 1950.

The End of America's Atomic Monopoly

On September 23, 1949, President Truman revealed that Russia had succeeded in exploding an atomic device. Russia's achievement of an atomic explosion at least three years ahead of American predictions was a serious blow to America's reliance upon retaliatory air power as a deterrent to Communist expansion; for, by raising the prospect of Soviet nuclear counter-retaliation, it greatly increased the magnitude of the stakes for which the United States would be warranted in employing its own retaliatory power, and, correspondingly, it reduced the military risk the Communists would incur from aggressions for limited stakes.

Therefore, except in the light of America's blindness to the threat of limited war, it is surprising in retrospect that government spokesmen should have adopted the official position that this momentous event made no difference so far as the nation's military strategy and defense policies were concerned, because the government had long anticipated the contingency.[22] If these spokesmen meant that the end of America's atomic monopoly did not affect the adequacy of the existing military strategy, which depended overwhelmingly upon the maintenance of that monopoly, they were either dissembling their concern (which actually seems to have been the case), or else they were blind to the significance of this development (which was partly the case). If, on the other hand, they meant that the government was ready to alter its military strategy in accordance with plans previously devised in anticipation of the end of America's atomic monopoly, there was nothing in their actions or statements either before or after the explosion to indicate such readiness.

The only immediate impact of the Russian achievement upon American military policies was to lead the President, his military advisers, and some influential congressmen to urge the acceleration of America's development of a "super" bomb.[23] This reaction was, apparently, no more than an automatic reflex, conditioned by the nation's long-standing faith in the efficacy of the atomic bomb; it did not spring from any new military or political evaluation of the usefulness of air-nuclear retaliation as an instrument of national policy.[24] And as far as the nation's top military minds were concerned, Russia's atomic explosion apparently failed to alter in the slightest way the prevailing preoccupation with preparing for a total nuclear war against the Soviet Union. The aforementioned hearings on the unification of the services, which were an extension of the B-36 controversy, took place in October, 1949; yet the whole lengthy discussion about military strategy and defense policies was carried on as though the United States still possessed a monopoly of the atomic bomb. Much was said about what the United States might or might not do to the Soviet Union by strategic nuclear bombing, but nothing was said about what the Soviet Union might before long do, in return, to the United States by the same means; and no one suggested that this new Soviet capability need alter America's existing strategy in any way.

In practice, the prevailing American interpretation of the strategic significance of Russia's atomic explosion simply led to an even greater emphasis upon America's nuclear-retaliatory capacity. Thus congressmen who had been pressing the government to expand the Air Force long before September, 1949, found the Russian explosion a welcome additional argument of considerable persuasiveness. Their conclusion that the United States must now redouble its efforts to maintain strategic air-nuclear superiority was, in fact, the logical inference to be drawn from the report of the President's own Air Policy Commission (known as the Finletter report for its chairman, Thomas K. Finletter), which had been published on January 1, 1948. According to this report it was for the very reason that the Soviet Union would probably achieve a substantial air-nuclear capacity of its own by 1952 that the United States should develop by 1950 a seventy-group Air Force in order to support a "new strategic concept" built upon America's ability to protect the air space and launch a counterattack of "utmost violence." For "the attack which we must anticipate determines the kind of force which will be needed to meet it," the commission reasoned; and in its view, although there was a possibility that war might not open with a direct assault by the main enemy and that it might even remain localized "on the model of the practice war between Germany and Russia in the Spanish Civil War," this was "not likely, and certainly we must not count on it." Instead, "We must assume, in making our plans, that if the enemy can do it he will make a direct air assault on the United States mainland regardless how or where the first shooting starts."[25]

In retrospect we can see that the real strategic importance of Russia's detonation of an atomic bomb lay in the fact that it foretold a time not far off when the United States would have to anticipate that atomic retaliation upon Russia might be answered by Russia's obliteration of American military installations and American cities. Therefore, Communist strategists could be confident that the United States would not rationally employ its retaliatory air power against any aggression that did not constitute the most serious immediate threat to American security. This situation clearly encouraged the kind of Communist aggression that did not impose such an immediate threat and did not offer a sufficient pretext for atomic retaliation, such as an attack for limited objectives in an area of secondary strategic importance by some Communist power other than Russia.

Here was a new strategic problem—or rather an old one brought to a head—that could not be alleviated by the accumulation of more atomic bombs or by the acquisition of the immensely more powerful thermonuclear bomb. For as the Soviet Union, as well as the United States, increased its air-nuclear power, the value of the American lead in these weapons would diminish. When both powers had acquired such large stocks of bombs and such great delivery capabilities that neither could prevent the other from devastating its homeland, then the United States would gain little additional deterrent value by acquiring the ability to obliterate the major Russian cities twice over, and even an inferior Russian counter-retaliatory power would be an effective deterrent to American nuclear retaliation. Only a great and sudden increase in the defensive or offensive superiority of one of the two powers or the overwhelming superiority of defensive over offensive capabilities on the part of both powers could alter the resulting atomic stalemate, barring the special contingencies considered in the preceding chapter.

Therefore, unless the United States were able to contain lesser aggressions locally by measures short of total war, it could only meet such aggression by total war, non-resistance, or ineffective resistance. If the nation were repeatedly confronted with this choice by overt aggression or the threat of aggression, it might suffer such serious international reverses and such grievous internal strains that total war would seem like the least disastrous course. But if Communist strategists preferred not to take the risk of pushing the United States to this extremity—which was more likely—their very ability to force the nation to choose between these three disastrous courses would still give them great diplomatic leverage, while it tended to undermine America's political relations with the rest of the world. For as all nations, including the United States, grew increasingly apprehensive of their vulnerability to nuclear attack, the Communist bloc would acquire a formidable means of diplomatic blackmail against the whole non-Communist world. And unless the United States could persuade other nations that it was prepared to contain Communist aggression without turning a small war into an unlimited war—that it was prepared to defend them, not just liberate them after an atomic war—it would rapidly lose the confidence of allies and the respect of neutrals.

In order to deter and check lesser aggressions by limited war, the United States would have to expand its woefully weak ground forces. There was no cheap and easy way to avoid this fact. For without adequate ground forces, the nation possessed no credible means of retaliation for anything but a major aggression; and the fewer ground forces it possessed, the more reluctant American leaders would be to expend them in peripheral contests, at the sacrifice of the ability to meet what they had come to regard as the major military task, the defense of Europe against a Russian invasion. And yet how could the United States and its allies hope to match the Soviet Union and its allies in ground troops, and how could it hope to hold the line of containment in any of a half-dozen critical areas around the vast perimeter of Communist power? Russia's detonation of an atomic bomb gave new urgency to this military problem, which had been implicit in the Truman Doctrine; but it took the Korean War to force that problem upon the attention of a nation so preoccupied with total war.

The Eastward Shift of Communist Pressure

The end of America's atomic monopoly may have only reinforced a shift in Communist strategy that political developments would have brought about anyway. For it is logical to expect that the very success of containment in Europe would have led the Communist bloc to seek fields of expansion elsewhere. Despite many sources of weakness around the European and Mediterranean periphery of Soviety power, by 1950 the Greek-Turkish Aid Program, the Marshall Plan, and NATO had helped to create situations of sufficient military and political strength to prevent Communist expansion by subversion or by military coups. Russia's heavy-handed attempts to weaken this area had only succeeded in consolidating it politically and strengthening it militarily. Ideologically, the appeal of communism had reached its peak by 1947, and the defection of Yugoslavia in 1948 even suggested the possibility of heresy within the satellites. By 1950 the two great coalitions seemed to have staked out such well-established spheres of influence that there was little room for further maneuvers except by the long-term processes of political activity.

America's retaliatory air power, buttressed by her demonstrated willingness to resist local incursions like the Greek civil war and the Berlin blockade, must have made the whole NATO area seem like a risky and unprofitable field for either direct or indirect aggression. But as long as there were other opportunities for expansion, the Communist leaders were not ones to pursue an inflexible strategy in the face of unreasonable obstacles. Communist China's unexpected success in gaining complete control of the mainland during 1949 opened up a whole new field or opportunities.

All around the Eurasian rimlands from Iran to Korea there remained a vast region contiguous to the Communist sphere of power that was ripe for Communist expansion. In these "gray areas" the Communists could exploit numerous situations of economic, social, and political weakness, and they could appeal to powerful nationalist and anti-Western sentiments.[26] Here Communist pressure would tend to divide rather than to consolidate the United States and its European allies. At the same time, it would tend to weaken the American coalition in Europe by diverting its energy and resources to secondary areas. In the gray areas there was no adequate local military resistance to check a determined Communist attack; yet America's retaliatory air power was an ineffective deterrent. It was ineffective because of the fruitful opportunities for indirect aggression and because the area was not of sufficient strategic importance to warrant turning local resistance into total war.

The gray areas could be termed a "secondary" strategic area only in comparison with the NATO area or the Middle East; and, certainly, Communist control of any substantial portion of the area, such as Southeast Asia, would be a major disaster for the West. Nevertheless, no single limited incursion in Southeast Asia would constitute as great an immediate blow to American security as, say, a Communist seizure of Turkey or West Germany; and it is likely that Communist strategists realized this fact as well as Americans. In any case the decisive determinant of the effectiveness of air power as a deterrent in the gray areas was not so much the areas' objective importance as what Americans *believed* their importance to be and what the Communists calculated that the Americans believed. And there was a wealth of evidence to show that on the stage of world politics Americans regarded Europe as the main show and the gray areas as, strategically speaking, a relatively small side show.

The Communists had before them a record of American policies and actions in the Far East that clearly demonstrated the peripheral nature of this area in American strategy. For a year and a half before the Greek civil war the United States had been faced with a determined Communist effort to take over the whole of China through civil war, but this situation, comparable in many respects to the Greek civil war, occasioned no talk of containment or of helping "free peoples" to "maintain their national integrity against aggressive movements that seek to impose upon them totalitarian regimes." The Communist conquest of China was the most serious blow to American interests since the end of World War II, but the administration that inaugurated containment in Greece and Turkey did not apply that strategy to China.[27] On the contrary, while it was assisting the Greek government to fight Communist insurgents, it was urging the government of China to unite with them in a coalition. To be sure, the United States gave Nationalist China substantial economic, military, and technical aid; but this aid was not granted for the purpose of containing communism; it was an outgrowth of the wartime policy of promoting a "strong, democratic, and united" China and the overriding military objective of securing the unconditional surrender of Japan. It is doubtful whether an extension of the economic and military measures applied in Greece to the much larger and more difficult problem of China could have kept that area out of Communist hands, once the Japanese were defeated. But the significant point is that the American government did not even envision the problem of China in terms of containment until the Nationalists had almost lost their foothold on the mainland;[28] and by then, if there had ever been any possibility of containing the Communists, the possibility had vanished.

One need not attribute any remarkable powers of divination to Communist leaders to see in Russia's atomic explosion and the changing configurations of world-wide power and interest the military and political conditions that aggressive, alert, and opportunistic revolutionaries might recognize and turn to their advantage. We may never know in detail what motives and perceptions led to the shift of Communist pressure from Europe and the Mediterranean area to the vulnerable rimlands of Asia; but, given the Communists' relentless and resourceful drive for power, it seems a reasonable speculation that, if they were at all attentive to the opportunities on the international chessboard, they must have regarded the military and political developments of 1947–49 as an invitation to probe the rimland areas—the ripest field for exploitation on the face of the globe.

Chapter Eight

THE KOREAN WAR

Communist Aggression and American Intervention

The Korean War is the single most significant event in the development of American postwar strategy. When the full history of the cold war is written, it may loom as one of the truly decisive events that shaped the pattern of war and politics in our era. However, we cannot wait so long to discern the lessons of limited war that it holds for us today. For the urgent purposes of contemporary American strategy it is none too soon to make our own imperfect appraisal of the war in Korea. The logical place to start is at the beginning. Why did the Communists attack, and why did the United States intervene?

In retrospect, as we observed in the preceding chapter, nothing seems more logical than the shift of the main thrust of Communist expansion from an area of relative Western strength, where expansion entailed large risks of total war, to an area of great vulnerability and weakness, where the West had scarcely applied the strategy of containment, where the risks of total war were minimized, and where neither local resistance nor massive retaliation was an effective deterrent. But why did the Communists choose a direct invasion of South Korea to test the vulnerability of the gray areas? And exactly what was the role and the motive of the Kremlin or of different factions within the Kremlin in this move? We may never know the complete answer. However, it seems reasonable to suppose that, whatever the intentions of those responsible for the invasion may have been, they could not fail to be encouraged in this course by American actions and pronouncements concerning Korea.

In September, 1947, the Joint Chiefs of Staff decided that on purely military grounds the two American divisions stationed in South Korea should be withdrawn.[1] They seem to have reached this decision by reasoning, first, that the United States did not have sufficient military interest in defending South Korea and, second, that in the light of the severe

163

over-all shortage of American manpower, the divisions in Korea could be better used elsewhere. It is significant that the first estimate, having been reached in a political vacuum, was based upon the importance of Korea in a total war. In terms of total war the defense of Korea and Formosa was regarded as a strategic liability.

On the basis of the Joint Chiefs' estimate, and in light of the establishment of the UN-sponsored Republic of Korea, coupled with the Russian announcement of troop withdrawal in North Korea, President Truman on the advice of the National Security Council decided in the spring of 1949 to withdraw American troops from South Korea and to base the protection of the new country on the development of indigenous security forces. American troops were promptly withdrawn. On the other hand, despite intelligence reports of the build-up of a formidable North Korean army, the United States limited itself to creating little more than a police force in South Korea—partly from fear that a larger army would march northward in an attempt to unify Korea.

The American government's low estimate of Korea's strategic importance was reflected in the words of high military and political authorities as well as in the disposition of forces. In the spring of 1949, before the National Security Council had reviewed the situation in Korea, General MacArthur, Supreme Commander for the Allied Powers, outlined in a newspaper interview an American "line of defense" in the Far East that omitted the Korean peninsula.[2] On January 12, 1950, Secretary of State Acheson, in a speech before the National Press Club, delineated the same American "defensive perimeter," from which he also omitted Korea.[3]

However, it did not even take the withdrawal of American troops or the statements of MacArthur and Acheson to assure the Communists that they might safely attack South Korea. The severe shortage of American ground troops, combined with America's repeated stress upon preparing to meet the Russians in a total war in Europe, ought to have been enough to convince them that the United States would not divert precious troops from major strategic areas for the defense of Korea. As General Marshall recalled during the MacArthur hearings in 1951, America's military establishment in the years before the Korean War was so inadequate that there was only one full Army division in the United States, and the Chiefs of Staff were concerned about obtaining enough men to guard air strips at Fairbanks, Alaska. "We had literally almost no military forces outside of our Navy and outside of an effective but not too large Air Force, except the occupation garrisons, and . . . even in Japan they were only at about sixty per cent strength."[4]

Therefore, Communist strategists had ample evidence that the American government would not consider it worthwhile to defend South Korea; and if they interpreted America's conduct of foreign policy in terms of their own standards, they could hardly have reached any other conclusion than that the United States would acquiesce in a limited move of a satellite army into a minor strategic position, just as a chess player must accept the maneuver of a pawn when he is in no position to prevent it. And yet when the North Korean army poured across the thirty-eighth parallel in June, 1950, the United States found compelling reasons for intervening to stop it. Why did the United States shift its strategy?

From the standpoint of pure power politics it is easier to explain the Communist invasion than American intervention. But, as one familiar with the sources of American conduct might have predicted, it was not purely on the grounds of power politics that the United States intervened. Despite the fact that President Truman and his advisers had ruled out American defense of South Korea on military strategic grounds, when aggression actually occurred, they unanimously agreed that larger political considerations made this defense unavoidable. What were these considerations?

Countless private and public statements of American policy-makers indicate that at the time of American intervention and throughout the war the dominant motive in their minds for fighting was the fear that if this aggression went unchecked, it would be the first of a chain of aggressions that would destroy the foundations of international security and eventually cause a third world war. This reasoning was based on an analogy with the events of the 1930's. It reflected the common assumption, heavily tinged with guilt feelings, that World War II had resulted from the democracies' failure to check the chain of totalitarian aggression that began with Japan's invasion of Manchuria in 1931.[5] If now the Communists should be allowed to launch aggression with impunity, the administration reasoned, they would be encouraged to think that no obstacle lay in their path to world domination; and eventually the free world would be forced to meet the Soviet Union in a total war, just as it had been forced to meet the Fascist powers.

This line of reasoning reflected more than a long-term view of American interests. It reflected a typical combination of national self-interest and supranational idealism. As self-interest, this reasoning anticipated deterring more serious future threats to American security by checking a limited threat in the present. Here the administration was tacitly following the imperatives of the strategy of containment, which had been excluded from over-all strategic planning by virtue of the prevailing political blindness and preoccupation with total war. As idealism, the compelling consideration in American minds was the image of the United States leading the civilized world in preventing a chain of aggression that violated the universal principles of law and order championed by America.

Actually, the decision to intervene in Korea did not depend on UN sanction. It is true that on June 25, 1950, the UN Security Council, minus the boycotting Soviet delegate, passed a resolution calling for an immediate end of the fighting and for the assistance of all members in restoring peace. And on June 27, after the Communists had defied this resolution, the Council recommended that member-nations aid the Republic of Korea. But American action was determined, independently of the UN, by the rapidly developing military situation. Thus on the day of the first resolution, President Truman ordered the Seventh Fleet into the Formosa Strait to repel attacks on Formosa and prevent the Nationalists from invading the mainland; and he instructed MacArthur to evacuate Americans from Korea and to supply the Korean army, while using American air and naval cover. On June 26, in response to the increasing military urgency, the President instructed MacArthur to use air and naval forces in support of South Korea. Finally, on June 30 he authorized MacArthur to use the ground forces in his command.

Nevertheless, UN sanction gave American intervention the color of a crusade. As leader of the UN forces, Americans could envision themselves as missionaries for the principle of collective security. In this role they would be above power politics. As upholders of the integrity of the United Nations they would be fighting for the peace and welfare of all mankind, not for their purely selfish national advantage. Because this combination of egoistic and idealistic motives is a recurrent and decisive feature of American foreign policy, we should appraise its effects upon American strategic thinking in this instance more closely.

The trouble with our action in Korea was not that we intervened in the war—which was necessary from the standpoint of containment—or that we intervened under the aegis of the United Nations—which probably facilitated more than it hampered the achievement of American objectives —but, rather, that our eagerness to represent American intervention as an altruistic act of pure collective security tended to obscure the underlying basis of *Realpolitik* without which intervention, regardless of UN sanction, would have been unjustified.

It is natural that nations should justify their actions on the highest possible grounds, especially when they must endure the sacrifices of war; but the danger in this is that they may lose sight of the peculiar circumstances of self-interest which enable them to claim those grounds and that, consequently, they will lack a consistent basis of action under circumstances in which the same happy coincidence of idealism and self-interest does not exist. Clearly, some quite special circumstances enabled the United States to fight the Korean War in the name of the United Nations.

In the first place, the Republic of Korea had been established by free elections held under UN supervision and had been recognized by the United Nations as the lawful government in the area south of the thirty-eighth parallel. In the second place, the Communists chose an overt attack on the Republic of Korea, so that the UN's special obligations as well as its charter were directly violated. In the third place, soon after the North Korean attack the Security Council was able to pass a resolution calling for an immediate end to the fighting and the assistance of all members in restoring peace, which would not have been possible without the Soviet delegate's absence during Russia's boycott of the UN.

In the Korean War, as in the Greek civil war, the problem of containment was obscured by broader and more palatable motives for intervention, which happened to correspond to the dictates of American security. In the urge to envision American resistance to Communist aggression on the highest moral plane, it was easy to overlook the power-political basis of our action and to overgeneralize its determining objectives. In this way we somewhat misled ourselves as to the true basis of our interests. One might have concluded from the announcement of the Truman Doctrine that the United States had adopted a policy of helping free peoples to resist totalitarian aggression, but Secretary Acheson had had to explain that it all depended on how the circumstances affected American interests. Similarly, one might have inferred from official explanations of American intervention in the Korean War that the United States would henceforth resist Communist aggression according to the collective will of peace-loving nations, as manifested in the councils of the UN. But a moment's reflection would indicate that neither resistance to aggression nor the collective will of peace-loving nations would always correspond with America's security interests in containing the Communist sphere; and it would be folly to suppose that the United States should always resist aggression, regardless of the consequences.

Would we have intervened in Korea if the South Koreans instead of the North Koreans had struck across the thirty-eighth parallel? If so, we certainly would not have intervened in behalf of the Communists or under the auspices of the United Nations. Moreover, aside from the special circumstances that permitted the United States to obtain UN sanction for its intervention and despite a desire to check a chain of aggression in the interests of international peace, one must suppose that American leaders would have foregone intervention if intervention had not been practicable from the standpoint of American interests. One circumstance that made intervention practicable in Korea was the existence of a clear-cut act of military aggression. Another was the fact that a large part of the American ground and air force in the Pacific area was stationed near the scene of action, in Japan. But certainly one could not count upon these fortunate circumstances recurring in future Communist aggressions.

The Korean War raised grave problems concerning the methods of containing lesser aggressions by limited war. These problems could not be resolved in terms of the general goals of defeating aggression and upholding collective security. They were strategic problems—the problems of managing national power according to an over-all plan for achieving security objectives. They would have to be appraised in the light of concrete military and political circumstances bearing upon America's power position. But the strategic lessons of the Korean War were partially concealed by the nation's instinctive depreciation of containment and its attempt to reconcile intervention in a limited war with the traditional image of the United States as a crusader above power politics.

At the same time, the disparity between the dictates of containment and America's traditional approach to war made this whole venture a traumatic experience from which the nation would not soon recover. Something of the accompanying strain and confusion erupted in the intense controversy over the conduct of the war that followed President Truman's recall of General MacArthur in April, 1951. Of all the foreign-policy debates that have marked the evolution of America's postwar strategy, the debate over the conduct of the Korean War has been the most profound and revealing. Therefore, the lessons of the Korean War lie not only in its military and political events, for what they show of the objective requirements of a strategy of limited war, but, equally, in the controversy surrounding those events, for what it shows of America's adjustment to these requirements. In order to appraise these lessons we must reconstruct from the substance of this controversy the methods and conceptions that governed the Truman administration's conduct of the war, on the one hand, and General MacArthur's, on the other hand.

The Administration's Conduct of the War

The administration's position was from first to last dedicated to keeping the war in Korea limited. Whether or not it conducted the war in the most effective manner, there can be no doubt that it was impressed with the need for limiting the ends and means of warfare and that it succeeded in this endeavor.

The overriding consideration that led the administration to limit the war in Korea was the fear of provoking Russian intervention and bringing about a third world war. As President Truman has written, "Every decision I made in connection with the Korean conflict had this one aim in mind: to prevent a third world war and the terrible destruction it would bring to the civilized world. This meant that we should not do anything that would provide the excuse to the Soviets and plunge the free nations into full-scale all-out war."[6] From the beginning of the war the Truman administration believed that the North Korean invasion was a Russian maneuver, and it operated largely on the prevailing assumption among its counsels that the Kremlin was probing the West's positions on the Communist periphery in order to discover and exploit weak points. However, at the same time, it could never entirely abandon the fear, which was especially strong at the outset of the war, that the invasion might really be part of a Russian plan to distract the United States preliminary to a general assault on the non-Communist world. It was determined not to fall into this trap by offering the Russians the slightest pretext for direct intervention.

A second decisive consideration was the fear of overcommitment, of allowing the war in Korea to expand to such an extent as to render the United States incapable of meeting aggression in any of a half-dozen other potential trouble-spots. The administration was not only keenly conscious of the danger of depleting the defense of western Europe and thereby encouraging major aggression in that vital area; it was also apprehensive of a Russian attack on Japan and of pressure of a more limited nature on Berlin, Yugoslavia, Iran, and Indochina.[7] President Truman assumed from the first that, whether or not the Korean War was the immediate prelude to a general assault, the Kremlin aimed to destroy America's capacity to meet her principal adversary by drawing her into military conflicts with a satellite in Asia. Therefore, he believed that "we could not afford to squander our reawakening strength as long as that enemy was not committed in the field but only pulling the strings behind the scenes."[8] This reasoning was in accord with the Central Intelligence Agency's estimate that "the Russians were not themselves willing to go to war but that they wanted to involve us as heavily as possible in Asia so that they might gain a free hand in Europe."[9] It was also consistent with the assumption, which the President and his advisers had considered from the outbreak of the war, that the Russians might be merely probing the West's defenses, as in Iran, Greece, and Berlin, but did not intend the action in Korea as a prelude to total war.[10]

Beyond these two determining considerations in limiting the war, the administration was also restrained by its relations with other nations. It was particularly anxious to maintain unity with America's European allies; and it believed that unity required a certain deference to their wishes—as in the case of forbidding air pursuit over the Yalu—in order to allay their fear of a total war. However, the decisive limitations which the American government placed upon the conduct of the war seem to have arisen from considerations affecting the United States directly, rather than from solicitude for allied sensibilities.

In order to avoid precipitating a third world war or overcommitting American resources in Korea the administration explicitly limited its political objectives and endeavored to keep military means and political objectives in proportion as the circumstances of the war changed. The principal restrictions it imposed upon military operations entailed confining both air and ground action to the Korean peninsula, withholding the employment of Chinese Nationalist troops, and rejecting measures, like the blockade of the Chinese mainland, which in the opinion of the Joint

Chiefs of Staff carried a risk of expanding the war disproportionate to the possible military advantages.

Tracing the process of limitation through the various stages of the war, one sees that in the first stage, when the American-led forces were on the defensive, the United Nations command confined its political objective to restoring peace and recovering the border at the thirty-eighth parallel—an objective which was announced in the UN resolutions of June 25 and June 27. Correspondingly, it took the position that military operations above the border should aim only to destroy military supplies; and although the Air Force was not restricted by the thirty-eighth parallel, precautions were taken to avoid carrying air action beyond the boundaries of Korea. But in the next stage of the war, when it became possible to take the offensive in Korea, the political limitations were reappraised. As a result of this reappraisal the Joint Chiefs of Staff, on the basis of recommendations of the National Security Council, sent a new directive to General MacArthur on September 15, 1950, the day of his brilliant assault on Inchon. This directive authorized ground operations *north* of the thirty-eighth parallel, but only if there were no indication of Soviet or Chinese Communist intervention in force. After the success of the Inchon landing, the government authorized MacArthur to destroy the North Korean armed forces within Korea, on the same condition, but specifically prohibited him from employing non-Korean ground forces in the provinces along the northern border and from employing air or naval action against Manchuria.[11] (As MacArthur approached the border, he failed to comply with the directive concerning the use of non-Korean forces, because, as he replied to the Joint Chiefs' anxious inquiry, he did not believe that compliance was militarily feasible.) Furthermore, in response to the brightening military prospect, the government formally and explicitly altered the political objective of the war. Since nothing seemed to stop the UN forces from achieving the long-standing goal, embodied originally in the Cairo agreement of 1943, of a free, independent, and united Korea, the UN General Assembly on October 7 was persuaded to pass a resolution that in effect authorized General MacArthur to employ the forces under his command for this larger purpose. Actually, by that time units of the Republic of Korea had already passed the thirty-eighth parallel.

From the beginning of the war the American government had been aware of the possibility of Chinese intervention. Now, as UN forces poured into North Korea, it received reports from several sources that the Chinese Communists would send troops to help the North Koreans if the "imperialists" advanced north of the thirty-eighth parallel. The Communist regime delivered direct warnings to this effect on the radio and indirect warnings through Panikkar, the Indian ambassador in Peiping. At this point some members of the State Department were in favor of trying to secure a settlement of the war at the thirty-eighth parallel before advancing northward to the "narrow neck" of Korea at Pyongyang and Wonsan. However, President Truman and most of his advisers did not regard the Chinese threat of intervention as serious enough to warrant stopping at the thirty-eighth parallel or imposing military or political limitations beyond the existing ones. General MacArthur, at his Wake Island meeting with President Truman on October 15, discounted the chances of Chinese intervention. Nevertheless, the government took pains to announce its intention to confine the war to Korea and to limit its political objective to creating a free, independent, and united Korea; and, at the same time, it left no doubt that it would consider Chinese intervention an act of aggression.

Actually, Chinese units had crossed the Yalu at least as early as October 16, one day after the Wake Island conference; but it was not until the end of the first week in November that General MacArthur and the CIA reported, independently of each other, that the Chinese had intervened in strength. On the basis of these reports the State Department was prompted to explore the possibility of negotiating with the Chinese for the establishment of a demilitarized zone ten miles on each side of the Yalu. General MacArthur's directives were not changed; but on November 24 the Joint Chiefs, becoming increasingly concerned over the danger of Chinese intervention, advised the General to hold his forces in terrain dominating the approaches to the valley of the Yalu. However, on that same day MacArthur announced "a general offensive" to "win the war" and instructed one of his commanders to tell the troops they would be home by Christmas. Four days later it was clear that the Tenth Corps had run up against vastly larger forces, and as the UN forces fell back in retreat MacArthur announced that "we face an entirely new war."[12]

In the face of a massive Chinese attack the UN forces retreated below the thirty-eighth parallel once again, but the retreat was checked. Under General Ridgway's direction UN forces mounted a limited offensive in January, 1951, and succeeded in stabilizing a line near the thirty-eighth parallel. With the war turned into a stalemate, the administration once more altered its operational political objective in the light of military circumstances, because it believed that to attain the objective announced by the UN on October 7, 1950, would entail an extension of the war effort and a risk of total war out of proportion to the objective's importance. Accordingly, in June, 1951, Secretary of State Acheson, testifying before the House Committee on Foreign Affairs, let it be known that, whereas the ultimate objective of unifying Korea remained in effect, the United States no longer favored pursuing that objective by military means but would be satisfied to revert to the original UN objective of repelling the aggression and restoring South Korea.[18] On the basis of this political adjustment the administration began cease-fire negotiations in July, 1951.

Thus, by limiting the ends and means of war and by balancing military and political objectives in the light of their effect on the scale of war and on the risk of total war, the United States, with the help of token foreign contingents succeeded in containing Communist aggression short of total war. This was a most significant and praiseworthy achievement, especially for a nation disposed to fight to the full extent of its physical capabilities. Yet the achievement in itself leaves unanswered the question of whether the government waged the war in the most effective manner consistent with the limitation of war—whether the particular limitations it imposed upon the ends and means of war were the wisest ones, compatible with the objectives at stake. This question was raised by the public dispute between the Truman administration and General MacArthur over the conduct of the war. At the same time, the deeper significance of that dispute lies in the fact that it went beyond questions of method and execution, to the very idea of limited war.

MacArthur's Conduct of the War

On April 10, 1951, President Truman finally relieved General MacArthur of his commands in Korea and Japan, after repeated evidence of the General's unwillingness to accept the administration's policies for conducting the war and after a series of public moves by which the General sought to promote his own policies, contrary to instructions. Instantaneously a furious controversy convulsed the nation. It culminated in the Senate investigation of MacArthur's recall and the Far Eastern situation during May and June, 1951. Yet a striking feature of this controversy was that the adherents of MacArthur's position, as well as the supporters of the administration, advocated not the kind of war the United States had undertaken in 1917 and 1941 but a limited war.

In his Senate testimony MacArthur repeatedly asserted that the objective he favored was confined to stopping the aggression in Korea, securing a cease-fire agreement, and negotiating a settlement consistent with the stated UN objective of an independent and United Korea.[14] Nor did he favor unlimited military measures to achieve this objective. He expressed the strongest opposition to engaging Chinese ground forces on the mainland beyond the Korean peninsula. He did not propose to strike with air power at the purported center of aggression in Russia; in fact, he disclaimed any knowledge of where the center of aggression was. He was not even in favor of bombing the Chinese supply lines leading to Russia. What he proposed was bombing Manchurian airfields, blockading the coast of China, and employing Chinese Nationalist troops in Korea and South China; but he proposed these measures only on the ground that they would achieve the UN's limited political objective more quickly, with fewer casualties, and with more chance of avoiding a third world war. And, if these measures were not taken, he advocated two other means of limiting the war, as alternatives to certain defeat: In the first stage of the war, he advocated the negotiation of an armistice on the basis of the thirty-eighth parallel; in the last stage of the war, he proposed a complete withdrawal from Korea.[15]

The decisive difference between MacArthur and the administration concerning the three principal measures he advocated arose from divergent estimates of their military advantage and of the risk of total war and overcommitment which they entailed. MacArthur declared that the course he recommended would quickly bring the war to a victorious close. The Joint Chiefs of Staff, while not directly disputing the military efficacy of these measures, maintained that they would expand the war and increase the risk of total war without giving any commensurate assurance of a quicker, less costly military decision. As long as the UN command could preserve a foothold in Korea while observing its self-imposed restrictions, the administration did not believe that it would be either militarily or politically worthwhile to abandon those restrictions—although in the early stages of Chinese intervention the Joint Chiefs tentatively approved the measures MacArthur advocated, when they anticipated that the UN forces might be compelled to evacuate the peninsula.[16]

MacArthur insisted that the risk of Chinese and Russian intervention was inherent in the decision to intervene in the first place and implied that this risk could not be increased by anything the UN forces did. After the Chinese intervened, he believed that there was no sense in restraining ourselves for fear of provoking them to take further measures, since they were already fighting the war to the limit of their capacity. As for the Russians, he was not sure that they would not intervene; but he thought that this was unlikely, since it was not to their advantage. In any case, he said that they would intervene according to their own designs, regardless of what the United States did.

The administration, on the other hand, believed that the introduction of Nationalist troops into South China or the bombing of Manchurian bases might lead China to move into full-scale war with Russian help. MacArthur could view this contingency with equanimity because he believed that communism—not any particular Communist power—was the main enemy and that the central objective of American counterforce should be to crush communism wherever it strikes. But the administration was conscious of America's limited military power and of a definite scale of priorities among the threats to American security upon which that power could be wisely expended, and in its scale of priorities a war with China did not figure at all. As General Bradley put it, "So long as we regarded the Soviet Union as the main antagonist and western Europe as the main prize," the measures MacArthur advocated "would involve us in the wrong war, at the wrong place, at the wrong time, and with the wrong enemy."[17]

Furthermore, the administration feared that MacArthur's course would involve us in the wrong war with the "right enemy" by provoking Russian intervention; and, as Acheson observed, the Russians had a variety of courses of intervention they might take, ranging from the use of "volunteer" air crews and ground troops to the launching of an all-out war.[18] Administration spokesmen have not publicly explained in any detail exactly how they arrived at their estimate of the risk of Russian intervention—if, indeed, they based it upon any systematic analysis at all. In the MacArthur hearings they pointed in general terms to Russia's self-interest, to her prestige, and to her obligations under the Sino-Soviet treaty; but, equally important, they revealed that, although the government operated chiefly on the assumption that the Russians were merely probing for soft spots and testing America's will and capacity for resistance, it was never sure that the Korean venture was not the prelude to a general offensive or that the Russians had not laid a trap in order to tie us down in Korea while they struck somewhere else. However, if the administration based its speculations about Russia's specific intentions in Korea largely on hunches, MacArthur was inclined to exclude such speculations altogether, as being out of the sphere of his competence as an area commander.

Aside from these decisive differences of estimates on the military and political consequences of a more vigorous prosecution of the war in Korea, MacArthur and the administration also differed over the importance of allied unity. The administration, having based American intervention so strongly upon the ideal of collective security, felt bound to preserve at least the appearance of unanimity in the conduct of the war; and it recognized that the bare hint of MacArthur's measures sent chills down the spines of America's UN allies. Therefore, it was unwilling to increase American risks and commitments in the Far East by measures which threatened to disrupt America's coalition in the NATO area. MacArthur, on the other hand, was quite willing to "go it alone," where American interests and American troops were so deeply involved, if our allies would not support the measures that he believed were the only alternative to national disaster.

As important as these differences of policy were, they indicated a much more profound difference concerning the very conception of war. Despite the General's affirmations of limited ends and limited means, he was, in fact, motivated by a conception of war that was antithetical to all such limits. Whereas the administration, implicitly operating upon the basis of Clausewitz' conception of war, imposed definite restraints upon the military effort in the light of superior political considerations, MacArthur was temperamentally incapable of tolerating these restraints if they conflicted with his single-minded determination to meet force with "maximum counterforce" in order to secure a clear-cut military victory. The administration entered, fought, and ended the Korean War for political objectives which took precedence, in its mind, over the conduct of battle; but MacArthur, from first to last, regarded the whole purpose of war as "destroying the enemy's military power and bringing the conflict to a decisive close in the minimum of time and with a minimum of loss."[19] Any deviation from that indispensable military objective for political reasons constituted "appeasement" in his mind. Far from accepting the primacy of politics, he fervently believed, as he stated in his testimony, that "the minute you reach the killing stage," politics has failed, "and the military takes over." Otherwise, he declared, you would have the Soviet system of the political commissar. "I do unquestionably state that when men become locked in battle . . . there should be no artifice under the name of politics, which should handicap your own men, decrease their chances for winning, and increase their losses."[20]

Motivated by this one-sided conception of the relation between force and politics, MacArthur was willing to accept the limitations that the administration placed upon the political objectives and military operations of the war only so long as they were compatible with the achievement of victory through complete destruction of the Communist capacity to fight. When these limitations interfered with the attainment of total military victory, his only thought was to get rid of them; and he naturally disparaged any argument that would preserve them. All of MacArthur's statements leave the distinct impression that his opposition to the administration's policies and his advocacy of his own measures stemmed less from a reasoned weighing of the consequences and risks involved in various alternative courses of action than from a profoundly emotional conviction that all such considerations were of minor importance compared to the overriding necessity of crushing the enemy.

In a sense, MacArthur's preoccupation with military victory made him a truer exponent of the guiding ideals which the administration adduced for fighting the war than the administration itself could afford to be, simply because he was unequivocally committed to putting them into practice. Thus he could not have been in more complete agreement with the administration's thesis that the Korean aggression had to be halted in order to prevent further aggression; but, whereas the administration felt compelled, in practice, to qualify its thesis by considering strategic priorities and the relation between commitments and available power, MacArthur simply refused to admit that Communist aggression could not be stopped everywhere in the world.[21] Similarly, MacArthur was ardently convinced that the principles of justice and democracy required a free, independent, and unified Korea, as the administration itself avowed; but whereas the administration found it necessary to settle for something less in order to keep political objectives within range of military measures that were compatible with limited war, MacArthur brushed aside all the perplexing problems of balancing the ends and means of war in an inflexible determination to unite Korea by crushing the enemy. Although he reconciled his view with limited war, to his own satisfaction, by staunchly maintaining that the measures he proposed would achieve the UN objective without expanding the conflict or precipitating unlimited war, there is a strong presumption, judging from his basic conception of war, that if his measures had not resulted in the victory he anticipated, he would not have been restrained by political considerations from resorting to even more ambitious measures and that if a general war had resulted, he would have regarded it merely as the inevitable unfolding of Russia's original intentions. But the administration, acutely conscious of its global commitments and the exorbitant costs of unlimited war, could afford no such indifference to the effect of American actions upon the enemy's conduct of the war. No matter how pure its principles might be in the abstract, it was compelled to limit and qualify its resistance to aggression, in practice, by the inescapable logic of its unwillingness to follow any other strategy than containment.

The Lessons of Korea

One can hardly overestimate the importance of the United States achievement in containing the Communist attack on South Korea without precipitating total war. By this achievement the nation went a long way toward demonstrating that it could successfully resist direct military aggression locally by limited war in the secondary strategic areas, where a demonstrated capacity for local resistance was the only effective deterrent to Communist military expansion. As a result, the United States placed itself in a much stronger position to contain the Communist sphere of control than if it had stood passively aside and fretfully watched the Communists swallow Korea. If it had stood aside, one can scarcely doubt that Peiping and the Kremlin would have been encouraged to engineer other attacks at vulnerable points along the Sino-Soviet periphery. In any event, the resulting blow to America's prestige might have fatally weakened the NATO coalition. It would certainly have encouraged neutralism in Japan and Germany and a massive swing to the Communist bloc throughout the defenseless areas of Asia. Unfortunately, by fighting a limited war in Korea the United States incurred serious internal schisms that weakened the national will to fight future limited wars. Yet this penalty was incidental to the main achievement, and it was mild compared to the turmoil and confusion, the cross-purposes and the extremism, that would have attended passive acquiescence in a blatant Communist aggression that the United States might have halted.

However, granting the American achievement in Korea, we must still wonder whether it was sufficient, whether we could have achieved much more at a tolerable cost. By repelling the Communist aggression through limited war we struck an effective blow for containment; but by leaving the Communists in control of North Korea we incurred some serious liabilities. We permitted the Chinese to gain great prestige throughout the vulnerable populations and wavering governments of Asia, while we raised serious doubts in the minds of those peoples about our ability to defend them. At the same time, we committed ourselves to defend a strategically profitless area under difficult circumstances, and we left a thorn in our Pacific flank; for the Communists, who have flagrantly disregarded the truce restrictions in Korea, could at any time force us to live up to our commitment. (This same disadvantage would exist if we had unified Korea, since Communist forces beyond the border would still hold a sword over the peninsula, but the problem of creating local defensive strength would be eased considerably.) In addition, we incurred the vexing liability of restraining an impetuous South Korean government led by an aging patriot whose whole life has revolved about the consuming ambition to unify Korea.

Strategically, politically, and in terms of our prestige, it is difficult to deny that we would be in a much better position now if we had soundly defeated the Chinese Communists and made a generous settlement on the basis of the UN's objective of unification. Thus the real question is whether we could have achieved this larger objective by a scale of military action and with a risk of total war commensurate with the potential political advantages to be gained. The answer to this question is obscured by our inability to plumb the minds of the Communists or to gauge the consequences of alternative methods of conducting the war that were never tried. Nevertheless, if we are to read the lessons of Korea correctly, we must speculate about these incalculable matters, just as the government was forced to do. Our speculations fall logically into several key questions about the administration's conduct of the war and the thinking that lay behind it.

Did the government correctly estimate the danger of total war resulting from Russian intervention? The Truman administration was never sure that the Korean War was not a premeditated prelude to a general Soviet attack on the West, leading to a third world war. This fear was the major consideration inducing the government to impose upon itself the restrictions that were so contrary to MacArthur's entreaties. Therefore, it is important to determine whether the administration estimated the risk of general war correctly or not.

In retrospect, it seems extremely doubtful that the Russians—especially before they had acquired great air-atomic capabilities—would have taken anything less than a direct attack upon their immediate sphere of control as the occasion for deliberately precipitating a total war. Total war would have meant the devastation of their homeland and the forfeiting of many less risky and more profitable opportunities for gaining Soviet objectives. It seems much more likely that the Russians—assuming that they bore the major responsibility for the North Korean invasion—regarded the Korean venture as a limited testing or probing action, which they were ready to write off as a loss if necessary but which they would not have found worth pursuing at the cost of an all-out nuclear war under any circumstances, as long as American objectives were confined to the Korean peninsula. This hypothesis is in accord with the American government's own interpretation of Soviet conduct in general, with the prevailing official analysis of Russia's specific motive for intervening in the Korean War, with the views of the senior military commanders in the Far East,[22] and with intelligence reports the government received throughout the war. Therefore, it seems quite improbable that the Kremlin would have deliberately intervened in such a way as to cause total war, merely for the sake of upholding China's position in Korea, as long as it believed that the UN command coveted no territorial objectives beyond Korea. It is especially improbable that the Kremlin would have chosen to attack in the NATO area in retaliation against the bombing of Manchuria or any other measure that MacArthur advocated.

But might not a third world war have resulted accidentally from limited Russian intervention? The Russians did not have to launch an immediate full-scale intervention in order to precipitate all-out war. Would they not have undertaken measures of limited and covert intervention—such as the sending of additional personnel, equipment, and aircraft to Korea and the resort to submarine and air attacks against

American naval units, ostensibly by the Chinese—rather than acquiesce in China's defeat by the measures MacArthur advocated? Perhaps China was too valuable an ally for the Kremlin to have acted otherwise. If so, such limited measures of indirect intervention might have led to a general war by successive steps of retaliation and counter-retaliation, especially if the United States had discovered that the bombing of Manchurian bases was not sufficient to contain Chinese troops and that the Soviet Union constituted a more formidable privileged sanctuary than Manchuria. At least this contingency was more likely than deliberate all-out Soviet intervention.

One can reason that, considering the compelling reasons for the Soviet Union and the United States avoiding total war, it was unlikely that either power would have decided to destroy major targets so vital to the other as to lead to total war. Moreover, the decision to destroy vital targets was not likely to be a matter of accident or miscalculation. On the other hand, this line of reasoning assumes a degree of rationality and predictability in the conduct of war that would have constituted extremely dubious grounds on which to base decisions which carried such disastrous penalties in the event of miscalculation. In reappraising the administration's fear of Russian intervention and total war, we must reckon with the element of uncertainty in all calculations concerning war. No sane and cautious person could have been sure of Russian intentions or of Russian reactions to various American measures. Many of our assumptions about Soviet conduct are still highly conjectural. Moreover, strategists cannot properly consider the dimensions of the risks involved apart from the importance and feasibility of obtaining the objectives for which the risks are taken. Therefore, the question confronting American strategists was not, simply, whether various measures carried a certain risk of precipitating total war but whether the risk was tolerable or intolerable in terms of the political stakes and the potential military advantages that might have accrued. In calculating this more complex equation, the Joint Chiefs of Staff not only believed that the risk of total war was much greater than MacArthur estimated, but they also believed that the military efficacy of the measures he advocated would have been far less than he estimated. In their view the bombing of Manchurian bases would not only have done little to stop the flow of men and material into Korea but would also have incurred the grave disadvantage of unleashing Communist air attacks upon our vulnerable ports and naval supply lines. Faced with this military predicament, the political leaders of the nation were, quite logically, willing to settle for less than the maximum UN objective.

It is difficult to disagree with the administration's conclusion if the measures MacArthur advocated would only have succeeded in expanding the war without advancing our ability to unify Korea. But if bombing the targets north of the Yalu would really have been as effective in defeating the Chinese in Korea as a number of commanders maintained, then the resulting boon to containment would have been worth the relatively small risk of total war this measure would have entailed.

The outsider is not in a position to gauge the military consequence of MacArthur's recommendations, but one can scarcely deny that the administration overrated the risk of Russia's deliberately precipitating a total war as the result of them. It overrated the risk because it had been consistently preoccupied with the threat of all-out Russian aggression, almost to the exclusion of considering more limited threats, and at the same time because it was inadequately prepared to fight anything less than a total war. If the administration had been more attuned to the threat of limited war, and if it had been less dependent upon strategic air power and the atomic bomb, it might even have given more weight to the military value of MacArthur's recommendations in comparison to the risk of total war they entailed. Perhaps by concentrating on the problem of retaliating against a major Russian aggression and depreciating the problem of meeting lesser Communist aggressions by limited war, American policy-makers and military planners incurred a kind of paralysis of reason and will, which led them to magnify the risk of measures short of massive retaliation beyond the objective indications of existing military and political conditions. Nevertheless, this would not refute the administration's contention that the risks related to MacArthur's recommendations were incommensurate with the limited political objectives at stake. It would only emphasize the lesson of military and psychological preparedness for limited war, demonstrated by the very occurrence of the Korean struggle.

Did the government correctly estimate the danger of overcommitting American power in Korea? Aside from the threat of total war, the administration was restrained in its conduct of the Korean War by its fear of committing such a great part of its military resources as to leave the United States dangerously exposed in other parts of the world, including many parts of far greater military strategic significance. This was undoubtedly a legitimate fear, given the low state of America's military establishment. As it was, the United States committed about 80 per cent of its effective armed forces to Korea and was forced to conduct its operations on a perilously thin logistical margin. If the administration had expanded the war by bombing Manchurian bases, the Russians and the Chinese with Russian help had a number of ways of retaliating by means short of total war, which probably would have increased the scale and scope of warfare beyond America's ability to sustain the fight at a reasonable cost in men, money, and equipment.

But if we concede that the government wisely estimated the danger of overcommitment, this only emphasizes the baneful effect of America's lack of preparedness for conducting limited warfare. The United States would have been in a far better position to achieve its objectives in Korea if it had had a military establishment capable of handling an expanded war without rendering itself defenseless in every other part of the world. With another four divisions to expend, the UN forces might even have succeeded in unifying Korea without bombing Manchurian bases; for the Chinese were committed to their full capacity, and when they finally agreed to armistice negotiations in the summer of 1951, they were near the end of their reservoir of trained manpower. Certainly the lesson here is that the greater our capacity for local defense, the more capable we shall be of resisting aggression at a cost commensurate with limited political objectives.

In the light of Chinese intervention, should the United States have crossed north of the thirty-eighth parallel and enlarged its objective to the unification of Korea? In terms of American prestige and future containment of communism the United States would have gained considerably more from the Korean War if it had soundly defeated the Chinese and negotiated the unification of Korea. On the other hand, since the United States had to settle for the thirty-eighth parallel anyway, it can be argued that American forces might better have stopped there in the first place.

On the assumption that our drive for the whole of North Korea after the Inchon landing needlessly expanded the war by provoking Chinese intervention, a few Americans—George Kennan among them—and many foreign observers held, at the time of the Inchon victory, that it was a great mistake not to stabilize a line at the thirty-eighth parallel or the "narrow neck" of Korea and to negotiate a political settlement on that basis. But one must wonder, in that case, whether the Chinese would have abstained from intervention. Or were they determined to intervene anyway, once we had entered the Korean War and neutralized Formosa? Assuming that the Chinese had not intervened, could we have negotiated any more stable and satisfactory a peace, with the Chinese still uncommitted and able to occupy North Korea at will? Even now we do not know enough about Chinese and Russian intentions in Korea to answer these questions. The only thing that is clear is that we badly misjudged Chinese intentions and Chinese strength and that we were poorly prepared to achieve the unification of Korea under the consequences.

But could we have reasonably avoided the miscalculation of Red China's intention to intervene? This question goes beyond the technical competence of our intelligence service and the adequacy of our secret information. It asks whether we fully understood the significance of the objectives of limited war and the proportionate relationship between the objectives and the scale of war. The original restriction of military operations below the thirty-eighth parallel concretely showed that our political objective was limited to repelling North Korean aggression and restoring the independence of South Korea. We do not know whether the Chinese would have been content to see the UN restore the status quo ante bellum without intervening; but it seems obvious that this objective threatened Chinese interests far less, and therefore called for a much lower order of resistance, than the unification of Korea. Similarly, when UN forces crossed the parallel and their objective was extended to the unification of Korea, this larger threat to Chinese interests called for an entirely different scale of resistance. Instead of merely giving up South Korea, which they did not hold in the first place, the Chinese were faced with the prospect of the whole peninsula passing into hostile hands, which would have eliminated the buffer zone protecting the center of Chinese industry in Manchuria. It is not surprising that China was unwilling to acquiesce in this loss when she had the means of preventing it. What is surprising is that we so badly underestimated the risk of Chinese intervention under these circumstances. Perhaps the miscalculation is understandable in terms of our unfamiliarity with the conduct of limited war, but it points to a lesson in the relation between political objectives and the scale of war that we dare not overlook again.

After the Chinese had intervened, should we have been content to recover the thirty-eighth parallel, or should we have continued to fight for a larger objective? When the Chinese intervened, the objective of both belligerents was nothing less than the control of the entire peninsula. Yet because neither side was willing or able to expend the effort necessary to obtain this objective, both were eventually willing to settle for the cease-fire agreement. General Van Fleet and other military commanders in Korea have criticized the government for entering into peace negotiations when, in their view, we could have defeated the Communists with a little more effort and at least restored our prestige and obtained better peace terms.[23] On the other hand, General Ridgway, while conceding that we could have marched to the Yalu if we had been willing to pay the price in dead and wounded, has written that from the purely military standpoint the effort would not have been worth the cost.

A drive to the line of the Yalu and the Tumen would have cleared Korea of the Chinese enemy. But he would have still been facing us in great strength beyond those rivers. The seizure of the land between the truce line and the Yalu would have merely meant the seizure of more real estate. It would have greatly shortened the enemy's supply lines by pushing him right up against his main supply bases in Manchuria. It would have greatly lengthened our own supply routes, and widened our battlefront from 110 miles to 420. Would the American people have been willing to support the great army that would have been required to hold that line?[24]

Both the Truman and Eisenhower administrations decided that the political advantages to be gained by defeating the Chinese in Korea were not worth the military cost. Under the circumstances, they were content to have repelled the aggression upon South Korea.

It is difficult to appraise the wisdom of the government's decision to agree to a truce on the basis of the thirty-eighth parallel without knowing the military cost and consequences of the effort to achieve more favorable terms. If we could have soundly defeated the Chinese without greatly expanding our effort and without bringing about formidable indirect Russian intervention, then the achievement of the unification of Korea or even of more limited objectives would have been well worth the extra effort. On the other hand, the government's decision was clearly the least objectionable alternative if the effort to achieve more favorable terms would have required such a drain upon our military capacity as to leave us impotent to contain the Communist sphere in other, more vital areas. Perhaps the light of history will show that the government, in its anxiety to end an unpopular war, underestimated the long-run political advantages of obtaining more favorable terms of settlement; but we shall never know whether the military cost of pursuing these advantages would have been as reasonable as some of the government's critics have assumed. In any case, we can safely conclude that we would have been in a much better position to make a wise political decision if we had possessed a military capacity more nearly commensurate with the requirements of limited war.

Did the administration in its concern for "collective security" place too much weight on the need for deferring to other members of the UN? Despite the administration's public deference to the other members of the United Nations, there is no evidence that it refrained from taking any measure that would have substantially affected the course of the war on account of the views of foreign governments. Nevertheless, in considering the general lessons of the Korean War, it is important to ask whether the American government adopted the wisest public position toward relations with its allies. Here it does seem that in stressing the need for unanimity among the free-world nations resisting aggression, American spokesmen exaggerated the moral justification for making allied approval a condition of American action. After all, the United States intervened unilaterally in Korea to promote what it regarded as a vital national interest. It sought UN support of this action as a sanction, not as a precondition. Since the United States would not have intervened, and should not have intervened, unless the government had believed that a compelling national interest was at stake, there could be no virtue in sacrificing this interest, once the decision had been made, in order to satisfy nations the government had not consulted in the first place. Moreover, the United States, together with the ROK army, bore over 90 per cent of the burden of the fighting. On grounds of national sacrifice, as well as national interest, there was far less moral justification for deferring to the fifteen UN members who sent troops—much less to the fifty-three who indorsed the UN position—than to South Korea, whose very survival was at stake and who contributed much more than all the UN nations put together.[25]

The political justification for deferring to our allies is another matter. But the political consideration would have existed regardless of whether we had fought the war under UN auspices. How important was it, in terms of holding a coalition together and maintaining fruitful political relations with UN members outside the coalition, to conduct the war in a manner agreeable to America's allies? One may concede that this was very important indeed and still not believe that it was so vital as to warrant sacrificing military and political objectives of primary and immediate importance to the United States. The answer to such a question can be determined only on the basis of a careful weighing of one kind of consideration against another in the light of the particular circumstances. But in weighing these considerations it is essential that the political question should not be confused with either the moral or the military question. The administration, in striving to give the color of altruism to an action that could not have been justified except primarily on grounds of national self-interest, tended to mix all these questions together and thereby obscure the legitimate basis of its decisions; and this was a process that in some measure misled foreign governments, the American public, and the administration itself.

Such questions as these are not much easier to answer in retrospect than they were at the time. Yet even if we could now be absolutely sure of the wisest way to have conducted the Korean War, this would not be a conclusive guide for meeting all future military contingencies. For example, granting the contribution to containment of the decision to intervene in Korea, it certainly did not prove that the nation should try to resist aggression everywhere under any circumstance, as General MacArthur maintained and as the administration's blanket indorsement of the ideal of collective security implied. If the United States had been twice as powerful, it still could not have afforded to check every possible aggression, regardless of the importance of the strategic stakes or the military and political feasibility of intervention. And there are few places around the Sino-Soviet periphery in which intervention would be as feasible as it was in Korea.

Nor did the halting of aggression in Korea provide any assurance that the Communists, having been taught a lesson, would renounce all further aggression. According to the common interpretation of the events leading to World War II, the chain of aggression would have been broken as soon as the democracies stood up to the aggressors; but whether or not this hypothesis applied to the chain of Fascist aggression, it is inapplicable to the persistent pressure of international communism. The strategy of containment is, in fact, based on the contrary assumption that Communist power, in Kennan's words, "is a fluid stream which moves constantly, wherever it is permitted to move, toward a given goal." It follows that if you succeed in damming it up in one place, it flows into another whenever the opportunity occurs.

In its persistent but flexible pursuit of expansion the Communist bloc had many opportunities for aggression by means and at places which would rule out the conditions that made American resistance feasible in Korea. Even while the Korean War was in progress, this fact was demonstrated when the Chinese openly appropriated Tibet and Communist guerillas continued to wage irregular warfare in Indochina, Burma, and Malaya. However, in the aftermath of the Korean War the challenge to containment was not only overt military aggression but also political, psychological, and economic penetration, in which Communist military strength served as a silent but, for that reason, all the more effective threat.

In Korea, as in Europe, military containment was feasible because the inhabitants perceived its necessity and were willing to sacrifice their lives for it if necessary. But throughout most of the rest of the gray areas the people and their governments were inclined to look upon containment as the exclusive concern of Western powers, who were trying to preserve the remnants of colonialism by manufacturing the threat of Communist aggression. They did not share our sense of urgency about the external threat of communism. They regarded our strategy of counterforce as dangerous "militarism," which could only entangle them in a struggle for power among foreign governments with interests quite alien to their own.

In order to capitalize upon this indigenous nationalism and anti-Westernism in the rimlands of Eurasia, the Soviet Union developed in the aftermath of the active fighting in Korea a tactic of "peaceful coexistence," which was shrewdly calculated to promote Communist influence in these sensitive areas and to diminish the influence of the West by portraying American strategy as the instrument of imperialism and an incitement to thermonuclear catastrophe. In some respects Russia's "new course" was merely the logical extension of a shift of attention to the periphery of Eurasia, which had begun, in response to the nuclear stalemate in Europe and the growth of the indigenous revolution in Asia, even before the Korean War.

In contrast to the Soviet Union's tactical shift, the American response to the Korean War seemed to be determined more by an interpretation of the postwar military exigencies than by an awareness of the changing international political context within which these exigencies occurred. In reaching their interpretation of the requirements of military strategy American leaders were now conscious of a troublesome dilemma, which had been inherent, from the first, in the effort to confront the Communist powers with unalterable counterforce at a series of shifting points by means short of total war. If the United States did nothing to check future Communist aggressions, then the deterrent effect of the Korean War would be largely nullified. But if the United States intervened and failed, or if it wasted away its resources in a series of inconclusive contests, it might suffer a greater loss of prestige and security than if it had remained aloof. The American reaction to this dilemma demonstrated that, whatever the true lessons of limited war the Korean struggle might contain, they were destined to have far less effect upon the shape of America's post-Korean strategy than the effort to escape the problem of limited war altogether.

The Psychological Aftermath

Perhaps the clearest lesson of the Korean War was this: that America's capacity to retaliate directly upon the Soviet Union could not deter Communist aggression in the gray areas but that the United States was inadequately prepared to contain Communist aggression by any other means. However, this lesson of physical preparedness cannot be separated from the lesson of psychological preparedness. For containment, like any strategy, is not only a matter of physical capacity; it is also a matter of will. If the nation as a whole is unwilling to expend its lives and resources upon limited military engagements that promise no clear-cut resolution of the struggle for power, then no military establishment will be adequate to sustain a successful strategy of containment. The Korean War, like previous American wars, showed that the American people will do what is essential to deal with novel and adverse circumstances when there appears to be no alternative; but the psychological aftermath, like the aftermath of other wars, raised serious doubts about their willingness to prepare for similar contingencies before it would be too late. This psychological aftermath was partly a result of the way in which the government represented the Korean War to the American people in order to elicit a united national effort.

The United States has never fought a war more unpopular than the Korean War. The American people rose admirably to meet the Communist challenge, while rejecting unlimited force or unconditional surrender; nevertheless, the experience was an exceedingly frustrating and bewildering one that left the nation in a querulous mood. The United States had suffered over 130,000 casualties in a war that brought no decisive victory. With one hand tied behind its back it had been forced to acquiesce in a stalemate, when persuasive voices said it could have readily won the war if the hand had been released. This was the first war that Americans had failed to win since the War of 1812 (and that war could at least be considered a political victory). What was more galling, it had been fought against the very power that had shattered America's old and cherished dream of a strong, democratic, Christian China. Yet throughout this whole inconclusive struggle America's principal adversary, the Soviet Union, remained uncommitted and inviolate, while the United States spent its precious manpower killing hordes of Chinese. And throughout the war the United States bore the major burden of the fighting while it deferred to allies who regarded American lives as less important than their fears of total war. No wonder that the end of hostilities brought contention, dissatisfaction, and anxiety instead of the uninhibited relief and exhilaration of previous armistices.

The Korean War, with brutal clarity, brought home to the nation as a whole the disparity between America's traditional image of her role in the world and the actual requirements of containment in a period of cold war and limited war. No one grasped this fact more keenly than John Foster Dulles, who in these years was a consultant to the State Department. To an audience in June, 1951, he explained that the world was in the situation that Trotsky had described as "not war, not peace." This was a novel and trying situation for the American people, as Dulles said.

> Heretofore, we have either had peace or we have had war. When we have had peace we have had a large degree of individual freedom and an absence of regimentation and militarism. When we have had war there has been an enemy to conquer, by all possible violence, and a considerable surrender of individual choice in order better to marshal our strength for a victory which would restore peace and freedom. There was an end that was in sight and a sure knowledge of how to reach that end.

In an appeal for patience and perseverance Dulles concluded:

> To sum it up, we are engaged in a gigantic sacrificial effort, of a kind which, in the past, we have made only in the face of obvious and dire peril and only to force an early decision which would end the necessity for such sacrifices. Today, the

peril to our homeland seems to many to be somewhat speculative, while continuance of our present measures could impair the very foundations of our American way of life without forcing an abandonment of Soviet strategy.[26]

Dulles' own growing dissatisfaction with containment suggested that Americans would not readily persevere in a strategy that promised no more than "a gigantic sacrificial effort." The Korean War showed once more that, although the nation might be unwilling to follow any alternative to containment, it was also deeply reluctant to adhere to a strategy so antithetical to its traditional outlook. The strains attending this contradictory state of affairs took many forms—from demands for withdrawal to "fortress America" to advocacy of "preventive" atomic war. They appeared in the bitter attacks upon Secretary Acheson and in the phenomenon of McCarthyism. They erupted in an astounding display of national passion upon the return of General MacArthur. In the end, the strategy of containment remained intact; but in the process psychological scars were created to the serious detriment of America's will to meet the problem of limited war.

The psychological aftermath of the Korean War was perhaps an inevitable incident of America's adjustment to unprecedented circumstances; but it certainly was not mitigated by the administration's reluctance to acknowledge, candidly and explicitly, its adherence to the strategy of containment—a reluctance which sprang as much from inner doubts as from a sensitivity to public opinion. The administration, like Americans in general, sensed the unprecedented nature of the nation's course in world politics, and it was disturbed by its inability to reconcile this course with America's traditional image of itself as a bold and idealistic nation untrammeled by the moral ambiguities, the restraints and frustrations, of controlling, balancing, and moderating national power. Its response to this contradiction between reality and predisposition was to try to maintain a rhetorical bridge between them by invoking the inspirational phrases of "collective security" while depreciating the strategy that actually created an unbridgeable gulf. This placed it at the double disadvantage of raising expectations that did not correspond with the facts and then defending the facts by throwing cold water on the expectations. The effect was not to build a bridge between reality and predisposition but rather to create the illusion of a bridge, which only compounded public frustration and bewilderment.

It is true that Dean Acheson, one of the most articulate Secretaries of

State of modern times, publicly elucidated all the elements of American strategy, at one time or another and in one form or another, with uncommon eloquence and sagacity. Yet the import of Acheson's elucidations was clouded by his failure to place the separate elements within the whole by acknowledging the government's adherence to the strategy which all the world knew as containment. Instead, Acheson, like all administration spokesmen, was apologetic and defensive about containment; and he seemed to go out of his way to present American policy in other terms, as though containment were indecent. Unfortunately, what came through to the general public was not the carefully formulated elements of a comprehensible national strategy but the weary generalities of collective security.

The chief trouble with the administration's rationalizations of American policy was not that they were out of line with popular aspirations and predispositions but that they were too much in line with public opinion to enable the public to accommodate itself to contradictory facts. The principle of collective security—the image of a nation impartially executing the will of the peace-loving, democratic community of nations by punishing aggression in behalf of the United Nations—simply did not fit the facts of a nation up to its neck in power politics, aligned with undemocratic and democratic powers alike, and forced to pick and choose its resistance to aggression according to the configurations of power and the dictates of its own national self-interest. The only way the actual course of American foreign policy could have been rationally explained was in terms of a national strategy, whether one called it "containment" or by any other name. In the long run, the attempt to escape this fact only deepened public confusion and anxiety, as it led the administration to overgeneralize its policies only to explain them away, to raise unrealistic expectations only to have events refute them.

Not until the MacArthur hearings forced the government to justify its actions in concrete terms and in the context of an over-all plan did the nation begin to receive a clear exposition of the true nature of American strategy; but, even then, administration spokesmen were excessively vague about it. Their only strong card in the debate seemed to be their determination to avoid a third world war; but so far as providing a positive rationalization for the Korean action, they relied chiefly upon analogies to the chain of aggression in the 1930's and upon general affirmations of the need for supporting the United Nations and the principle of collective security. Only once did an official spokesman briefly venture to associate the administration's actions with containment.[27] To be sure, for students of international relations the administration's testimony contains a full and able exposition of the central assumptions underlying American strategy, but for the ordinary informed citizen the essence of that strategy was blurred by the administration's own ambivalent attitude toward it—on the one hand, implicitly defending containment in terms of concrete actions but, on the other hand, half apologizing for it and almost pretending that it did not exist. Under these circumstances, the government's case was bound to be vulnerable to MacArthur's ringing charge, "There is no policy—there is nothing, I tell you, no plan, or anything."[28]

Perhaps a candid, explicit defense of containment would have been too great a shock for a nation just feeling its way through the adversities of power politics. But how long can a nation be expected to pursue a strategy which its leaders are ashamed to acknowledge, even to themselves?

Chapter Nine

CONTAINMENT AFTER KOREA

The Democratic Administration's Response to Korea

The Korean War confronted the nation with a serious strategic problem it had scarcely recognized before: the problem of containing peripheral Communist incursions by means short of total war. The Truman administration sensed a new and dangerous state of affairs, but it is doubtful whether it understood the real nature of the strategic problem or met it with an adequate response. The Republican administration, which came into office in the wake of mounting dissatisfaction with the Korean War, was acutely conscious of the strategic problem; but its attempt to find a clear-cut solution compatible with American traditions and predispositions led, ironically, to a return to the Democratic administration's pre-Korean reliance upon strategic nuclear retaliation, which now became increasingly inadequate as Russia's nuclear counter-retaliatory power grew at a surprising pace. The political effect of this strategic reversion was to accelerate the disintegration of the Western coalition and the disaffection of the uncommitted nations, which had begun with the crystallization of a nuclear stalemate in Europe and the shift of Communist power to the gray areas even before the Korean War.

The Democratic administration's most significant military response to the Korean War—a response that began when the war was at its height—was the launching of a "crash" rearmament and remobilization program designed to prepare the United States for total war at a theoretical point of maximum danger in 1953. Accordingly, Secretary of Defense Louis Johnson, who had stood for budgetary economy in defense planning, became a casualty of the war when he was replaced by General Marshall in September, 1950; and the Budget Bureau was forced to yield its preponderant influence in setting force levels to the National Security Council. Under the impetus of the Korean crisis the administra-

194

tion planned on expanding the army from 10 to 21 divisions. By the spring of 1951 it was talking in terms of a 95-group Air Force, whereas only eighteen months before it had refused to approve an increase beyond 48 groups to the 70-group level favored by Congress. Before the end of 1951 it had raised its sights to 143 groups by 1956. In addition, it called for a Navy with 408 major active combatant vessels and 16 carrier air groups, plus the construction of the giant aircraft carrier "Forrestal." It planned to maintain a Marine Corps of 3 divisions. Large sums were requested for military assistance and economic aid to foreign countries, in the name of "defense support." Under the presidential instruction of January 20, 1950, "to continue . . . work on all forms of atomic weapons, including the so-called hydrogen or super-bomb," the government more than doubled estimates of expenditures for the Atomic Energy Commission. This rearmament program was substantially approved by Congress, with the exception of the "defense support" items.

Undoubtedly, the enactment of this program made the United States better prepared for limited war than it had been before the Korean War. And yet it does not seem to have reflected any significant change in strategic thinking. It was primarily a response to immediate military needs in Korea and to heightened fears of Russian aggression and total war in Europe, not to a new recognition of the threat of limited war in the gray areas.

The increase in American ground troops can be considered the belated fulfilment of a National Security Council plan, originally formulated early in 1950 on the basis of Russia's detonation of an atomic bomb, which had reached the conclusion that, with the growth of Russia's atomic capacity, the United States would have to rely not only on its retaliatory air power but proportionately more upon ground troops in order to deter a Russian attack in Europe or elsewhere. Budgetary restrictions had precluded the implementation of this plan at the time, but the Korean War removed them; for now that the Communists had refuted American expectations by showing that they would not hesitate to use direct military action to gain their ends, the administration concluded that the danger of the Russians or of Russian satellites moving into Europe had greatly increased.

This same reasoning led the administration in the winter of 1950/51 to plan the transfer of four American divisions to Europe, in conjunction with a scheme for building up an "integrated" European army, and to explore methods for putting German armed units at the disposal of the West. From the government's effort to build a ground force actually capable of defending Europe, rather than one serving merely as the trip-wire to set off the alarm for air-nuclear retaliation, was to emerge most of the wracking conflicts within NATO over military and economic integration and the terms of a German contribution.

The persistent emphasis of American strategy upon deterring a Russian attack in Europe was manifest in the arguments of all the administration spokesmen who participated in the "Great Debate" over the troops-for-Europe issue in the winter of 1951. The hearings and the debates in Congress on the defense measures submitted to it during the Korean War reveal that the great majority of congressmen were also thinking almost exclusively in terms of deterring a major war with Russia. The only difference was that most congressmen placed more emphasis on strategic atomic retaliation and less on ground troops, and a few highly vocal congressmen were more ardently in favor of expanded military aid to the Far East. But these differences of emphasis were nothing new; they had existed ever since the fall of Nationalist China and the formation of NATO.

The administration did show that it was responsive to the shift of Communist pressure to Asia by entering into mutual security treaties with the Philippines, Australia, and New Zealand in the summer of 1951 and by making a peace treaty and a security treaty with Japan in September, 1951. But this rudimentary Pacific security system was aimed at the protection of America's defensive perimeter, not at the containment of communism in the gray areas. It envisioned defense by strategic retaliation, not by local resistance.

Still another direct response to the Korean War was the Uniting for Peace Resolution, sponsored by the American government and approved by the UN General Assembly in November, 1950. This resolution was a device for securing UN sanction for resistance to future Koreas by bypassing the Russian veto in the Security Council and permitting the General Assembly to recommend collective measures by a two-thirds vote. However, this blow for "collective security" appeared to accomplish far more than it actually accomplished, as far as implementing containment was concerned. In the event of an actual Communist aggression, a two-thirds vote for collective action would depend, not, primarily, on abstract moral or legal principles, but rather on the extent to which the nations represented in the General Assembly identified their concrete interests with American interests in checking the particular instance of aggression. Considering the growing split between the United States and even its major ally, Great Britain, over policy toward Nationalist and Communist China, it was unlikely that two-thirds of the General Assembly nations would sufficiently identify their interests with American interests to join the kind of collective effort they had supported in resisting aggression upon the UN-sponsored Republic of Korea. The growth of an Asian-African "neutralist" bloc in the Assembly foreboded increasing difficulties in obtaining the support of the group of nations who were the most likely victims of aggression. In any case, America's ability to organize collective defense was pre-eminently a political problem, then a military problem, and only lastly and to a minor extent a legal problem. The Uniting for Peace Resolution did nothing in itself to promote a political or military basis for concerted action. At most, it was an instrumentality for bringing an existing collective will into operation under UN auspices.

The measures by which the administration dealt directly with the threat of Communist expansion in the gray areas were the same measures it had relied upon before the North Korean invasion, that is, granting military equipment, economic aid, and technical assistance. The bulk of America's military aid outside Korea continued to go to the French and Vietnamese troops in Indochina, as before the Korean War. The administration was conscious of the political liability of appearing to support a colonial regime and Vietnam's unsavory Emperor Bao Dai, but it believed that American pressure could induce France to execute a graceful political departure, while American material aid sustained the French-led military resistance against the Vietminh insurgents.

Evidently mindful of the consequences of having failed to give clear advance notice of America's intention to resist aggression in Korea, the State Department took the lead in securing a joint declaration in 1952 with France and Great Britain, warning that the signatories would regard direct Chinese Communist intervention in Southeast Asia as a matter requiring urgent consideration by the United Nations. But, outside Indochina, the United States continued to intrust military resistance to indigenous forces and British anti-guerilla warfare.

The Truman administration hoped that these military expedients in Asia would be sufficient to "hold the line"; but it was also aware that, in the long run, containment in the gray areas would depend in large measure upon the will and the capability of the inhabitants to defend themselves against infiltration, subversion, and insurrection, as well as against overt military attacks. At the same time, it had to recognize that many of the nations of these areas lacked the minimum conditions of internal cohesion upon which situations of strength could be built with the help of American economic and military assistance. Secretary Acheson pointed to this fact in his remarks before the National Press Club on January 12, 1950, when he said, "American assistance can be effective when it is the missing component in a situation which might otherwise be solved. It can not furnish the will, and it can not furnish the loyalty of a people to its government."[1]

Notwithstanding this obstacle, the administration, even before the Korean War, had initiated a program of economic and technical aid to "underdeveloped" areas on the supposition that higher standards of living might keep the inhabitants from turning to communism. Some such scheme as this had been under consideration ever since the inauguration of the Marshall Plan, but in its scale and scope the plan that emerged in 1949 bore no resemblance to the European Recovery Program. When President Truman initiated the so-called "Point Four Program" in his inaugural address of January 20, 1949, he spoke of a "bold new program" that would "help the free people of the world, through their own efforts, to produce more food, more clothing, more materials for housing, and more mechanical power to lighten their burdens."[2] But the modest scale of aid which he envisioned—not more than forty-five million dollars— made it clear that the major effort would have to come from the inhabitants of these areas over a long period of time. Moreover, experience in operating the program threw doubts upon the original optimistic assumption of a simple and direct correlation between the level of a nation's economy, its growth of democratic values and institutions, its political stability, and its vulnerability or invulnerability to communism. A nation's vulnerability or invulnerability to Communist penetration seemed to depend upon a variety of internal social and political conditions, as well as upon external political and military developments, which were beyond any predictable effect of economic and technical aid. In any case, after the outbreak of the Korean War the government was forced to assign an even lower priority to this long-run problem of containment in the gray areas. The economic and technical aspects of American aid inevitably became increasingly subordinate to short-run military requirements, especially to the requirements of the French and Vietnamese armies in Indochina.

The Republican Challenge to Containment

Before the Democratic administration ended its term of office in 1952, it had responded to Russia's growing atomic capacity and the shift of Communist pressure toward limited aggression in secondary strategic areas principally in the following ways: expanding the military establishment in all services; placing greater emphasis upon ground troops in the defense of Europe; establishing a Pacific security system for the protection of America's Far Eastern defensive perimeter; stepping up military aid to France and Vietnam in Indochina and to the Nationalist Chinese in Formosa; and continuing, on a reduced scale, economic and technical aid to underdeveloped countries. None of these measures nor all of them put together represented any significant change in strategic thinking. Despite America's experience with limited war in Korea, the administration continued to place preponderant emphasis upon what it regarded as the overriding task of containment: preventing a third world war by deterring an overt Russian attack on Europe.

It is doubtful that this response to Korea was objectively adequate to deal with the actual strategic situation; but, manifestly, it was subjectively incapable of satisfying the great mass of Americans who yearned for a clear-cut solution to the problems of containment revealed in Korea. The Korean War suddenly made the nation acutely conscious of the frustrations attending the application of containment in secondary strategic areas. For the first time it revealed the great scope of the problem of confronting the Communists with "unalterable counterforce at every point where they show signs of encroaching upon the interests of a free and stable world." Yet the administration seemed to have no new ideas for banishing these frustrations or for solving the strategic dilemma, other than increasing American military commitments and expenditures.

It was a foregone conclusion that the Republican party, which had been out of office throughout the cold war, the "loss of China," and the Korean War, would become the rallying point for the mounting dissatisfaction with American foreign policy. The party came into power convinced that it had a mandate from the people to reverse the disastrous tide of events and buoyantly confident that it had the policies to fulfil that mandate. What was the nature of this mandate, and how did the new administration intend to fulfil it?

The popular mandate was somewhat contradictory. Excluding the persistent strain of "liberal" criticism of containment, because it was not significant as part of the public sentiment to which the Republicans appealed, the mandate was twofold. On the one hand, there was a strong current of public opinion calling for a "tougher" policy toward communism, both at home and abroad. The adherents of this position believed that the United States had been losing the cold war through softness and appeasement. They charged that Dean Acheson—"this proud priest of 'coexistence,' " as *Life* magazine called him—was too anxious to get along with international communism and not determined enough to get rid of it. As far as specific recommendations were concerned, the advocates of a tougher policy urged a wide range of measures, from "preventive" war to a "moral offensive." But, in reality, this current of protest was more of a mood than a set of policies. People just felt that somehow American prestige had to be restored and American initiative regained; that it was not sufficient merely to contain communism in an endless series of defensive moves; that it was time for Americans to be true to their national heritage and adopt a "positive" policy.

On the other hand, an equally strong current of opinion, frequently existing beside this one within the same individual, called for a reduction of American commitments and expenditures and a withdrawal from military and political entanglements. The adherents of this position were weary of placating allies and pouring aid into foreign lands. They charged that containment had involved the nation in an impossible task of holding a Maginot Line all around the 20,000-mile periphery of Communist power, while the Soviet Union, secure in its interior position, merely pulled the strings that unleashed one satellite here or another there.

In a direct way this contradictory mandate was stimulated by the Korean War; but in a deeper sense, it was a legacy of the nation's ambivalent approach to war—the confluence of pacifism and pugnacity. On the one hand, Americans yearned to isolate themselves from conflict and violence; but, on the other hand, if they could not withdraw, they wanted to participate in a straightforward manner, boldly wielding the initiative and marshaling all the nation's energy toward some clearly conclusive end. American ambivalence came to a head in the impulse either to win the Korean War or to pull out of it altogether, but this all-or-nothing impulse was only the particular manifestation of a general attitude that infused the nation's whole approach to the cold war with a gnawing sense of frustration.

The Republican party was sensitive to the popular dissatisfaction with containment, and it was confident that it had a strategic alternative. The recognized spokesman for Republican strategy was John Foster Dulles. Almost from the beginning of the Korean War Dulles had expressed his mounting dissatisfaction with the course of American strategy. In numerous articles and speeches his criticism of containment reached a crescendo in the 1952 presidential campaign. The Republican platform, which he largely drafted, called containment a "negative, futile and immoral policy."[3] As Dulles interpreted it, containment consumed the nation's resources in a futile attempt to suppress a series of local incursions that the Communists, taking advantage of their interior lines of communication in the heartland of Eurasia, initiated and fought on their own terms.

As it applied to Europe, Dulles believed that containment was correct as far as it went, but he said that it did not go far enough. The United States should not be satisfied merely to keep the Communists from enlarging their sphere of control, he thought; it should also look forward to the contraction of that sphere. However, it was outside of Europe that Dulles found containment particularly deficient. NATO was a good thing for Europe, he said, but it was inapplicable to Asia, where nations had neither the military tradition, the industrial capacity, nor the financial resources to organize effective mutual defense.[4] He warned that the United States would go bankrupt, alienate its political friends, and forsake its moral vitality trying to implement a strategy that promised nothing but a protracted series of local reactions to Communist aggressions in Asia while the area of freedom in the world steadily diminished. "Ours are treadmill policies," he charged, "which, at best, might perhaps keep us in the same place until we drop exhausted."[5]

The alternative to containment, as Dulles expounded it before he came into office, placed as much emphasis upon a change of mood or spirit as upon specific alternative courses of action. Consistent with a conception he had long held, Dulles asserted that in international relations, as in all spheres of human activity, the "dynamic" prevails over the "static," the spiritual over the material. Today, he said, communism represents the active, dynamic element and the free world the static, passive element.

These roles had to be reversed. But how? As Dulles explained it, communism's victories had been mostly through social ideas. Therefore, the free world had to seize the spiritual offensive from the Communists. There is a moral or natural law, he avowed, that determines right or wrong in the world. By conforming its policies to this natural law America could recapture the spiritual and dynamic element in the world, which it had traditionally represented.[6] And so he called for a "psychological and political offensive" in words that were echoed in General Eisenhower's announcement that his campaign would be conducted as "a great crusade—for freedom in America and freedom in the world."

> Our nation was dedicated, at birth, to serve not only its own welfare but the welfare of mankind. . . . If we get back into that mood, then we would not tremble before the menace of Soviet despotism. It would be the despots that would do the trembling. There comes a time in the life of any great people when their work of creation ends. They lose their sense of purpose and of mission in the world, seeking only to conserve what they have. Material things begin to seem more important than spiritual things and security seems more a matter of military defense than of a spiritual offense. Surely that hour has not struck for us.[7]

More specifically, Dulles asserted that the United States should not be forever content to confine Soviet communism within its present orbit but should instead openly declare that its goal was the liberation of the peoples enslaved behind the Iron Curtain and then take specific measures toward that end. However, aside from the declaration of the goal itself, the only major measure of liberation that Dulles mentioned during the 1952 campaign which the government had not already undertaken was the termination of diplomatic relations with Russian satellite states; and he recommended this only if and when it would promote his "freedom campaigns." Although other spokesmen of his party were less cautious in advocating liberation,[8] Dulles specifically stated, "We do not want a series of bloody uprisings and reprisals."[9]

During the presidential campaign liberation was the most prominent theme in Republican foreign-policy pronouncements. But as it turned out, this theme was less important when Dulles became Secretary of State than another alternative to containment, which he advocated during 1951 and 1952. This alternative was the strategy that came to be known as "massive retaliation." At General Eisenhower's insistence, Dulles' reference to atomic retaliation was deleted from the party platform, and as a presidential nominee Eisenhower explicitly criticized the notion of an exclusive reliance upon retaliatory air power.[10] Nevertheless, in his public statements Dulles laid heavy emphasis on strategic atomic retaliation as a deterrent to Communist expansion. Instead of trying to meet Communist aggression by local defense, the United States, he declared, was ready to retaliate instantly against open aggression by using its air and sea power so as to "hit an aggressor where it hurts" by "means of our choosing." Dulles laid particular stress upon the efficacy of giving advance warning to potential aggressors and repeatedly charged that, if the Communists had known that the United States would resist in Korea, they would not have attacked. "The only effective way to stop prospective aggressors," he said, "is to convince them in advance that if they commit aggression, they will be subjected to retaliatory blows so costly that their aggression will not be a profitable operation."[11] By organizing this retaliatory power within the framework of the UN Charter he believed that we would reduce, close to the vanishing point, the risk of open armed attack and avoid arousing fears that we might recklessly precipitate an atomic war in which others would be the principal victims.

Dulles indicated what this strategy of retaliation might mean for the defense of the gray areas in an address in Paris on May 5, 1952. Here he said that the best defense of Indochina and other parts of Asia would be the threat of retaliation against Communist China or the Soviet Union. "Is it not time," he asked, "that the Chinese Communists knew that if, for example, they sent their Red armies openly into Vietnam we will not be content merely to try to meet their armed forces at the point they select for their aggression but by retaliatory action of our own fashioning?" And he pointed out that "Siberia and much of China, notably Manchuria, are vulnerable from the standpoint of transport and communication."[12]

A psychological and political offensive, a policy of liberating the enslaved peoples, air retaliation upon aggressors at places "where it hurts" by means "of our choosing"—these measures, of which Mr. Dulles was the principal spokesman, seemed to call for a much more dynamic and offensive-minded strategy. However, in other Republican pronouncements these bold and affirmative alternatives to containment were joined with quite different measures, which seemed to lead in just the opposite direction from a "tougher" policy. Repeatedly, Republican spokesmen demanded relief from the burden of military commitments and defense expenditures, which they attributed to the blundering recklessness of the Democratic administration. The Communists, they asserted, were trying to force the United States to spend itself into "bankruptcy." Continually, they affirmed the maxim that an effective defense program depends upon a "sound domestic economy." Indignantly, they reiterated their long-standing condemnation of "New Deal–Fair Deal spending" and pointed with alarm to the unbalanced budget. General Eisenhower readily accommodated himself to this line of attack. He assured Senator Taft that national expenditures could be reduced by one-fourth within three or four years, and he placed himself squarely in line with the party platform's cautious view of foreign aid, expressed in its resolve not to "try to buy good will."

But probably the single most effective Republican appeal of the entire campaign was the implied promise of relief from the high casualties and taxes of the Korean War. This was a theme to which General Eisenhower lent the whole weight of his persuasive personality. In Eisenhower's mind withdrawal from Korea was not just an expedient for immediate relief from sacrifice. It was the application of his long-held strategic conception of a central mobile reserve, which, in turn, was an expression of his profound aversion to the employment of American ground troops in foreign struggles. As he saw it, the true purpose of the American Army was to serve as a "highly alert and highly mobile" reserve; and this required making the areas around the Communist periphery as independent of American troop support as possible, so that we could disengage ourselves from the Eurasian continent and rely primarily upon supporting indigenous forces with our superior air and sea power.[13] However, in the heat of the presidential campaign this strategic reasoning was overshadowed by the concentration of Republican fire on the immediate, highly charged emotional issue of Korea. Here General Eisenhower bore down heavily on the Truman administration's responsibility for the war. He repeatedly charged that Secretary Acheson's description of America's defensive perimeter had been as good as an invitation to the Communists to attack. As the emotional significance of the Korean issue in the campaign became apparent, he declared in a speech at Champaign, Illinois, on October 2:

> There is no sense in the United Nations, with America bearing the brunt of the thing, being constantly compelled to man those front lines. That is a job for

the Koreans. We do not want Asia to feel that the white man of the West is his enemy. If there must be a war there, let it be Asians against Asians, with our support on the side of freedom.[14]

Finally, on October 24, in a dramatic climax, Eisenhower delivered one of the most telling strokes of the campaign when he made a solemn pledge "to bring the Korean war to an early and honorable end" by making a personal trip to Korea.

Thus the new administration assumed the unfamiliar responsibilities of statesmanship pledged to satisfy two powerful popular desires that could not easily be reconciled in practice: the desire to oppose international communism more vigorously and the desire to reduce America's economic and military commitments. Corresponding with these two popular desires, the Republican leaders associated themselves with policies which promised to oppose Communist power more forcefully and effectively and even to diminish its sphere of control but which, at the same time, anticipated reducing defense expenditures and taxes and disengaging America's military strength from Asia. The appealing feature of a strategy that relied primarily upon retaliatory air power—aside from the fact that any plausible alternative to containment was welcome—was that it promised to reconcile these seemingly contradictory aims. Above all, it promised to prevent a repetition of the galling sacrifices of limited war.

Liberation, Disengagement, Massive Retaliation

After the new administration assumed the responsibilities of office, events soon proved that it could no more escape the problems of containment and limited war than the old administration. When it applied its formulas to the hard facts of the cold war, it found that the positive and negative aims were more difficult to reconcile in practice than in rhetoric. Yet the Republicans were even more reluctant than their predecessors to acknowledge the actual strategy which, in fact, they were forced to pursue. So, in effect, the negative aim—economic and military retrenchment—was put into action, and the positive aim—forthright, vigorous opposition to international communism—was put into words. As a result the American government, contrary to a previous Republican President's admonition, frequently found itself speaking loudly and carrying a small stick.

"Liberation" was the first casualty. Actually, neither Secretary

Dulles nor President Eisenhower had regarded liberation as the military "rollback" of Communist power. They had specifically counseled against stimulating insurrections. Neither had envisioned liberation as anything but an ultimate goal. Like their Democratic predecessors, they were never prepared to translate this aspiration into concrete policies and actions; and in publicly announcing the aspiration they did no more than the Democratic administration had done less conspicuously on a number of occasions.[15] Nevertheless, since Dulles had enthusiastically represented liberation as a dynamic alternative to containment, it is not surprising that even those familiar with the hyperbole of American political campaigns should have anticipated a fundamental departure in American strategy; and such a departure could only have meant a military rollback or the stimulation of insurrections. The resulting alarm was especially acute among America's European allies, who could well imagine their own countries becoming candidates for liberation as the result of a war precipitated by American recklessness. Democrats did not discourage these apprehensions in their eagerness to strike back at an effective campaign weapon.

The upshot of the matter was that the Eisenhower administration, after gauging the European and the American reaction, publicly swallowed the implications of its words. After earnestly disavowing any intention of inciting rebellion or of employing anything but peaceful means, it soon stopped talking about liberation altogether. When the anti-Communist riots in Berlin during June, 1953, presented to the American government its best opportunity since World War II to put liberation into practice, the Eisenhower administration confined itself to sending food packages to the beleaguered inhabitants.

However, the administration was more successful in its program of economic and military retrenchment. During his early months in office President Eisenhower stressed the view that one of the most important problems facing his administration was how to maintain indefinitely a strong military force without bankrupting the country. Anticipating the end of the Korean War and recognizing the economic inability of the NATO countries to sustain the emergency military expansion agreed upon at Lisbon in February, 1952, he gave his solution to the latter part of this problem when he announced at the end of April, 1953, that defense planning would henceforth be based on the "long pull" instead of the "year-of-crisis" plan in order to bring economic and military necessities "into some kind of realistic focus."[16] On the basis of this "long-pull" plan, Secretary of Defense Wilson directed the new Joint Chiefs of Staff to examine the Democratic defense budget and come up with a "new look." At first they did not succeed. President Truman's defense budget for the fiscal year 1953/54 already represented a substantial retrenchment from the previous post-Korea budgets; and the new Joint Chiefs of Staff were unable to cut it much further, since they recommended substantially the same force levels that the Truman administration had set. However, when the 1955 budget came up for consideration, the National Security Council, reflecting the views of Secretary of the Treasury Humphrey and Budget Director Dodge, considered this budget too high. Thus it imposed a considerably lower ceiling of about $31 billion on new appropriations. On the basis of this ceiling the Joint Chiefs of Staff revised their force levels and recommended military policies that the administration advertised as providing more defense for less money, or, as the phrase-makers would have it, "more bang for a buck."

This program of economic retrenchment had its logical concomitant in the administration's promise of disengagement; for, clearly, the maintenance of a large ground army to fight local contests was incompatible with the reduction of defense expenditures. Republican planners regarded the "crash program" occasioned by the Korean War as a special danger to the economic health of the country. In his first news conference after becoming Secretary of State, Dulles disclosed the administration's intention of achieving a more favorable balance of power with the Soviet Union in the Far East by disengaging American troops and stepping up military aid to indigenous forces, in line with the policy of relying on Asians to fight Asians.[17] After the tortuous negotiations with the Communists in Korea finally eventuated in an armistice on July 26, 1953, the administration was in a position to initiate such military withdrawal.

Economic and military retrenchment bore a logical connection with the other major element of the administration's purported alternative to containment: the so-called strategy of massive retaliation. The connection was roughly this: the lower defense ceiling, set by the National Security Council, necessitated a cut in manpower; the cut in manpower required new force levels; the new force levels, coupled with the policy of disengagement, required a revision of military strategy. For if a nation tries to maintain optimum military security while spending less money on defense, it must, inevitably, concentrate a greater proportion of its expenditures upon defending itself against the most serious threat to its security; and this meant placing more reliance on the means of deterring a major Russian attack and less reliance upon the means of fighting lesser engagements. This rule was as applicable to Republican military policies after the Korean War as to Democratic policies before the war.

Charged with devising force levels within the reduced budget, the Joint Chiefs of Staff planned a long-range program, which by June 30, 1957, would reduce the nation's total manpower by about 635,000 and increase the proportion of air to ground forces. The brunt of the man-power cuts (about 400,000 men) would be borne by the Army, necessitat-ing a reduction from 20 divisions to 17 or 18, while the Air Force would be built up to 137 groups. This increased emphasis upon air power, coupled with the policy of disengagement, logically implied a military strategy that placed less emphasis upon local ground defense and more emphasis upon retaliating by air against the center of aggression.

Secretary Dulles made the logic of this situation quite explicit when he delivered his famous massive-retaliation address before the Council on Foreign Relations on January 12, 1954.[18] In this address Dulles officially announced the strategy he had long advocated as a private citizen and as a special adviser to the State Department. President Eisenhower, in con-sultation with Dulles and Admiral Radford, had approved this strategy aboard the cruiser "Helena" and at Honolulu on the way back from his promised inspection of Korea in December, 1952. Because it became the foundation of the administration's effort to reconcile a strong military posture with defense economy, Dulles' formulation deserves a careful examination.

It is significant that, although this was a short address, it contained more than a half-dozen references to the objective of economy, which was so clearly uppermost in the minds of civilian planners. Dulles charged that the policies of the previous administration would saddle the country with military expenditures so vast as to lead to "practical bankruptcy," and he claimed that the new administration's policies would make it pos-sible "to get, and share, more basic security at less cost." However, it would be misleading to attribute to purely economic considerations a strategy which had grown out of a broader opposition to containment, of which a fear of high defense expenditures was only one aspect, though, admittedly, a compelling one in an election year.

The central point of Dulles' address was that the United States could get "a maximum deterrent at a bearable cost" by placing "more reliance on deterrent power, and less dependence on local defensive power." He acknowledged that local defense would always be important, but, he asserted, "There is no local defense which alone will contain the mighty landpower of the Communist world. Local defenses must be reinforced by the further deterrent of massive retaliatory power." The attempt to meet aggression "by being ready to fight everywhere . . . could not be continued for long without grave budgetary, economic, and social consequences." But before military planning could be changed, the government had to take "some basic policy decision." "The basic decision was to depend primarily upon a great capacity to retaliate, instantly, by means and at places of our choosing."

At face value, these words did not reveal just how, if at all, the new administration's strategy differed from the strategy of its predecessor, for the Truman administration had also placed primary reliance upon retaliatory air power to deter aggression in Europe. But since Dulles represented his policy as a new and cheaper one, it was reasonable to infer that he anticipated relying upon massive retaliation to deter aggression in the gray areas of Asia, whereas the Truman administration had been forced to abandon this approach, temporarily, by the Korean War. Yet other parts of his speech left even this inference ambiguous.

Dulles did not say, in so many words, that the United States should employ its massive retaliatory power against local aggression in Asia. In fact, at one point he implied that it might be wiser, in some circumstances, to forego resistance altogether. Disclaiming any "magic formula that insures against all forms of Communist successes," he stated:

It is normal that at some times and at some places there may be setbacks to the cause of freedom. What we do expect to insure is that any setbacks will have only temporary and local significance, because they will leave unimpaired those free world assets which in the long run will prevail. If we can deter such aggression as would mean general war, and that is our confident resolve, then we can let time and fundamentals work for us.

On the other hand, in a passage before this one, Dulles illustrated the application of his strategy by citing positions the Eisenhower administration had taken with respect to Korea and Indochina, which implied that the United States would retaliate upon Communist China in the event of direct Chinese intervention in local aggressions. In order to discern the full meaning of Dulles' words, we must examine them in the light of these positions.

His citation of the administration's position with respect to Korea referred to the following events: On July 27, 1953, within hours after the conclusion of the armistice in Korea, the United States and the other fifteen members who had sent troops to Korea signed a declaration warning that if there were a renewal of the armed attack on Korea, "we should again be united and prompt to resist," and adding, "The consequences of such a breach of the armistice would be so grave that, in all probability, it would not be possible to confine hostilities within the frontiers of Korea."[19] To this joint declaration Dulles had added a special American warning in an address to the American Legion Convention in St. Louis on September 2, 1953. Stressing the lesson that wars come about from miscalculation, he had termed the security treaty with the Republic of Korea a "clear warning" that would "prevent any recurrence of the enemy miscalculation of 1950." Then, citing the sixteen-nation joint declaration as an additional deterrent, he had warned that in a renewal of the war in Korea the Communists could no longer count on their "privileged sanctuary" north of the Yalu.[20]

The growing crisis in Indochina had led the administration to take a similar position in an effort to deter Chinese intervention in that quarter. These were the circumstances surrounding that position: As the mounting success of the Vietminh Communists in the summer of 1953 refuted the United States original optimistic appraisal of France's Navarre plan, the new administration was confronted with a dilemma. On the one hand, as it had stated with increasing urgency, it regarded Indochina as vital to the security of Southeast Asia, and Southeast Asia as vital to America's position in the Pacific and, in fact, to the whole balance of power throughout the world. But, on the other hand, like previous administrations, it was unalterably opposed to committing American troops to the Asian mainland. President Eisenhower declared that the Communist occupation of Indochina "would be of a most terrible significance to the United States of America";[21] but, having just fulfilled his campaign pledge to end the war in Korea, he was obviously not disposed to involve American forces in another war in Indochina. In the end, the administration reconciled its desire to contain communism with its unwillingness to resist local aggression locally by delivering the same kind of direct warning to the Chinese it had delivered with respect to Korea. In his address to the American Legion Secretary Dulles stated:

> Communist China has been and now is training, equipping and supplying the Communist forces in Indochina. There is the risk that, as in Korea, Red China might send its own army into Indochina. The Chinese Communist regime should realize that such a second aggression could not occur without grave consequences which might not be confined to Indochina. I say this soberly in the interest of peace and in the hope of preventing another aggressor miscalculation.

When one views Dulles' enunciation of the doctrine of massive retaliation in his address of January 12, 1954, in the light of the positions he cited with respect to Korea and Indochina, the doctrine emerges more clearly as an attempt to deter local aggression in the gray areas by threatening the Chinese Communists with exactly the kind of air retaliation which he had suggested in his speech in Paris on May 5, 1952. By citing the warnings contained in his American Legion speech as examples of the application of the administration's new strategy, Dulles merely affirmed an assumption he had stressed in his original exposition of strategy in the course of the presidential campaign. This assumption was, as he had stated on May 16, 1952, that "the only way to stop prospective aggressors is to convince them in advance that if they commit aggression, they will be subjected to retaliatory blows so costly that their aggression will not be a profitable operation."[22]

This assumption reflected Dulles' belief that the original invasion of South Korea had occurred because of miscalculation; but it was reinforced by what he regarded as additional evidence of the efficacy of an advance warning of retaliatory air action in the Communists' final agreement to an armistice in Korea. For he attributed the Communists' agreement to his oblique warning—which he said he had delivered to Peiping through Prime Minister Nehru in the third week of May, 1953, two months before the armistice—that, if the war continued, the United States would lift the self-imposed restrictions on its actions. James Shepley's account of this incident, which appeared in the January 16, 1956, issue of *Life* magazine and was based upon tape-recorded interviews with Dulles, stated that the Secretary's warning through Nehru reflected a decision, indorsed by President Eisenhower (an assertion which is in doubt), to carry the air attack to Manchuria if the Communists continued the stalemate and to use tactical atomic weapons if the hostilities should be renewed.[23] Explaining just what targets in Korea and Indochina the administration had planned to strike in retaliation, the article quoted Dulles as saying, "They were specific targets reasonably related to the area. They did not involve massive destruction of great population centers like Shanghai, Peking, or Canton. Retaliation must be on a selective basis."[24] There is no evidence that Dulles' warning had any effect upon the Chinese, but we may accept his word that the government was at least actively considering a decision similar to the one upon which he has said his warning was based.[25]

Summing up the import of Dulles' address of January 12, 1954, we may reasonably conclude that the administration intended to rely primarily upon the implicit threat of massive nuclear retaliation against strategic targets in the Soviet Union in order to deter aggression in Europe but that it would rely upon clear advance warnings of conventional or nuclear air retaliation against selected military targets not necessarily within the area of attack in order to deter direct Chinese Communist aggression in Asia. If the Chinese did not support aggression with their troops, the United States would apparently be content to support local resistance of indigenous forces with economic aid and military equipment. But if resistance were unfeasible and aggression would have only "temporary and local significance," the government was prepared to accept occasional "setbacks to the cause of freedom."

Clearly, the strategy that Dulles announced was not an alternative to containment. It differed from the previous administration's strategy only as a method of supporting containment in the gray areas. Whereas the Truman administration, despite its lopsided reliance upon retaliatory air power before the Korean War, had been forced to rely upon local ground resistance during that war, the Eisenhower administration now proposed to prevent another Korean-type war by threatening to remove the restraints against selective retaliation which the United States had imposed upon resistance to direct Chinese intervention in that instance. The qualified nature of the Eisenhower administration's revision of containment soon became apparent when Secretary Dulles explained and elaborated the doctrine of massive retaliation in response to the storm of controversy that followed its original announcement.

The first fruit of Dulles' address of January 12 was widespread alarm and protest. American critics—not entirely Democratic spokesmen— charged that the strategy would turn every local war into a big war, that it was an empty bluff, that it left us no choice except non-resistance or all-out atomic warfare, that it would undermine a coalition policy and violate the constitutional right of Congress to declare war. Foreign spokesmen, more politely apprehensive, expressed concern lest they become involved in an atomic holocaust without their consultation. In order to quiet the storm Dulles issued a series of restatements. These restatements did not alter the conclusion that a careful reading of the January 12 speech might have conveyed, but they did refute the more extreme inferences that the ambiguities of the speech had encouraged. Their net effect was to place more emphasis upon selective air retaliation.

Dulles explained that in some areas and circumstances, when an open Communist assault could only result in starting a general war, the United States, in consultation with its allies, would have to be prepared to reply with massive atomic and thermonuclear retaliation. However, this was by no means true of all circumstances. He emphasized the word "capacity" for massive retaliation, in his original phrase, and pointed out that "the possession of that capacity does not impose the necessity of using it in every instance of attack."[26] In other areas and circumstances, he said that the free world should retaliate with its "mobile deterrent power" on a selective basis and that in these areas indigenous local defense would be important.

Dulles reasserted the view that it was essential to give potential aggressors advance warning of the free world's intention to retaliate in the event of overt aggression; but he added the large qualification that the question of where, when, and how the free world retaliated was a matter to be dealt with in accordance with the facts of each situation, and the aggressor had best remain ignorant of these details.[27] Nevertheless, if the aggressor took Dulles' words at face value, he could be in no doubt that overt aggression, if it were answered at all, would be answered by American air strikes on targets within the aggressor's country. For Dulles reiterated his view that the important thing was to confront the aggressor with the certainty that he would suffer damage outweighing any possible gains from aggression, and he made it quite clear that in all areas "the main reliance must be on the power of the free community to retaliate with great force by mobile means at places of its own choice." Otherwise, the enemy "would be tempted to attack in places and by means where his manpower superiority was decisive and where at little cost he could impose upon us great burdens."[28] But even if Dulles had not re-emphasized America's primary reliance upon mobile striking power, the Communists could have readily deduced the point from the reduction of America's ground forces, from the policy of disengagement, and from statements counseling against the involvement of American troops on the mainland of Asia.

Since Dulles' elaborations and qualifications added little substantively to his original pronouncement, the real implications of the Republican administration's strategy could only emerge from the test of events, not from further exercises in formulation. The continuing success of the Chinese-supported Vietminh in Indochina provided that test. The Communist triumph in Indochina raised grave doubts as to whether retaliatory air power would be any more effective in containing communism in the gray areas after the Korean War than before. These doubts were given added point by the growing counter-retaliatory capacity of Communist forces.

The War in Indochina

In the spring of 1954 the Communist forces in Indochina mounted a crushing offensive that overwhelmed the desperate French resistance. This military humiliation was followed by armistice agreements, signed at Geneva in July, which gave the Communists possession of Indochina north of the seventeenth parallel and provided for general elections in 1956 to determine the fate of the remaining segment of the country, Vietnam. The reverse in Indochina demonstrated that successful containment in the gray areas depended upon a capacity for local ground defense that the United States could not provide. It also demonstrated the disastrous effect upon American prestige, diplomacy, and the credibility of her deterrent of trying to contain Communist aggression by military policies that purported to escape the necessity of local ground defense but that actually put the United States in the position of having its bluff called. Finally, it exposed the fatal ambivalence of American strategy—the practical impossibility of reconciling a more vigorous opposition to communism with economic and military retrenchment.

The American government disclaimed responsibility for the negotiations and eventual armistice that took place at Geneva. Nevertheless, it was unmistakably and inseparably linked with these unfortunate developments by having assumed a primary role in the war, virtually co-equal with the role of France itself. In assuming this role the government had asserted the vital importance of Indochina to American security; it had given the French the military equipment and economic assistance they needed to sustain the war; it had pressed them to continue the fight; it had tried to halt Chinese intervention through warnings of retaliation; and, finally, it had permitted the Chinese to ignore the warnings with impunity. There is no escaping the fact that American strategy and American power were pitted against Chinese strategy and Chinese power just as surely, if not as directly, as in Korea. The results of the struggle were a resounding defeat for the United States.

For years the United States had poured increasing quantities of money and material into the French-Vietnamese effort. In the fiscal year 1953/54 the American government added $385 million to the $400 million already earmarked for this purpose, so that it bore over a third of the cost of French operations, exclusive of Marshall Plan aid. Early in 1954 the American government responded to urgent French requests by sending twenty-five B-26 bombers and two hundred air technicians. Yet despite the optimistic statements about eventual victory Washington issued up to the eve of final defeat, the Vietminh insurgents continued to advance into the Red River Delta during the spring of 1954. At the same time, Communist China, free of the Korean entanglement, did exactly what the American government had warned her not to do: she shifted her efforts to Indochina by providing more aid to the Vietminh, more openly, than ever before.[29] Even while the Big Four, Communist China, and the other powers involved in the Korean and Indochinese wars attended the Geneva Conference in order to discuss the peaceful settlement of these conflicts, China boldly supplied the equipment and trained personnel that permitted the insurgents to transform their military effort into a massed assault. We have the word of Premier Laniel of France and of Secretary Dulles himself that the troops fighting under Ho Chi Minh were largely trained and equipped in Communist China, that China supplied them with artillery and ammunition and gave them military and technical guidance, and that Chinese advisers occupied key positions in the staff sections of the Vietminh high command, at the division level, and in the specialized units, such as signal, engineering, artillery, and transportation.[30]

Furthermore, China's mounting scale of intervention was in conspicuous defiance of repeated American threats of retaliation, both implicit and explicit. We have seen that Secretary Dulles in his American Legion address of September 2, 1953, warned the Chinese Communist regime that a repetition in Indochina of the aggression in Korea "could not occur without grave consequences which might not be confined to Indochina," and that President Eisenhower had declared that the loss of Indochina "would be of a most terrible significance to the United States of America." We have seen that Dulles referred to his previous warning and placed it in the context of the strategy of massive retaliation in his address to the Council on Foreign Relations on January 12, 1954. As the crisis deepened, the American government asserted its role as the chief protagonist of anti-Communist resistance still more forcefully. Although at the Berlin Conference in February, 1954, Dulles reluctantly agreed to include Red China among the other powers who were to gather at Geneva on April 26 in order to discuss the settlement of the Korean and Indochinese conflicts, he assured the American people that "the Communist regime will not come to Geneva to be honored by us, but rather to account before the bar of world opinion."[31] On March 13 the Communists launched an attack upon the French fortress of Dienbienphu, which in less than two months brought a virtual end to all French resistance in Indochina. In his news conference on March 24 President Eisenhower declared that the region of Southeast Asia was "of the most transcendent importance." That same week Admiral Radford and Secretary Dulles insisted once more that the French were going to win. Then on March 29 Dulles, taking note of the extent of Chinese intervention, issued another warning and called for "united action":

Under the conditions of today, the imposition on Southeast Asia of the political system of Communist Russia and its Chinese ally, by whatever means, would be a grave threat to the whole free community. The United States feels that that possibility should not be passively accepted, but should be met by united action. This might have serious risks, but these risks are far less than would face us a few years from now if we dare not be resolute today.[32]

In his press conference on April 7 President Eisenhower reiterated the vital importance of the war in Indochina to American security by comparing the effect of the loss of Indochina upon the rest of Southeast Asia to a row of falling dominoes.[33] On April 16 Vice-President Nixon, in an "off-the-record" talk before the American Society of Newspaper Editors, warned that if the French withdrew from Indochina, the United States might have to send its own troops there.[34]

The British, anxiously surveying the approaching disaster at Dienbienphu, were inclined to negotiate a settlement before the French resistance collapsed altogether. The French government was under great pressure to do the same. But the United States continued to exert all its influence to prevent any negotiations with the Chinese, while still maintaining that the French would win. Therefore, since the French were obviously incapable of defending Dienbienphu by themselves, and since outside aid could come only from the United States, the whole military and diplomatic position of the West depended upon the power which the United States could bring to bear upon the struggle. But what power could the United States dispose? Apparently, not the power of local ground resistance, as in Korea. For, in contrast to the forceful assertions of American opposition to Chinese intervention, the American government had also clearly expressed its unwillingness to turn Indochina into another Korea. Conscious of its role in terminating that most unpopular of all American wars, the Eisenhower administration was determined to avoid the galling sacrifices the Truman administration had incurred. Only a month before the attack on Dienbienphu President Eisenhower had said that no one could be more bitterly opposed to ever getting the United States involved in a hot war in Indochina than he was and that he could not conceive of a greater tragedy for America than to get heavily involved, especially with large units, in an all-out war in those regions.[35] Three days before the Communist assault on Dienbienphu, he had seemed to emphasize his opposition to intervention of any kind by asserting that America was not going to become involved in the war unless Congress exercised its constitutional right to declare war.[36] And even Republican majority leader Senator Knowland, the most ardent advocate of a "tough" Asian policy, had given "categorical assurances" that the United States would send no ground troops to fight in Indochina.[37] Furthermore, the United States was less able to rush adequate numbers of trained troops to Indochina in 1954 than it had been to rush them to Korea in 1950. Therefore, if the administration intended to support its objective of containment in Indochina by military means, it would, evidently, have to rely upon the "mobile striking power" which Dulles had described as the principal instrument of selective retaliation.[38]

Three times that spring—in the third week of March and in the first and last weeks of April—the French made desperate appeals to the United States for air strikes to save Dienbienphu. The American aircraft carriers "Boxer" and "Philippine Sea" stood by in the South China Sea.

Aboard were tactical air groups, armed with atomic weapons. Dulles was actively seeking political arrangements that would enable the United States to meet the French request. And yet the United States did not intervene—massively, selectively, or otherwise. On May 7 the Vietminh troops stormed the last outposts of Dienbienphu and extinguished the last sparks of resistance among its defenders. That same day the problem of Indochina came up for formal discussion at Geneva. The opportunity for effective American intervention, if there had ever been any, had passed. On June 11, the day before the French government fell, Dulles announced that the United States would consider intervention only as part of a collective effort of some of the other nations of the area and contingent on four other conditions, which he listed as an invitation from the French government; clear assurance of the complete independence of Laos, Cambodia, and Vietnam; evidence of concern by the United Nations; and assurance that France would not withdraw from the battle until victory were achieved.[39] Dulles added that if the Chinese regime "were to show in Indochina or elsewhere that it is determined to pursue the path of overt military aggression," that would constitute a threat to the United States itself, and the United States would then seek UN help and might even have to intervene unilaterally. But this faint echo of the Secretary's original warnings of immediate retaliation, coming after what was, in effect, a renunciation of American intervention in the existing contest, did nothing to conceal the fact from all the other nations at Geneva that the one nation who had the power to support France's bargaining position had decided to withhold it. In July the new French government of Mendès-France made the best of a hopeless situation and signed the armistice agreements that finally brought an uneasy peace to a divided Indochina.

What lessons of limited war can we draw from the conflict in Indochina? We must begin that inquiry by asking why the American government failed to back up its bold resolutions and firm warnings with action. For the major weakness of American policy toward the Indochinese crisis was the discrepancy between American words and actions. The full story of the factors determining the government's course in the critical weeks preceding the collapse of French resistance has not been published, but from the accounts that have been published we can at least reconstruct some of the principal elements in the administration's decision not to intervene.[40]

a) Superficially, the most obvious explanation of America's failure to intervene is that the primary stated condition of American intervention never existed. Dulles threatened retaliation against the direct employment of Chinese troops, as in the Korean War; but China did not find it necessary to resort to this kind of intervention. Undoubtedly, China's indirect support of an indigenous revolution made it embarrassing for the United States to undertake overt military intervention. Nevertheless, by the testimony of Dulles himself, the Chinese Communists provided the United States with about the clearest, most arrogant provocation for retaliation they could have devised short of direct, large-scale intervention of Chinese troops. If the fate of Indochina was as important as the administration said it was, it is difficult to imagine the government basing its decision to intervene or not to intervene primarily on the distinction between direct and indirect Chinese intervention. Moreover, Dulles' attempt to organize a basis for united action with the British and French in spite of the fact that China had not used its troops indicates that, in his mind at least, it was not for lack of provocation that the United States withheld intervention. Nor has he made any such claim. Rather, he has stressed his inability to secure the united action that he says was necessary to enable the United States to reply to China's provocation effectively.

b) After the Communist victory in Indochina, with his confidence in the efficacy of clear advance warnings of retaliation still apparently unshaken, Dulles complained that the British, by rejecting his scheme for united action, deprived the United States of the leverage that would probably have checked the Communists without resorting to actual military intervention. It is true that the British flatly refused to consider any plan for united action, at least not until the negotiation of a peaceful settlement had been given a fair trial at Geneva. And according to Robert J. Donovan's "inside story," Eisenhower made British approval, as well as several other unlikely conditions, a prerequisite for American intervention.[41] Thus one must agree with Dulles that the absence of British approval was an important factor in ruling out American intervention. However, it does not seem plausible that British approval or disapproval should have been an indispensable prerequisite for American action in a situation that the government considered of such transcendent importance from America's own standpoint. Would British support have made American intervention any more effective militarily or any more acceptable politically? There is some doubt as to exactly what sort of united action Dulles intended; [42] but, whatever he intended, it is extremely unlikely that an ultimatum, backed by British and French support, would have had any more effect upon the course of events than the series of unilateral warnings already issued by the American government. So even if Dulles had succeeded in securing British support of his scheme, the administration would still have been faced with some very hard practical considerations bearing upon the feasibility of military intervention. There is reason to think that these were the decisive considerations that determined the American decision to forego intervention.

c) Common sense and the existing evidence suggest that the most important considerations governing the Eisenhower administration's decision to forego intervention were the likelihood that effective intervention would require American troops, coupled with the unwillingness of the government to use American troops. As Chalmers Roberts has reconstructed the decisive events of the first week in April—obviously, on the basis of conversations with some of the participants—on April 3, the day after France's urgent request for American air strikes, Secretary Dulles and Admiral Radford, on the authority of President Eisenhower, called a secret emergency conference with members of the National Security Council and eight leaders of Congress in order to secure approval of a joint resolution by Congress authorizing the President to use air and naval power in Indochina. However, the congressional representatives were not persuaded. Three considerations are said to have weighed most heavily in their opposition to Dulles' and Radford's plan of intervention: (*a*) none of the other Joint Chiefs of Staff supported Radford's plan; (*b*) Dulles had not consulted America's allies; (*c*) Radford could give no assurances that air strikes would be successful without the use of American ground troops.

Considering the long-standing American opposition to the involvement of American troops on the mainland of Asia and the recent traumatic experience of the Korean War, we may reasonably speculate that the third consideration was sufficient in itself to have blocked Dulles' scheme of selective retaliation, insofar as American intervention depended upon congressional approval. But, even more important, that same consideration must have weighed heavily upon the President, considering his previous strong statement of opposition to the involvement of American troops in Indochina and his personal responsibility for ending the

Korean War. General Ridgway's account of his own part, as Army Chief of Staff, in opposing American intervention tends to confirm this supposition.[43]

According to Ridgway's account, as it became clear that the French garrison at Dienbienphu was doomed, he was deeply disturbed by the growing sentiment for American intervention, both inside the government and outside, because he believed it reflected the same dangerous delusion that marked the outset of the Korean War—"that we could do things the cheap and easy way, by going into Indochina with air and naval forces alone." In order to establish the real cost of intervention he sent a large team of Army experts to Indochina to study the military factors bearing upon the feasibility of American ground action. He found that effective military operations in Indochina would be every bit as costly and considerably more difficult than the campaign in Korea had been, and he lost no time communicating his conclusions to President Eisenhower. "The idea of intervening was abandoned," Ridgway writes, "and it is my belief that the analysis which the Army made and presented to higher authority played a considerable, perhaps a decisive, part in persuading our government not to embark on that tragic adventure."[44]

Clearly, the final decision on American intervention or non-intervention was President Eisenhower's. It seems equally clear that Eisenhower was very strongly opposed to involving American troops in Indochina and that, furthermore, he believed this "tragedy" might result from American intervention by air and sea power, as Ridgway predicted. It is true that the President nevertheless gave his conditional approval to a plan for united action that envisioned air strikes against China. If his unlikely conditions had been met, Indochina might have become the scene of a war more deadly than the Korean War. On the other hand, it is hard to believe that he would have insisted upon his conditions in the first place if he had thought that the United States could contain the Communists simply by air and sea action, without involving American troops in a war of intolerable cost in men and money.

In spite of circumstantial evidence, we do not know exactly what combination of motives and thoughts in the minds of various men governed the course of American policy toward Indochina in the spring of 1954. Yet, whatever the truth of that matter may be, it is unlikely that the revelation of further details will do anything but corroborate one significant lesson of American strategy, which is already patent: that containment requires a diversified and flexible military capacity capable of resisting Communist aggression locally, under a variety of circumstances, by means proportionate to limited political objectives. The United States lacked this capacity in Indochina, because it was almost wholly dependent upon air and naval power, which carried a risk of expanding the war that was out of proportion to its military effectiveness and which was incapable of attaining America's limited political objectives in the struggle, either militarily or diplomatically.

In the absence of a capacity for effective local ground resistance, an American decision to intervene would almost certainly have been more disastrous than the actual decision not to intervene. Even if the President, backed by a joint congressional resolution and a three-power military agreement, had authorized air strikes, would that have frightened the Communists into halting their advance? We have no way of knowing, but it seems quite implausible. Let us imagine, on the other hand, that we had actually delivered the air strikes the French called for; would we have come any closer to containing the Communists? Perhaps air strikes with tactical atomic weapons would have saved Dienbienphu, temporarily; but it is quite improbable that they could have halted the Vietminh advance without the support of American ground forces on a scale surpassing that of the Korean War. Air strikes alone were ineffective in stopping the Communist advance in Korea. They would have been even less effective in Indochina, considering the nature of the terrain, the collapse of indigenous resistance, and the ability of the Communists to advance by revolutionary means. And even if we assume that American air strikes would have been far more effective than we have reason to assume, would the Chinese and the Russians have withheld equally effective means of counter-retaliation? If the Chinese, for example, had sent large numbers of their troops into the battle, could we have hoped to repeat in the jungles and bogs of Indochina, a thousand miles from the nearest American base, the feat of the Eighth Army in checking the Chinese tide in Korea? It seems more likely that we would have been faced with the alternative of losing all of Indochina or precipitating a general war. Even without full-scale Chinese intervention it is doubtful that the United States, given the low state of its ground forces, could have successfully undertaken a ground war in Indochina at a cost commensurate with the political stakes and not incompatible with American security in other areas. American military leaders were reported to believe that such a war would have required from eight to ten divisions of American troops. Whether or not even these troops would have been sufficient to contain the Communist advance under the difficult conditions of combat and supply in Indochina, it is clear that the United States was not remotely prepared, militarily or psychologically, to undertake another Korean War under the much less advantageous circumstances of the struggle in Indochina.

However, to consider the lessons of the war in Indochina in these purely quantitative military terms is to conceal its full significance. After all, the French and Vietnamese armies did not fail for lack of manpower and equipment. In both respects they were actually superior to the enemy. They failed, partly, because of faulty military tactics—because of their dependence upon a static blockhouse defense system and upon mechanized equipment not suited to the primitive terrain. But, more fundamentally, they failed for lack of the proper political and psychological foundation for effective military action. The French-led armies fought under the prohibitive handicap of trying to defend a people who identified the Vietminh with national independence and progress and the French with colonialism and backwardness. This fact, combined with economic unrest and political anarchy, enabled Communist guerillas to melt into the villages during the day and raid the French positions at night. It sapped the will of indigenous resistance and led great numbers of Vietnamese soldiers to desert to the Communists.

Whatever effect clear advance warnings of American retaliation may have had in deterring overt Communist aggression, the significant feature of the Communist advance in Indochina was that the Chinese did not need to resort to direct intervention in order to attain their objective. Their capacity to support a successful insurrection indicates the crucial difference between the problem of containment in Asia and in Europe. In Europe, where the inhabitants have the will to defend themselves against insurrection and subversion, the Communists can expand only by direct military action; but in Asia, where the issue of Communist rule seems largely irrelevant to the prevailing ambitions and hatreds, the Communists can expand by indirect methods and by irregular warfare with the help of an indigenous revolution. One major lesson of Indochina, like the lesson of Korea, is that, unless we have the will and capacity to support local defense by limited war, our ability to drop bombs on China and the Soviet Union will not be sufficient to contain communism in areas which we are unwilling to defend at the cost of total war. But, equally important, the war in Indochina indicated that local military defense cannot succeed unless the inhabitants have a certain minimum will and ability to defend themselves.

Considering the unfavorable internal political and psychological conditions, as well as the disadvantageous physical conditions of combat, one must doubt whether the United States could have saved northern Indochina by an effort that was not disproportionate to the political stakes, even if American ground troops had been available on a scale far surpassing their actual availability. Under the existing military and political circumstances the United States probably lost far less by not intervening than it would have lost by intervening ineffectively. One can argue that, under the circumstances, the wisest course for the American government would have been actively to support the negotiations at Geneva with a show of Western unity in order to obtain the best bargain possible, instead of sullenly trying to dissociate itself from the bargaining and exposing Western disunity by dramatizing a scheme of united action that its allies would not support. There is something to be said for this argument, but there is no evidence that a course different from the one the government followed would have secured any more favorable terms of settlement; and there were disadvantages to any course that would have committed the United States to uphold a precarious settlement, which the Vietnamese would probably feel compelled not to observe. But however one may view this particular issue of diplomatic tactics, the most valid criticism of the Eisenhower administration's policy toward the war in Indochina is not that it failed to undertake military intervention but, rather, that it created the opposite expectation by relying upon the bold words of a strategy of retaliation which it was not willing to support with action. The net effect was not far from the acid appraisal of the Swiss analyst Herbert Luethy, who observed of the weeks before the Geneva conference:

Never was the difference between the verbal intransigence and the practical prudence of the new Republican team in Washington more disastrously demonstrated than during these feverish weeks, when threats in Washington of a preventive war against China alternated with assurances to the electorate that the United States would in no circumstances engage in "another Korean war." Never did the so-called strategy of "massive reprisals," that lame compromise between the crusading spirit and the spirit of budgetary economy, more strikingly demonstrate its incapacity to respond to the limited reversals, the local conflicts and the pin-pricks which constitute the daily fare of international politics. Reduced to the sole device of threatening apocalyptic war on every occasion, it sowed terror among America's allies and proteges without making much impression on her enemies, and finally ended in resounding inaction.[45]

In the light of the frustrations of the Korean War it was frequently said that what the United States really needed was more a change in the spirit or mood of its policies than a change in the policies themselves.[46] But the chief trouble with American policy toward the war in Indochina was precisely the spirit and mood it conveyed rather than the policy itself or even the literal content of its enunciation. What stuck in the minds of neutrals, allies, and many Americans as well, was the administration's dramatic affirmations of its determination to check Communist aggression in Asia by forceful new methods that would avoid the trials of local ground defense. The world paid little attention to the qualifications that Dulles affixed to these affirmations. Therefore, when the United States failed to respond to the Communist offensive in the spring of 1954, the government's bluff appeared to have been called just as clearly as though the Communists had defied an ultimatum. This was, of course, a serious blow to American prestige; but more than prestige was at stake. By having seemed to rely upon a threat it was not prepared to carry out, the government not only exposed its inability to contain indirect aggression but greatly reduced the credibility of the deterrent upon which it relied to contain direct aggression. Thus the government cast grave doubts upon its determination to back up the clear advance warnings, which Secretary Dulles had repeatedly declared were so essential to prevent the Communists from miscalculating.

The net result of the first big test of the Republican administration's conception of containment was the impairment of the government's capacity to deter Communist aggression in the areas most vulnerable to Communist expansion. At the same time, by sharpening the apprehensions of other nations that the United States was recklessly pursuing an "atomic diplomacy" that threatened to turn any local war into a general nuclear war, the administration's stress upon retaliatory air power weakened the Western coalition it had so sedulously cultivated and stimulated the very trend toward "neutralism" and anti-Westernism throughout the gray areas which it had sought to counteract. For, increasingly, the uncommitted nations were viewing the United States as the major threat to peace, while America's allies were coming to regard their ties with the United States as an incitement to their destruction in a nuclear war rather than as a source of protection against Soviet aggression. In accelerating this trend, American pronouncements combined strangely with Russia's own "new look," adopted in the aftermath of the Korean War; that is, the deliberate relaxation of international tensions and the pursuit of the tactic of "peaceful coexistence" in a well-planned campaign to split the Western coalition and gain the allegiance of the uncommitted nations of Asia, the Middle East, and Africa. Thus America's "tough" posture, combined with its "soft" action, in the Indochinese war incurred all the liabilities of the Soviet, as well as the American, "new look." In this respect Indochina was truly the "payoff" on the ambivalence that had characterized American policy from the beginning of containment and, most markedly, since the Korean War.

Same Strategy—New Weapons

After the Geneva settlement of the war in Indochina, the "soft" or negative side of the Eisenhower administration's strategy became more prominent. While administration policies continued to stress economic retrenchment and military disengagement, administration spokesmen publicized American policy in more moderate tones. Although a literal construction of Dulles' words did not reveal any substantive change in American strategy, noticeably he spoke of America's retaliatory power less frequently and more prudently, while stressing its flexibility and selectivity.[47] However, it was primarily President Eisenhower who set the tone of official pronouncements. Where Dulles had once proclaimed the efficacy of America's retaliatory air power, President Eisenhower solemnly affirmed the horror and irrationality of nuclear war. Where Dulles had publicly anticipated the recession or disintegration of Communist power, Eisenhower spoke of the need for coexistence and a *modus vivendi*. In what seemed like a deliberate effort to allay foreign apprehensions, the President avowed America's dedication to the concept of the "good partner." He counseled against truculence. He took a restrained stand on incidents involving American planes and aviators. He entered into great-power negotiations as though they were something of an opportunity rather than a pitfall. With great persuasiveness he proclaimed the government's determination to find a way to a more secure peace, and he took the lead in promoting the international control and inspection of nuclear weapons and the peaceful use of atomic energy.

To what extent this changed tone in American diplomacy resulted from the lessons of Indochina, one can only speculate. Perhaps it was less a response to the military and political failure of selective retaliation in Indochina than to a heightened sensitivity to Russia's growing nuclear capacity, following her achievement of a thermonuclear explosion in August, 1953, and her tactics of "peaceful coexistence" following the death of Stalin in March, 1953. In any case, the new approach went far to restore foreign confidence in America's pacific intentions and, at the same time, to quiet the extremists within the President's own party.

However, the administration's basic strategy remained the same as before the Geneva settlement. Force levels and the allocation of defense expenditures continued to reflect a decreasing reliance on local ground defense and an increasing reliance on air-atomic striking power from land and sea bases. The Air Force continued to expand toward the 137-group level while the Army, already reduced to about a million men, faced further cuts. At the same time, consistent with these military policies, the government continued to disengage American forces from Asia. Although as late as January, 1955, President Eisenhower envisioned mobile American ground units in nearby areas rushing to the support of indigenous troops,[48] the actual trend was to withdraw the few ground units remaining in nearby areas to make them part of the central reserve in the United States. On July 15, 1955, Army Chief of Staff General Maxwell D. Taylor predicted still further reductions of American ground forces in the Far East as a result of the administration's manpower cuts.[49] By 1956 all but two American divisions had been withdrawn from Korea. Despite the impression the administration's pronouncements sometimes conveyed, its "releashing" of the Nationalist government on Formosa indicated that it was as anxious to disengage itself from Formosa as from Korea, even if its ambiguous commitment to the defense of the coastal islands of Quemoy and Matsu threatened to have just the opposite effect, should the Chinese Communists choose to press the issue.[50]

Politically, the administration's major response to the Communist threat in Asia after the war in Indochina was the formation of "collective security" agreements with any Asian nation that would join, of which there were only three initially. In Manila on September 8, 1954, the governments of the United States, Great Britain, France, Australia, New Zealand, the Philippines, Pakistan, and Thailand signed the Southeast Asia Collective Defense Treaty, known as SEATO, which pledged the signatories to consult on common action in the event of external aggression or internal subversion. This treaty, however, merely provided a legal basis for intervening with "mobile striking power" against the sources of aggression.[51] Because it included only two small nations on the Asian mainland, because it merely obligated the signatories to consult in case of aggression, and because it embodied no organization, SEATO resembled NATO chiefly in its initials. The only local ground defense that the United States envisioned in connection with SEATO was the self-defense of the Asian signatories against insurrection and lesser disturbances. The idea of building up locally powerful armies, which the government once envisioned, was definitely abandoned by the administration; and so was the idea of establishing American reserves in key areas. In view of the small and dwindling numbers of American ground troops located in the Far East, the administration resisted requests from Australia, New Zealand, and the Philippines to scatter these troops at key points along the Asian periphery as mobile forces ready to reinforce nuclei of indigenous resistance. Instead, it held to its policy of concentrating American forces in the United States. Thus while expanding its political commitments, the government continued to reduce its military capacity to support them.

Along with SEATO and the mutual security agreements with the South Korean and Formosan governments, Secretary Dulles outlined the supplementary strategy of the "three fronts," which he and Eisenhower had first hit upon while returning from Korea in December, 1952, as a device for inducing the Chinese Communists to agree to an armistice.[52] According to this idea, as Dulles presented it at the Bangkok Conference of the SEATO powers in February, 1955, the United States would regard Southeast Asia, Formosa, and Korea as interdependent fronts for the purpose of resisting Communist aggression. Dulles believed that the very prospect of a three-front war would deter the Chinese from engaging in open armed aggression, on the theory that they would have to contend with a situation which they would supposedly feel incapable of meeting; namely, local war on more than one front at a time in areas where American sea and air power would have a relative advantage.[53] However, if the United States was unwilling to intervene in Southeast Asia by limited air strikes in order to check a local aggression in Indochina, it was difficult to believe that it would be willing to launch a general war for the same purpose; and the Chinese would probably reach the same conclusion. Nor was it likely that, without much greater ground strength, American air and sea action on three fronts would succeed in checking the Communists on any front; it might only compound America's military problems. Moreover, the plan does not seem politically feasible anyway. Dulles has conceded that attacks on Formosa and Korea would not activate the Southeast Asia Collective Defense Treaty—a point that Eden was careful to establish at the Bangkok Conference.[54] And it is equally unlikely that the SEATO powers would approve the unleashing of Syngman Rhee and Chiang Kai-shek in retaliation for a Communist attack upon Southeast Asia. Therefore, the "three-fronts" strategy would seem to add nothing to our deterrent to direct Chinese aggression, whereas it is no more suited for countering indirect aggression than the strategy we announced but did not dare to put into effect in the spring of 1954.

Despite a more moderate tone of enunciation, the formation of Asian and Far Eastern collective defense treaties, and such elaborations as the "three-fronts" conception, the Eisenhower administration continued to follow essentially the same strategy that Dulles and Eisenhower had described from the beginning of their term of office and even before: containment through disengagement and selective retaliation. However, the weapons to put this strategy into effect changed tremendously in both type and number. In addition to the great expansion in its stock of strategic atomic and thermonuclear bombs, the United States also acquired a large and varied arsenal of smaller tactical atomic weapons (developed even before the Korean War but made available in great quantity and diversity as operational battlefield weapons only in 1954 and 1955). These weapons held both new hope and new danger for a nation whose security depended increasingly upon containing Communist power by means compatible with limited war.

The immediate military significance of tactical atomic weapons lay, principally, in the fact that the administration relied heavily upon their concentrated firepower to compensate for a lack of manpower in containing the Soviet Union and Communist China. This reliance was reflected in military plans of great political significance. In Europe the NATO Council decided in December, 1954, to plan Western military strategy around the use of tactical and strategic nuclear artillery, bombs, and missiles; and Field Marshal Montgomery announced that nuclear weapons would certainly be used if the West were attacked. In Asia official statements left no doubt that military planning depended heavily upon the use of airborne tactical atomic weapons against selected military targets.

The hopeful aspect of America's arsenal of tactical atomic weapons is evident; for with the Communist superiority in trained manpower, magnified by our own reduction of ground troops, these weapons may be virtually the only effective means the West possesses for checking local Communist advances, short of massive strategic retaliation. Moreover, as our military training, military organization, and war planning become increasingly dependent on tactical atomic weapons, we may have no choice but to use them, except for the smallest police actions. In the opinion of some strategists these weapons hold promise of making good the administration's original claim of providing more security for less cost. One must hope that they are the solution to the forbidding problem of containment posed in Kennan's prescription for "the adroit and vigilant application of counterforce at a series of constantly shifting geographical and political points, corresponding to the shifts and maneuvers of Soviet policy."

But can a war with tactical atomic weapons be limited? Can tactical targets be distinguished from strategic targets? What would be the political repercussions of initiating the use of these weapons in Asia? What are the political consequences of depending upon them for the defense of Europe? Will they meet the problem of indirect aggression? Will they necessarily give us a military advantage if the enemy employs them also? Will they even necessarily permit us to economize in numbers of ground troops or in total defense expenditures? These are some of the hard questions that political and military planners must answer if tactical atomic weapons are to contribute to a sound strategy of limited war. The very posing of these questions assumes that we shall plan the use of tactical atomic weapons as a means of deterring and fighting limited wars, not as a means of escaping the problem; but here we must pause to wonder whether the United States has yet confronted the problem of limited war with sufficient candor and clarity of purpose to give assurance that national strategy controls weapons rather than the other way around.

Unless the use of nuclear weapons is scrupulously planned and controlled within the context of a sound strategy of limited war, their great military potentiality, instead of being our salvation, could easily become the very thing that would defeat our political objectives and even lead to our utter devastation. The government has wholeheartedly adopted a large and diversified atomic arsenal as an integral part of American strategy, but can we be sure that it has thought through the problem of limited war with equal energy and resourcefulness? For the outsider the answer to this question must lie chiefly in inferences drawn from scattered public statements. If one considers as a whole all official statements on tactical atomic weapons since President Eisenhower first publicly broached the subject in his press conference on January 12, 1955, it appears that the government does not anticipate that these weapons will "normally" be used as "police weapons" against "lesser hostile actions not broadened by the intervention of a major aggressor force." But, in other cases, it plans to use them where they can be delivered against "strictly military targets" without "endangering unrelated civilian centers" and where they are appropriate to the scale of the Communist attack and the political circumstances surrounding it.[55]

These statements indicate that the American government is, at least, conscious of the problem of adapting nuclear weapons to limited war and that it has formulated some general rules for that purpose. On the other hand, other statements convey the impression that our military and political leaders still regard the problem of preparing for limited war as a distraction from the nation's one true concern: preparing to defend the United States in a total war with the Soviet Union. They suggest that the government is still operating under a profound reluctance to confront the problem of limited war on anything but an *ad hoc* basis as crises may arise. Perhaps the United States will fight a limited war if it absolutely cannot avoid it, but the government gives the impression of preferring not to make any special preparations for the eventuality.

Thus in December, 1954, President Eisenhower told a press conference that he thought the distinction between little and big wars was a bit artificial. He said that, in the light of the necessity of carrying forward a defense establishment for perhaps fifty years under the free-enterprise system and with the full support of the population that knows it has to bear the necessary taxes, he preferred to mold the nation's security arrangements to meet the great threats and to rely on improvisation to meet the little wars; for his attitude was that if you can win a big one, you can certainly win a little one.[56]

The President's attitude was entirely consistent with his administration's defense policies. Having discovered that the creation of a selective retaliatory nuclear capacity was a great deal more expensive than anticipated, and that it would actually entail a considerable increase in the defense budget, the administration was forced to cut still more deeply into conventional and ground forces in order to maintain America's relative air-nuclear position in the race with Russia's astonishingly rapid quantitative and qualitative advances in this field.[57] Consequently, despite all the talk about selective retaliation and a flexible military establishment, the actual composition of America's military establishment compelled the government to rely upon deterring the little wars by the same means as the big wars. Secretary of the Air Force Donald A. Quarles frankly avowed this strategy before a congressional committee in June, 1956. Rebutting the Army's position that America's increasing reliance on nuclear retaliation threatened to deprive the nation of its capacity to deter or repel limited aggressions, Secretary Quarles said:

> If it were obvious that limited aggressions would be met with *the full force of atomic weapons*, I do not believe such aggressions would occur. As in the case of all-out war, if the Communist leadership were tempted toward limited aggression but were faced with the plain fact that the United States stood ready to use its best weapons to defend its vital interests, they would have to conclude that such aggression would be unprofitable. Again, as in respect to total war, air-atomic power becomes a convincing deterrent.[58]

Although administration spokesmen continued to talk about a flexible strategy adapted to fighting small wars as well as general wars, it was hard to avoid the conclusion in the fall of 1956 that the United States was actually progressively losing its capacity to fight anything but the smallest police action or the largest nuclear conflict. For this tendency the administration in office bore the direct responsibility. However, in its depreciation of the problem of limited war, which underlay the tendency, the Eisenhower administration, like the Truman administration before the Korean War, was in basic harmony with the prevailing public and congressional view. To be sure, its military strategy and defense policies were confronted with a mounting public protest on the part of a few military experts—mostly Army officers—and a small body of civilians interested in military affairs, which charged that the government's growing reliance upon massive nuclear retaliation left the United States unprepared to deal with the most likely military contingency: limited war. However, the technical complexity of the military issues, the costliness and political unpalatability of raising and maintaining ground forces, widespread confidence in President Eisenhower's wisdom in military affairs, and the general sense of well-being that pervaded the nation prevented this protest from capturing public or congressional imagination. A significant indication of this fact is that, although the continuing inter-service controversy over weapons, missions, and strategy reached an intensity and overtness during 1956 approaching the B-36 controversy of 1949, the only effective challenge to the administration's military policies came from an investigation of the alleged inadequacy of America's strategic bombing capacity. This investigation, conducted by a Senate Armed Services subcommittee led by Senator Symington (a former Secretary of the Air Force under President Truman in 1947–50), did not challenge the administration's strategy in the least; it only purported to expose the inability of one branch of the Air Force to fulfil that strategy. The concrete result of Symington's investigation was that once more, as in 1948 and 1949, the Senate added funds—some $900,000,000—to the Air Force budget against the President's wishes.[59] Meanwhile, the sputtering protest against an overreliance upon air-nuclear retaliation, spearheaded by General Ridgway's resignation and an Army campaign to halt the reduction of ground forces, faded into insignificance.

Chapter Ten

TOWARD A STRATEGY OF LIMITED WAR

The Need for Reappraisal

It is easier to discern the inadequacies of American strategy than it is to prescribe a remedy, but it is also easier to be contented with the status quo than it is to venture alternatives. For the most practicable alternatives to current policies seem to promise a larger military and economic effort, although they carry no compensating guarantee of improving America's position in the cold war. As long as no conspicuous catastrophe befalls us, the status quo has at least the appeal of something known, whereas the feasible alternatives to the status quo seem at best untested measures of avoiding speculative dangers.

Yet the history of America's foreign relations in recent decades is a succession of unanticipated crises preceded by general complacency and followed by widespread alarm and recrimination. One does not have to entertain an apocalyptic view of history to believe that the present international situation is replete with opportunities for a repetition of this pattern. Common prudence requires not only a critical reappraisal of existing military and political policies but also a systematic examination of possible alternatives.

The suggestions that follow are not intended to comprise a detailed military program or a strategic blueprint. They are of a general nature— partly because of the limited technical information available to the layman, and partly because the most important factor determining the adequacy or inadequacy of American strategy has been our ideas about basic strategic principles rather than our technical capacity for implementing these principles. The general requirements of an American strategy must necessarily be set out in terms of the military technology known at the present time, but one can try to analyze the important elements of this strategy broadly enough to allow for alterations of policies within the general requirements in response to unforeseen technological developments and a great variety of possible military contingencies.

Containment—A Question of Method

The logic of the cold war and the concrete experience of the last decade indicate that America's over-all strategy should be the containment of the Communist sphere of control by our readiness to oppose aggression with a variety of means under a variety of circumstances. Containment is based upon assumptions about the nature of Communist conduct that have been confirmed in practice. It is a feasible strategy, compatible with our basic political objectives and our power to attain them. No other strategy, under present circumstances, will fulfil the requirements of American security as adequately. The nation has tacitly acknowledged this fact by rejecting every opportunity to pursue an alternative.

The important question concerning American strategy is not its general objective, which is best described as containment, but rather the method of attaining that objective. Assuming that the capacity to oppose aggression—which includes the willingness as well as the physical capability—is the most effective deterrent to Communist military expansion, the real question that has faced us since 1947 is: By what means should we be prepared to oppose different forms of Communist aggression in different areas under a variety of circumstances?

In the most general way, we can answer the question by saying that containment requires a capacity to wage both total and limited war. The capacity to wage one kind of war is insufficient without the capacity to wage the other.

Capacity for Total War and Limited War

America's capacity to wage a total war should be adequate to serve the following ends: to deter the Communists from undertaking major aggression in areas essential to our security; to induce them to refrain from taking measures that would be incompatible with limited war; and, if these deterrents fail, to fight a large-scale war in a manner that will maximize our chance of achieving basic security objectives at the end of the war.

In order to command a military capacity adequate for these purposes the United States must maintain at least offensive and defensive parity in strategic nuclear weapons and delivery capabilities with the Communist bloc. However, effective parity does not require numerical equality. Moreover, unless defensive techniques should attain an overwhelming superiority over offensive techniques, gains in our strategic nuclear weapons and delivery capabilities seem likely to reach the point of diminishing returns before long, since neither the United States nor the Soviet Union will be able to prevent the other from imposing intolerable destruction upon its tactical and strategic facilities, regardless of how the enemy's blows are countered.

It can be argued that for this reason ground forces will come to play a more decisive role in the military balance. But considering the extent of destruction that would follow a total nuclear war, even if we assume that the adversaries quickly eliminated each other's capacity to maintain such a war, increases in our capacity for ground war are not likely to contribute much toward preventing the deliberate resort to total war. On the other hand, if all deterrents proved ineffective and a total war, a war of desperation, actually did occur, then the side with a military superiority on the ground would be in a much better position to occupy and control territory; and to that extent it would have a substantial advantage in achieving its own political objectives and obstructing the enemy's.

Nevertheless, in terms of the relative urgency of military dangers confronting the United States, there can be little doubt that the greatest strategic dividends to be derived from a given expansion of our ground forces lie in the direction of preparing the free world for the contingency of limited war. In view of the superior numbers of trained manpower available to the Communist bloc, our capacity for total war is likely to be promoted most effectively and at a tolerable cost by maintaining an offensive-defensive superiority—or, at least, parity—in the ability to strike directly at the tactical and strategic capability of the Soviet Union. As the offensive capabilities of the Soviet Union increase, the relative importance of American and allied defensive capabilities—both in terms of air defense and a dispersed base system—will increase, unless or until both nations attain offensive capabilities so vast as to be beyond the power of the defense to nullify in any significant measure.

Assuming that the United States maintains an adequate capacity for total war and that the Communists continue to conduct a rational and cautious foreign policy, designed to gain their ends by indirection and limited ventures rather than by massive military assault, the chief function of our capacity for total war will be to keep war limited and to strengthen our diplomacy against the blackmail that a strong and unscrupulous power can wield. However, the fulfilment of this function will not be sufficient for the purposes of containment unless it is accompanied by a ready capacity to resist lesser aggressions by limited war. Otherwise the Communists can confront us with the choice between total war, non-resistance, and ineffective resistance; and the results of that situation would probably be piecemeal Communist expansion, the paralysis of Western diplomacy, and the further disaffection of uncommitted peoples.

Therefore, preparation for limited war is as vital to American security as preparation for total war. It is a matter for thorough and systematic planning, not for improvisation. After all, in developing our capacity for total war we are preparing for the least likely contingency; its principal justification lies in the fact that it may never be used. But in developing a capacity for limited war we would be preparing to meet the most likely contingency; we would be maintaining the only credible military deterrent to Communist advances in the most vulnerable areas of the world.

The Limitation of Political Objectives

The specific requirements of a strategy that will enable the United States and its allies to deter and fight limited wars must be determined in the light of the many forms such wars can assume and the great variety of circumstances under which they may occur. These wars may vary in character from guerilla actions to a massive clash of modern arms. They may result from clandestine Communist support of an indigenous revolution, from the intervention of Communist "volunteers" in a war between smaller powers, or from a direct invasion across a well-defined boundary. As an increasing number of smaller powers acquire the will and strength to act according to their independent designs, the United States may have to consider intervention in wars that do not directly involve Communist powers at all. One can readily imagine the different means by which limited wars might have to be fought in the Formosa Straits, the jungles and swamps of Southeast Asia, the mountains of Afghanistan, or the deserts of the Middle East.

The detailed military plans to meet these varied requirements are beyond the scope of this study; but we can properly formulate the essential guidelines for these plans. These guidelines extend from the framework of the two general prerequisites of limited war: the limitation of political objectives and the limitation of military means. What do these prerequisites mean in terms of a strategy of limited war under contemporary military and political conditions? Let us examine the question of limited objectives first.

Clearly, the over-all strategic objective of containment requires that the specific political objectives for which the United States must be prepared to fight limited wars will not entail radical changes in the status quo. The very fact that a war remains limited although the belligerents are physically capable of imposing a much greater scale of destruction assumes that neither of the belligerents' objectives constitute such a serious challenge to the status quo as to warrant expanding the war greatly or taking large risks of precipitating total war. However, this does not mean that we must necessarily confine our war objectives to the exact territorial boundaries and the other political conditions that existed prior to aggression. This kind of mechanical requirement, making no allowance for the dynamic, unpredictable elements of war, would impose rigid political constraints, unrelated to the actual balance of military power and the enemy's response. Moreover, if potential aggressors could count upon ending a war in at least no worse position than they began it, they might come to regard this situation as an irresistible invitation to launch a series of limited incursions at a minimal risk in proportion to the possible gain.

In the final analysis the precise objectives of a war can be determined only in the light of the specific circumstances in which it occurs. However, this does not mean that the objectives should be left entirely to improvisation. They should be derived from a pre-existing framework of concrete political aims, expressing the particular power interests of the United States throughout the various strategic areas of the world. This is a matter of balancing power and commitments, of combining force with policy, in advance of crises, so that when crises occur, the government will not be forced to formulate under the pressure of the moment the kind of basic judgments of strategic priority and enemy intent that are essential to the rational conduct of war.

The Korean War illustrates the dangers of ignoring this rule. Although we did manage to improvise limited objectives once the war broke out, these objectives had no clear relation to our strategic planning before the war. Throughout the war the government gave the unfortunate impression of being in doubt about its own aims, as well as the aims of the adversary. Our objectives during the war suffered unnecessary ambiguity because they seemed to be more the product of intuition and changing military fortunes than of firm military and political policies formulated in the light of an over-all national strategy. Clearly, our general commitment to the Truman Doctrine and the principle of collective security was no substitute for strategic forethought; in fact, our reliance upon these generalities tended to obscure rather than to clarify the determining objectives of the war.

This is not to say that wartime political objectives should or can be formulated with the precision of legal documents prescribing binding rules in perpetuity. What is necessary is that the government establish concrete, feasible objectives, sufficiently well defined yet flexible enough to provide a rational guide for the conduct of military operations, and that it communicate the general import of these objectives—above all, the fact that they are limited—to the enemy. The importance of this requirement is evident in view of the fact that one of the essential elements of limited war is the operation of some kind of system of mutual self-restraint based upon the belligerents' observance of a reasonable proportion between the dimensions of war and the value of the objectives at stake.

Political objectives need not be made explicit at all times in order to serve their proper function of limiting and controlling war. The method of conducting military operations, especially the particular military restraints observed, may convey the nature of determining political objectives more effectively than explicit announcements. But since the political character of limited war is all-important, diplomacy—the public statement of positions, the private exchange of official views, the bargaining over terms—is an indispensable instrument of limitation, not only for communicating objectives but for terminating hostilities on the basis of accommodation. However, diplomacy is not something that nations can readily turn on and off. It operates best when it is in continual use. Diplomacy is not apt to serve its moderating function during war unless there exists in advance of war an expectation that neither side will push things too far without recourse to political accommodation.

Admittedly, there are grave difficulties in conducting useful diplomatic relations with Communist powers. The Communists do not regard diplomacy as a means of ironing out conflicting positions among nations sharing a fundamental harmony of interests. They regard it, rather, as a device and a tactic for pursuing an inevitable conflict of interests. Nevertheless, there is nothing to indicate that they are unwilling to strike bargains of mutual advantage. They neither make nor accept concessions as a tender of good will, but we should not on that account exclude compromises that advance our interests as well as theirs. They understand better than we that diplomacy, like force, cannot properly be divorced from power; rather it is a function of power. If we were to comprehend the function of diplomacy as an instrument for attaining limited political objectives in conjunction with military force, rather than as an alternative to force, we would be in a better position to cultivate useful channels of communication for keeping the present struggle for power cold and limited.

When one considers the general requirement of the formulation and communication of limited objectives, one must also take into account the method of promulgating strategic objectives. For the impression of its objectives that the government seeks to convey through diplomacy can be undone by the way in which it publicly announces its strategy. The essential requirement here is that the government announce its strategy in such a way as to make credible its limitation of objectives and its ability to back them up with proportionate force. This is not a matter of giving fuller publicity to the details of American strategy but rather of publicizing strategy in words that correspond with capabilities and intentions and that avoid raising false expectations. It would be foolish to try to relieve potential aggressors of all their doubts about our intentions under every conceivable circumstance, even if we could know those intentions ourselves. But it would be dangerous to leave them with the impression that our conduct is reckless, capricious, and unrelated to our words. And the point is equally applicable to the impression we convey to allied and uncommitted nations.

Unfortunately, much of the hyperbole we use to convince ourselves that we are conducting our strategy in the American way convinces others that we are incurably aggressive. Foreign states are peculiarly sensitive to our emphasis upon military considerations and the ideological aspects of the cold war. The bold phrases which, presumably, give us courage make our allies shiver. It is ridiculous that we should be the ones to bear the onus of militarism and imperialism when it is the Communists who have the huge armies and who have been the determined expansionists while we have had to be begged and frightened into making the minimum effort necessary to defend even the positions essential to our security. But if our bellicose talk is the obverse of our pacific inclinations, we cannot expect other nations to appreciate that paradox. Sometimes we even fool ourselves into taking this talk at face value. Perhaps if we were clear in our own minds about the limited nature of our strategic objectives, we would be in a better position to clarify the thoughts of others. And then we could place the onus of militarism and imperialism where it belongs.

The Limitation of Military Means

The problem of limiting the political objectives of war and national strategy is inseparable from the problem of devising limited military means. Unless we have military policies, weapons, techniques, and tactics capable of supporting limited objectives, we cannot have an effective strategy of limited war; for containment depends less upon what we say than upon what we are ready to do. An effective strategy requires more than the mere formulation of objectives; it requires a balance between objectives and means, such that the objectives are within range of the means and the means are commensurate with the objectives. Otherwise, we shall have to intrust our security to bluff, improvisation, and sheer luck.

One great difficulty in developing a military establishment and a military strategy and tactics capable of meeting the threat of limited war lies in the fact that the requirements for limiting war do not necessarily correspond with the requirements of fighting limited wars effectively; and yet the fulfilment of one requirement is incomplete without the other. Therefore, nations must be ready to weigh the risk of expanding wars against the need for military success. In balancing these two factors the importance of the political stakes must be the crucial determinant.

At the same time, the requirements of both military limitation and effectiveness are, in themselves, complicated by the great variety of circumstances under which limited wars might have to be fought. The kind of measures that would be effective in fighting a limited war in the Formosa Straits might be ineffective in Thailand or incompatible with limited war in Iran. Moreover, both the limitation and the effectiveness of military operations embrace a number of separate but related criteria, which are not susceptible to precise measurement. The scale of war, for example, can be limited in area, weapons, targets, manpower, the number of belligerents, the duration of war, or its intensity. And military effectiveness must be measured not only by physical capabilities on the battlefield but also by the political and psychological consequences of various measures and the relation of these measures to the general resources of the United States and its allies, especially manpower and economic potential.

The proper blending and balancing of all these considerations in a coherent strategy assumes an accurate anticipation of the response of potential adversaries to a wide range of measures and circumstances. Such an anticipation will depend upon calculating the value that the potential adversaries attach to various objectives and the proportionate effort they are willing to expend upon achieving them or upon preventing us from jeopardizing them. And this sort of calculation must rest upon a sound appraisal of their intentions, strategy, and general international behavior.

Moreover, we must anticipate the response to our policies and actions in terms of a two-way interaction, calculating that the adversary will respond on the basis of his own anticipation of our counter-response. In other words, the course of action—the means of resistance and deterrence —upon which we plan to rely under different circumstances must be determined in the light of the same kind of complex calculation of response and counter-response that chess players or boxers must make. Therefore, it is too simple to operate on the principle that successful deterrence depends merely upon letting potential aggressors know that they will suffer damage outweighing any possible gains from aggression; for the same measure might also cause the potential aggressor to respond in a way that would impose intolerable penalties upon our own interests. Calculating the deterrent effect of this risk upon our own actions, the aggressor might well conclude that he could safely ignore our threat. The Chinese Communists seem to have done this very thing in supporting the Vietminh seizure of Dienbienphu.

Thus the first requirement of deterrence is that it be credible to the potential aggressor; and credibility, in turn, requires that the means of deterrence be proportionate to the objective at stake. This commensurability may be difficult to achieve in practice, but the underlying principle is simple enough: it is the principle of economy of force, without which the reciprocal self-restraints essential to limited war cannot exist.

Even this elementary outline of the general considerations concerning the limitation of military means should leave no doubt that the different factors involved and the complexity of their relationship to one another confront American strategists with a perplexing problem of military planning. Nevertheless, if we are at least aware of the various elements that enter into the military equation, it should not be beyond our ingenuity to devise means of preparing the nation for the most serious contingencies of limited war. After all, there are only a limited number of areas in which such wars might occur, and there are only a limited number of circumstances, or kinds of circumstances, from which they are likely to arise.

The history of American strategy since 1947 strongly suggests that we have excluded from our military planning some of the central elements in the equation of limitation, that we have obscured them with handy but misleading generalizations, simply because our aversion to the very idea of limited war has inhibited us from approaching the problem objectively and systematically. One might almost say that the things we have failed to consider in the realm of military preparation have been less of a handicap than the things we have taken for granted; for it is the major unexamined premises of our approach to force and policy that have established the pattern and focus of our strategic thinking.

Geographical Limitation

Under the military and political conditions of the foreseeable future the decisive limitations upon military operations that are within the power of belligerents to control would seem to be limitations upon the area of combat, upon weapons, and upon targets. Without these three kinds of limitations, it is difficult to imagine a war remaining limited. With them, the other limitations would probably follow, and wars might remain limited even if they did not follow. Therefore the heart of the problem of developing a strategy of limited war lies in devising methods of conducting military operations that are compatible with these three limitations and yet militarily effective in terms of supporting America's security objectives.

The importance of geographical limitation is obvious. Without the localization of war, hostilities involving the United States and the Communist bloc, directly or indirectly, would almost certainly exceed the scale of practicable limitation, given the existing military potentials of major powers. For a war not fought within well-defined geographical limits would probably pose such a massive threat to American and Russian security that both powers would feel compelled to strike at the center of opposition. The same thing can be said of the simultaneous occurrence of several local wars, for both the Soviet Union and the United States would probably regard such wars as the sign of a general contest that it could not afford to counter on a local and piecemeal basis. Geographical limitation is all the more important because it is the easiest, most practicable limitation to establish, to observe, and to communicate.

However, like any other limitation designed to control the dynamics of warfare, limitation of the area of combat must not be construed in an absolute sense. Thus it need not under all circumstances preclude naval action or tactical air retaliation beyond the immediate area of attack. Whether the extension of a war by air and sea action is warranted must be judged in the light of the danger of enlarging the scope of war beyond the bounds of control, balanced against the political urgency and the military efficacy of the measures involved. For example, if important political objectives are at stake in a peripheral contest supported by Communist China, and if they can only be attained by bombing Chinese bases and supply lines supporting the aggression, then this measure might be worth the additional risk of enlarging the scale of war that it would entail. However, if the military efficacy of such a measure is dubious, if bombing Chinese bases would probably lead to retaliation by countermeasures that would nullify the anticipated military advantage or that would entail a risk of total war disproportionate to the importance of the objective at stake, then the least objectionable course might be to adhere to existing limitations and make the best of them.

Ideally, we should like to be able to contain every possible Communist aggression on a strictly local basis, for then we could avoid the choice between undertaking ineffective resistance and risking total war or, at least, war on a scale beyond our ability to sustain at a tolerable cost—a dilemma that would probably result in non-resistance unless aggression occurred in the most vital strategic area. However, we must recognize that in some highly industrialized and economically integrated areas—certainly the core of the NATO area—even limited military incursions would constitute such a serious threat to our security interests (and would be so difficult to check on a purely local basis) that we could not afford to confine our resistance to the immediate combat area. This might be true even if the topography, the industrial and transport linkages, and other physical features made restriction theoretically feasible. Therefore, in these areas, except in cases of insurrection and minor military coups, we shall have to continue to rely primarily upon our capability to strike at the center of aggression to deter Communist advances.

But the American government, especially under the Eisenhower administration, has frequently argued another reason for the unfeasibility of relying upon purely local defense, a reason with much less claim to validity. It has argued that because of the Communists' central geographical position and their numerical superiority in manpower the free world cannot afford the expenditure of men and money necessary to resist aggression locally at every possible point along the Sino-Soviet periphery. American strategists have been frightened by this theoretical situation ever since the inauguration of containment. What they have envisioned is the Russians and Chinese, secure in the heartland of Eurasia and enjoying the advantages of inexhaustible manpower and interior lines of communication, striking out at will at a series of soft spots along the periphery, remote from the center of our own strength, while the American coalition dissipates its precious manpower and resources in endless futile efforts to hold a kind of Maginot Line against assaults initiated by the Communists at places and with weapons of their choosing. The prospect is, indeed, a disturbing one; but how realistic is it?

In the first place, the image of trying to hold every point on a 20,000-mile Maginot Line is, to say the least, exaggerated. It is true that in the European sector of such a line we would certainly operate at an irrevocable disadvantage in trying to contain Communist assaults on a local basis, since the West suffers such substantial numerical inferiority in mobilizable manpower.[1] But, as we have observed, the defense of the part of the Communist perimeter that adjoins the NATO area does not depend primarily upon local resistance. Furthermore, other sectors of the perimeter are less vulnerable than a simple line drawn on a map suggests. India and Pakistan are protected by a formidable mountain barrier. Political considerations may protect other segments equally effectively. For example, India's close interest in Burma and the reluctance of Communist China to turn India from a neutral power into a dangerous competitor in Southeast Asia may deter an attack on Burma—and, perhaps, on Laos, Cambodia, and Thailand too—far more effectively than a large local garrison, providing that these nations have a minimum capacity to police their territories.

The Middle Eastern and Asian rimlands are undoubtedly vulnerable but not so vulnerable as the purely spatial relation between the heartlands and the rimlands implies. We shall deal with the methods of defending these rimlands when we examine the specific problem of applying containment to the gray areas; but it can be noted now that the image of Sino-Soviet interior lines of communication facilitating the rapid transfer of great masses of troops from one peripheral point to another is not supported by the logistical realities of the situation. The tremendous length of those lines, their distance from major supplies, their sparseness, and the poor transportation facilities refute any analogy with our own elaborate and highly developed network of communications. And as for transferring troops rapidly from one peripheral point to another, the Communists are in no better position to do that than we are; for the Asian rimland is not a continuous open field but actually a series of terrain compartments, between which communication is far easier by sea and air than by land. In a contest with the Sino-Soviet heartland for this Asian rimland we and our allies have the tremendous advantage of easy access to the sea and control of the sea, as well as a large number of naval and air bases encircling Eurasia and the technical capability of transporting great quantities of men and equipment to various points on the Sino-Soviet periphery. The Korean War was an impressive illustration of this fact.

As for a number of more or less simultaneous attacks on the periphery of Communist power, there is no reason to think that the Communists are in a better position to fight more than one local war at a time than we, providing that we take full advantage of our superior mobility, our geographical position, and our logistical advantages. Moreover, assuming that the Communists continue to conduct a strategy of caution and limited risk, they will realize that a series of small wars could constitute such a serious threat to our prestige and security as to incur an inordinate risk of precipitating a full-scale war; for their simultaneous attacks would be a signal to us that they had deliberately accepted the grave risk of a general war, and we would have to accept the same risks. If we could not contain these attacks locally, we probably could not afford to confine our resistance to the combat area; nor would the American people tolerate piecemeal defeat under this circumstance. Presumably, the Communists would know this.

Therefore, with the exceptions and qualifications noted above, it seems both feasible and essential that the United States develop its strategy around the conception of local defense that has been implicit in containment from the first. Of course, the particular geographical restrictions upon a war must be determined in the light of such factors as the direction and scope of the aggression and the geographical features of the area. Clearly, island and peninsular wars will be easier to localize than wars in areas with no clear physical demarcations; and small-scale attacks directed at well-defined territorial objectives will be easier to localize than large-scale assaults or general insurrectionary activity unaccompanied by clear indications of military and political intent.

However, we must also recognize that alliances may inject a complicating factor into geographical limitation of warfare; for by creating an obligation for many nations to come to the aid of one, they also create the danger that an attack on one country will result in spreading the war to several. Thus we might find it difficult to resist the demands of an ally under attack that other allies share the burden of the war in their own territories. We must remember that such an ally will not feel the same restraints as we. For the war which we strive to confine geographically may, in effect, be unlimited from the standpoint of the ally whose country happens to be the scene of battle. He may already have reached that stage of desperation that we are trying to avoid. This situation will afford him considerable bargaining power, especially if the adversary offers him conditional surrender. If this hard-pressed ally should also have a nuclear capacity, he could increase his bargaining power that much more by threatening to expand the war on his own.

For this reason alone, it would be a mistake to seek in other parts of the world, where local resistance is both feasible and essential, the kind of tight, inflexible commitments that the North Atlantic Treaty embodies. By the same token, we should avoid trying to make every local action in which we are involved a UN action. At least we shall have to weigh whatever onus may attach to unilateral action against the advantage of controlling the scope and conduct of war more readily. And that calculation should not be colored by a false assumption of the moral superiority of "collective security." If the divergent interests and the growing independence of the non-Communist powers should preclude their joining rigid alliances or UN defense commitments anyway, that is all the more reason, then, to avoid needless irritations and misunderstandings by importuning them to participate in conflicts in which we shall have to bear the lion's share of the fighting.

Weapons and Targets Limitation

Before the momentous economic and technological expansion of the Industrial Revolution, the severely restricted physical capacity for war which states could draw upon made limited war virtually an automatic by-product of limited objectives. But, with the tremendous capacity for destruction available to modern nations, the limitation of war demands a deliberate restriction not only of the area of combat but also of weapons and targets. For it is doubtful that any war could be controlled for limited political purposes, no matter how narrowly and precisely a belligerent might try to define his objectives, if all the present means of destruction were employed indiscriminately, even though they were employed initially within a narrowly circumscribed area.

At the same time, it would be a mistake to assume that there is a mathematical correlation between the destructiveness or firepower of weapons and the scale and scope of warfare. The effect that use of a certain weapon exerts on the dimensions of warfare depends largely upon the seriousness with which the enemy regards the resulting threat to national values. The careful limitation and clarification of objectives can go far to keep that threat ordinate, even when the most powerful weapons are employed. Therefore, nothing inherent in a wide range of atomic weapons renders them incompatible with limited war, apart from the targets toward which they are directed and the political context in which they are employed. For this reason it is a serious mistake to equate nuclear warfare with total warfare and oppose them both to "conventional" warfare. Of course, we must reckon with the fact that weapons as destructive as the multi-megaton nuclear bombs are pre-eminently instruments for obliterating large centers of population. Consequently, the employment of these weapons under almost any conceivable circumstance would be a signal that a general war upon strategic targets had begun. But there is a vast difference between the multi-megaton bomb and the variety of "low-yield" kiloton weapons—a much greater difference than between the most powerful

World War II "block-busters" and conventional artillery shells. A two-kiloton bomb has a maximum damage radius of several hundred yards; its radioactive fallout is negligible. A twenty-megaton H-bomb, by no means the largest available, would virtually obliterate everything within a radius of ten miles and dust a downwind area with deadly or harmful fallout for hundreds of miles (unless it were exploded at a great height). Since the enemy's exact response to the use of certain weapons against certain targets under particular circumstances is difficult to anticipate, it would be dangerous not to allow for a considerable margin of error in planning our weapons system and our military strategy and tactics; but it would be equally dangerous to assume that the powerful new weapons that have recently become available are necessarily and under all circumstances less compatible with limited war than the conventional weapons of World War II.

The essential requirement in adapting weapons to a strategy of limited war is that we have a flexible weapons system and flexible military strategies and tactics capable of supporting limited objectives under a wide variety of conditions. Clearly, all the weapons and measures that are suitable for total war are not suitable for limited war. For example, it is almost inconceivable that any war in which air power were employed against major strategic targets would remain limited; nor would the indiscriminate employment of air power necessarily promote local defense even if the war did remain limited. The special technological requirements of limited war are particularly marked in the realm of mobile, airborne troops capable of employing low-yield nuclear weapons and the most advanced conventional weapons with precision against military targets. Therefore, we cannot simply devise our military policies to meet the threat of major aggression and total war and expect to deter and repel lesser aggressions by improvising resistance with whatever can be spared from the total-war arsenal. Precisely because the requirements of reconciling the limitation of war with military effectiveness are so varied and complex, we cannot afford to rely too heavily upon any single weapon or any single tactic. We need to have a weapons-and-delivery system as flexible as the probable military contingencies are varied, lest the range of measures from which we can select our response in the event of an attack be so narrow as to deprive us of an intermediate response between total war and non-resistance. For, even though the Communists may never force us to choose between nuclear suicide and acquiescence, we shall have to act as though they might; and our diplomatic position will profit or suffer in proportion as we are prepared or unprepared to avoid the dilemma. By the same token, in proportion as our range of military capabilities increases, the flexibility of our diplomacy will be enhanced; and as the flexibility of our diplomacy is enhanced, we shall be that much better able to advance our bargaining power with Communist nations and to promote our relations with non-Communist nations.

Ground Troops

Under existing technological conditions, one essential requirement of a flexible military establishment is sufficient numbers of ready combat troops to check Communist aggression locally. If we cannot check aggression locally, we shall be compelled to run larger risks of total war by striking at targets beyond the area of combat that support the aggression, unless, of course, we choose to acquiesce in defeat. It follows that the greater our capacity for local military containment, the better we shall be able to minimize the risk of total war. Some advocates of tactical air power notwithstanding, there is little military support for the view that "mobile striking power" can provide this capacity in the absence of substantial ground strength—except, perhaps, in a very few island and peninsular positions, such as the Formosa Straits, with naval support. The Korean War is only the latest war to demonstrate this fact.

However, if we recognize the desirability of possessing ground strength capable of checking aggression locally, we must also recognize that we cannot realistically expect to achieve this condition of limitation in all areas of potential aggression, since we cannot count on the free world mobilizing sufficient manpower for the purpose. However, this drawback is rendered somewhat less significant by the fact that western Europe, the area in which local ground defense is least likely to be feasible, is of such great strategic importance and so uncongenial to limitation on other grounds that we shall have to rely primarily upon the deterrent of massive retaliation for its defense anyway.[2]

At the same time, we need not conclude that our relative numerical deficiency in ready, mobilized manpower precludes successful local ground defense in all areas. That would be true only if we had to match the Communists man for man. But the experience in Korea confirmed the lesson of other wars that troops with superior firepower, technical skill, and logistical support can hold forces several times as numerous. Throughout the gray areas our superior mobility and our superior ability to train, equip, and supply troops can go a long way toward compensating for numerical inferiority. Indeed, in the light of this superiority, considered in conjunction with the growth of Communist air power, some students of military strategy have suggested that we may actually enjoy our greatest potential advantage in ground warfare.[3]

Tactical Nuclear Weapons

In considering the requirements of a flexible military establishment, the role of tactical nuclear weapons looms large; for the adaptation of these weapons to limited war is probably the most crucial problem of weapons and targets limitation that American strategists face today.[4] At some future time the role of other kinds of weapons—perhaps weapons that have not as yet been designed—may be equally important, but for the foreseeable future the peculiar importance of tactical nuclear weapons lies in the fact that they carry greater promise than any other weapon of enabling us to fight limited wars on an equal basis against numerically superior forces. And yet we know very little about their actual effects on the battlefield. Therefore, what follows, in an attempt to assess the role of tactical nuclear weapons, is necessarily speculative.

In official statements dealing with the military efficacy of tactical nuclear weapons, it has frequently been claimed that they will compensate for our numerical inferiority in ground troops. When the Truman administration made this claim, it seemed to be thinking primarily in terms of supplementing the firepower of the ground troops in Europe; whereas the Eisenhower administration stressed the substitution of "mobile striking power"—that is, air and sea action—for ground forces in Asia. We have just observed that the validity of the latter conception is dubious, except under very special circumstances. As for tactical nuclear weapons being used in conjunction with ground troops, it is undoubtedly true that they will provide a given number of troops with more firepower than conventional weapons; and to this extent they compensate for our numerical inferiority in comparison with Communist ground forces. However, they do not obviate the necessity of having a minimum number of troops available to compel the enemy to concentrate his forces, to cover the routes of attack, to provide for a strategic reserve, and to perform many other tactical functions that conventional forces would have to perform. Although the tactical employment of atomic weapons is still in an experimental stage, the experience so far does not indicate that the minimum number of troops needed to defend any particular theater of operations will be substantially smaller than would be necessary in the absence of atomic weapons;[5] and some authorities, like General Ridgway, even believe that the successful exploitation of these weapons will require more, not fewer, troops.[6]

Aside from these considerations, there are other reasons for taking a qualified view of the military efficacy of tactical nuclear weapons. For one thing, they are no answer to irregular warfare—to the kind of insurrectionary and guerilla activity upon which the Communists prefer to rely in the early stages of a campaign of expansion. Nor do they meet the needs of intervention in a war fought by non-Communist powers, such as might occur in the Middle East. Furthermore, even in the case of orthodox, direct Communist assaults it is by no means certain that it will always be to our advantage to use tactical nuclear weapons if, by doing so, we lead the enemy to use them also. There can be no doubt that the Soviet Union and perhaps China as well will acquire a large and varied arsenal of tactical nuclear weapons. When that time arrives, even though we shall probably still retain quantitative superiority, we shall face the serious question of who has the most to gain by using these weapons. Who would be more vulnerable to these weapons in the event of a Chinese attack on Formosa? Who would have most to gain or lose by using them in a war in Southeast Asia? Here again we encounter questions that are difficult for even the military expert to answer with any assurance. But at least it seems safe to say that the questions are not foreclosed by what little is known in the absence of battlefield experience. And precisely because it is so difficult to gauge the exact military efficacy of tactical nuclear weapons, it would be foolhardy to rely on them to solve all the problems of limited war. That would be committing the same mistake that we committed in our over-reliance on the atomic bomb.

Much of the recent discussion of tactical nuclear weapons has started by assuming that they will necessarily give us a great military advantage and then has addressed itself to the question of their compatibility with limited war. But the two questions cannot properly be separated, because if these weapons cannot be used in ways commensurate with limited objectives, then, regardless of their superior firepower, they will not meet the standards of flexibility that an effective strategy of limited war demands.

Clearly, weapons with a range of destructiveness extending as high as the explosive power of the bombs dropped on Hiroshima and Nagasaki must be used in a highly selective fashion in order to remain compatible with limited war. Of course, it is conceivable that a war in which these weapons were used indiscriminately could still be settled for limited objectives before the belligerents reached the stage of utter exhaustion or mutual annihilation; but the physical, economic, and social impact of a war like this would almost certainly extend beyond the limits within which it could be controlled as an instrument for attaining predictable political results. Therefore, given the tremendous destructive potential of even the smaller tactical nuclear weapons, their utility as rational and effective instruments of national policy will depend upon the belligerents observing rules of self-restraint that relieve them of the fear of the extreme devastation and the radical alteration of national power which would occur if these weapons were employed indiscriminately.

The possibility of using tactical nuclear weapons in a manner proportionate to limited objectives would seem to depend largely upon the feasibility of two methods of limitation: (a) confining the use of these weapons to a limited geographical area and (b) using them with precision against military targets without destroying strategic targets and the large centers of population. Geographical limitation without target restrictions would be effective in keeping warfare limited only under three conditions: (a) if the battle area is one within which the United States and its Communist adversary are willing to accept virtually total destruction of all physical facilities without retaliating upon targets beyond the area; (b) if the Americans and the Communists believe they can fight the war effectively enough by confining their operations to the area without striking at targets beyond the area which facilitate these operations; (c) if the area does not belong to a nation that possesses an independent atomic arsenal, the use of which it would be unwilling to confine to its own territory at the cost of what would amount to total national destruction. The last condition may exist for a decade or longer, but we cannot safely count on the other two even now. It follows that in the use of tactical nuclear weapons geographical restrictions must be combined with target restrictions in order to fulfil the minimum requirements of limitation.

The successful restriction of targets depends largely upon the feasibility of distinguishing between tactical and strategic targets—that is, between targets directly related to military operations (such as the actively employed armed forces, the supporting air bases and naval units, and the supply and transportation facilities of direct service to the field armies) and targets directly related to the economy and the civilian morale of a nation (principally, industrial facilities, central supply depots, and urban population centers). For if this distinction were feasible, it could be the basis for a rule of mutual self-restraint that would minimize the threat to national values and enable the belligerents to employ a graduated scale of force proportionate to a wide range of objectives and contingencies.

Theoretically, the distinction is feasible on three major conditions: (*a*) if tactical targets can be distinguished logically and physically from strategic targets in a manner that both belligerents recognize as legitimate; (*b*) if nuclear weapons can be used with sufficient precision to destroy specific tactical targets and those targets only; (*c*) if the belligerents are willing to tolerate strikes upon occasional strategic targets as accidental or as incidental to attacks upon legitimate tactical targets.

There is a good prospect that the condition of precision could be met by the smaller nuclear bombs and missiles and by further development of low-yield atomic artillery weapons of from two to ten kilotons' power, designed for use against enemy troops on the battlefield. The low-yield weapons, which were designed but not in production in 1956, seem especially well suited for limited warfare; for they promise not only great mobility and firepower but also the requisite accuracy to confine destruction to well-defined military targets.[7]

The condition of mutual definition of tactical targets is more doubtful. Certainly, in heavily industrialized areas and areas with great concentrations of population it will be difficult to draw a distinction between tactical and strategic targets—especially with respect to supply depots and the communications and transportation network—that both sides will recognize as legitimate in the heat of battle; and even if the distinction is logically feasible, the two kinds of targets may be so closely associated in physical space as to preclude the destruction of tactical targets without also devastating large urban centers. The great number of tactical targets (consider merely the 150 or so airfields) that would be subject to attack in an area like western Europe would, by itself, almost preclude the possibility of establishing significant limits upon the scale of destruction. On the other hand, areas like this are unlikely scenes of limited war anyway, because the strategic stakes are so high and the interdependence of the geographical components render localization so difficult. In the areas of less immediate strategic importance, where Communist military incursions are most likely and area limitation is more practicable, the distinction between tactical and strategic targets is a good deal more feasible, because of the relatively undeveloped state of the indigenous economies. Moreover, the distinction between targets does not require the logical clarity of a legal document in order to serve as a practical basis for limiting warfare. The important requirements are two: first, every belligerent involved should believe that the other belligerents intend and are able to limit military destruction in a manner commensurate with the limited objectives at stake; and, second, on the basis of this belief every belligerent should observe definite target restrictions, which will serve as effective tokens of limited intentions, however difficult it may be to formulate those restrictions in terms of discrete strategic and tactical categories.

But this raises the question of the condition of tolerating accidental or incidental destruction; for since it would be too much to expect the belligerents invariably to be capable of confining destruction to tactical targets with complete accuracy and precision, the limitation of war may depend upon the willingness of the belligerents to tolerate occasional destruction of non-tactical targets on the assumption that such destruction is contrary to the intentions of the adversary. The existence of this requisite degree of tolerance is plausible, provided the belligerents share a confidence in each other's willingness and ability to discriminate between different kinds of targets. Therefore, where other conditions of target and area restriction exist, the limitation of war may depend upon the ability of each belligerent to establish in the mind of the others a presumption that it is conducting the war according to definite and practicable restraints that are contingent upon the adversary doing likewise. Indeed, without the existence of this fundamental condition, it is hard to conceive of the successful operation of any other condition for target or area restriction.

Considering the incentive for avoiding thermonuclear war, and assuming that the belligerents possess flexible military capabilities, the public announcement of a general policy of so-called "graduated deterrence" might well promote the measure of confidence needed to sustain effective mutual restraints.[8] This would simply amount to a public acknowledgment of our adherence to the principle of the economy of force, according to which we would employ a range of military measures proportionate to the enemy's threat to our security, as determined by the kind of targets he attacks and the weapons he uses against us. An advance declaration of our intention to observe, on a reciprocal basis, a distinction between tactical and strategic targets (except perhaps in the NATO area) would be a reasonable way of giving this general policy sufficient content to make it susceptible of verification. We might also state that we had no intention of dropping nuclear bombs on large cities in the event of a war in any area unless our own cities were bombed first.

These advance commitments would go no further than recognizing the restrictions which we could count upon being to our advantage and, with the possible exception of the implicit restriction upon bombing our large port cities, to the Communists' advantage as well. Any further explicit commitments to specific self-imposed restrictions would be of doubtful value, because we could not be sure of adhering to them; and a violated commitment would be infinitely worse than no commitment at all, since it would undermine confidence in the whole system of reciprocal restraints. Plainly, if self-imposed restraints turned out to jeopardize national security, neither we nor the Communists would feel bound to observe them in the heat of war. The diverse circumstances of war, the multitude of unpredictable elements, including the rapid rate of technological change, would seem to preclude advance knowledge of specific restrictions that we could safely observe in the event of war, beyond the minimum ones mentioned above. And it is doubly difficult to foresee what reciprocal restrictions the Communists might feel that they could safely observe; for, clearly, the same restrictions that were to the advantage of one belligerent might be a serious disadvantage to the other.

An examination of the role of tactical nuclear weapons would be incomplete without considering their psychological consequences, which are so closely related to the requirements of effectiveness and limitation. We cannot doubt that the strange and terrible power of any nuclear explosion raises a peculiar moral revulsion in the popular mind today. If the Communists launched an attack for limited objectives with conventional weapons and we retaliated with nuclear weapons, we would incur the onus of initiating nuclear warfare. If the people of the world were convinced that any kind of nuclear weapon is so horrible that the nation that uses it first is worse than an aggressor, then the military advantages of using tactical nuclear weapons to check Communist aggression by conventional means might be outweighed by the political disadvantages—especially if we initiated their use in Asia, where the cold war turns so largely upon a struggle for the respect and allegiance of the inhabitants.

On the other hand, if these weapons are really a vital military asset to our capacity for limited war, we cannot afford to renounce them simply because of widespread misunderstanding of their effects. Instead, we should find ways of counteracting their adverse psychological impact. Actually, there are no rational grounds for regarding low-yield atomic battlefield warheads as any more horrible and inhumane than napalm or, for that matter, TNT. To the extent that the world has come to regard nuclear weapons as a peculiar form of terror, that popular impression is derived from the devastation of Hiroshima and Nagasaki and from the well-publicized American tests of even more powerful atomic and thermonuclear bombs. But the apprehensions raised by these instruments of total war need not be irrevocably associated with all nuclear weapons. Of course, if we talk in words that suggest virtually an exclusive reliance upon massive retaliation and if our military establishment reflects this strategic imbalance, all nuclear weapons will be likely to carry the stigma of the super-bombs. But if the American government were to adapt tactical nuclear weapons to a well-conceived strategy of limited war, based upon a policy of graduated deterrence, then it should not be difficult to erase this stigma by publicizing the facts in a sober and candid fashion.

Finally, in considering the role of tactical nuclear weapons in a strategy of limited war, we must reckon with the fact that before long the Communists will also acquire an arsenal of these weapons. Their achievement will probably mark the time when nuclear weapons will be considered conventional. Then we may be compelled to plan our military policies on the assumption that tactical nuclear weapons will be used whether we desire their use or not; and once war is so planned, it is more than likely to be fought that way. If the Soviet arsenal is not yet as diverse and numerous as ours, at least it will soon be sufficient to compel us to plan our training, equipment, and tactics to fight wars in which both sides will use tactical nuclear weapons; for, although there may be circumstances in which it would not be to our advantage to meet conventional forces with nuclear weapons, it is hard to imagine circumstances in which we would not suffer serious disadvantages if the enemy used them and we did not. Indeed, the United States is already far advanced in this process of adaptation.

As the variety and quantity of tactical atomic weapons increase and the process of military adaptation is refined and elaborated, it will become increasingly difficult for troops prepared for nuclear war to fight strictly conventional wars effectively. The military materiel, the size and deployment of troop units, and other measures of preparedness suited to nuclear warfare will be ineffective and probably a positive liability in fighting purely conventional warfare.[9] This very prospect will make a war in which only conventional weapons are used increasingly unlikely, except in the case of insurrections, guerilla activity, and police actions. Therefore, although there will still be sound reasons for withholding the use of nuclear weapons in some military and political situations—preeminently in the case of non-nuclear aggression in the gray areas—we must count upon these weapons becoming an integral part of our military policies and our national strategy.

In summary, tactical nuclear weapons, especially the low-yield battlefield weapons, can play a decisive role in supporting containment by giving the United States an adequate capacity for limited war at a tolerable cost. In anticipation of the Communists' growing tactical nuclear capacity, as well as our own needs, we shall have to plan our training, equipment, and tactics around the use of these weapons. However, in the light of the requirements of a flexible military establishment, we shall also have to retain a capacity to fight non-nuclear wars in areas and under circumstances in which the political and psychological disadvantages of nuclear war, as well as the added risk of total war, outweigh the possible military advantages of employing tactical nuclear weapons. Furthermore, we cannot safely assume that our growing nuclear capacity will enable us to reduce our ground forces; it may actually require an increase in ground forces.

But regardless of the composition of our military establishment, it is essential that American strategists plan the use of tactical nuclear weapons in accordance with a policy of graduated deterrence, based upon the distinction between tactical and strategic targets. Above all, these weapons must be employed within a carefully defined political context of limited objectives, susceptible to the process of diplomatic accommodation.

Limited War in the NATO Area

These appear to be some of the general requirements concerning the ends and means of a strategy of limited war. It remains to be seen how they might apply to specific areas of the world in the light of the diverse military and non-military conditions that American strategy actually encounters.

At the outset it is well to recognize that no strategy, no military program, can provide absolute security against Communist expansion. It is too much to expect that any strategy can successfully contain the Communists everywhere under all conceivable circumstances. The Communist powers have non-military means of expansion available to them, especially in the vulnerable areas of Southeast Asia, which cannot be met by counterforce, and there are undoubtedly points on the Sino-Soviet perimeter which we could not protect against outright military seizure. Therefore, we should not allow an exaggerated commitment to collective security or overdrawn analogies to the Fascist aggression of the thirties to plunge us into despair in the face of occasional reverses of a limited nature. To be sure, we cannot safely tolerate more than a very few such reverses; but, for that matter, the free world is not so vulnerable as to present more than a very few opportunities; nor is it in such desperate straits that our security and prestige require us to rush to the scene of aggression regardless of the location and circumstances. A national strategy requires that statesmen pick and choose the exercise of power according to a scheme of priorities and a calculus of risks. This being the case, we ought to assume a position of firmness, tempered with flexibility, that will enable us to minimize the shock of occasional reverses, and avoid working ourselves into a rigid posture of absolute resistance to aggression, which we cannot support with action.

When one considers the application of a strategy of limited war to specific geographical areas, one must recognize formidable obstacles to the successful conduct of limited war in the NATO area and especially in western Europe. The advanced and integrated economic development, the heavy urban concentrations of population, the profusion of military installations, the tight mutual defense commitments among allies—these features of the area render the geographical restriction of combat and the discrimination between tactical and strategic targets extremely difficult; and in the absence of geographical and target restrictions, the effective limitation of weapons is virtually precluded. Moreover, a war in the NATO area would almost certainly be fought with nuclear weapons, if only because all defense plans are built upon that assumption, in accordance with the NATO Council decision of December, 1954.

However, the most serious obstacle to limited war in the area is the vital immediate importance of the political objectives that would be at stake, combined with the inability of the NATO powers to check Communist aggression effectively on a local basis. The technical difficulty of establishing geographical, weapons, and targets limitations only exacerbates this fundamental obstacle to the operation of reciprocal restraints. Let us suppose that there were a Communist attack in Europe. American security and prestige would be so heavily involved in the defense of Europe, and a Communist seizure would cause such a radical alteration in the cold-war distribution of power, that neither side would be willing to countenance restrictions upon its conduct of the war at the cost of defeat, and both would be driven to assume large risks of total war rather than forfeit their objectives. At the same time, because of their numerical inferiority the NATO ground forces could not hope to contain a Communist attack (except perhaps a small-scale military coup) without using air-nuclear power to strike at targets beyond the battle area. Theoretically, these air strikes might distinguish between tactical and strategic targets; the first order of priority would in any case be airfields and supply lines rather than production facilities. But, considering the importance of the political stakes, it is quite improbable that the Russians would spare the hundreds of air bases outside the immediate battle area. And if NATO retaliation proved effective at all, the Soviet air force would almost certainly strike at the European ports, which would be so vital to NATO operations, even though they understood that this might remove the restrictions upon their own strategic targets; for to spare the ports would be to grant a far disproportionate advantage of mutual self-restraint. In this situation the more effective the measures that one belligerent took, the less the other would feel safe in observing self-imposed limitations, until soon the scale of destruction in Europe would surpass any effective bounds of limitation.

Of course, it is conceivable that the major antagonists, Russia and the United States, might still be spared the brunt of such a war. In that case the western tongue of the Eurasian continent would be comparable to one vast Korean peninsula. However, it is doubtful that our European allies would be willing to see the war confined to the destruction of their homelands while the American Strategic Air Command merely served as a deterrent to attacks upon the United States. In that event, they could be excused for ignoring the American restrictions or for withdrawing from the contest if the Russians offered attractive terms of settlement. They would be even less likely to tolerate one-sided limitations if they possessed nuclear weapons themselves.[10]

The chances of total war resulting from Communist attacks in less vital parts of the NATO area than western Europe—that is, on the Mediterranean or Scandinavian wings—are somewhat less, providing that we can contain such attacks locally. But if we cannot contain them locally, depending upon their scale and location, then we probably cannot afford to surrender even small territorial objectives there without carrying the war beyond the area of aggression. In any case, unless such attacks took the form of guerilla activity or civil war, they would, at the least, result in limited wars of a scale and intensity far surpassing the Korean War.

Under present conditions, then, it is difficult to imagine a limited war in the NATO area, and it is almost equally difficult to imagine a total or nearly total war remaining confined to this area. Nevertheless, the catastrophic consequences of all-out nuclear war compel us to examine every opportunity, however meager, for limiting warfare in any area. Of course, one can argue that this problem is not really so important, since the greater the risk of total war in Europe, the less likely Soviet aggression becomes. But where the consequences of war are so momentous, we cannot discount even the least likely contingency. Moreover, even though that contingency may never occur, the mere anticipation of it can exert a fateful impact upon our diplomatic bargaining power and our political relations with European allies; for unless we can anticipate meeting Soviet aggression with something less than a thermonuclear holocaust we shall hand the Kremlin a powerful instrument of blackmail, which it may wield to great advantage without so much as a threatening word.

As long as we adhere to a military strategy that convinces our allies that any war in the NATO area must inevitably become a total war and, hence, a total disaster for them, it will be extremely difficult to counter a Soviet tactic that holds the silent threat of annihilation in one hand and the tempting prospect of conciliation in the other.

There is another consideration that we must take into account lest we assume that war must necessarily be total in the NATO area. Although we tell ourselves and the world that we will oppose a Communist attack in Europe by massive retaliation upon the Soviet Union, can we be sure that if the event actually occurred, we would find resistance to aggression worth the fearful price of thermonuclear war? Perhaps we would have no choice if the Soviet leaders, in the manner of Hitler, were so rash as to launch a massive assault by Russian forces. But, certainly, this is the least likely form of aggression. Suppose, instead, that a force of East Germans or some other satellite force undertook a swift seizure of some limited point, using only conventional weapons, while announcing its willingness to negotiate a moderate settlement and conveying its determination to keep the action limited unless we should choose to strike at targets outside the area of attack. Would we then prefer to precipitate a war of mass obliteration rather than acquiesce in a limited loss? It is difficult to say; but as time goes on, it seems safe to predict that Americans are likely to become less willing rather than more willing to make the decision that would turn the awful specter of mutual destruction into a reality. Thus whether or not the threat of massive retaliation is ever put to the test, if the United States has no other method of resisting aggression, it runs the risk—even in the most vital strategic area—of incurring a paralysis of decision, which a resourceful adversary will exploit to the utmost.

For these reasons we must earnestly seek some method of applying the strategy of limited war to the NATO area, however improbable it may be that we shall have to act upon it. Otherwise, the best we can do is provide a nuclear capacity to our European allies and concentrate heavily upon measures of air defense, while placing less emphasis on the military aspects and more on the economic and political aspects, in order to mitigate the apprehension of thermonuclear disaster implicit in our present military strategy.

Perhaps the greatest single obstacle (within our physical capacity to remove) to limitation of warfare in the NATO area is our present inability to check a Communist attack locally. If we could check aggression on the ground without expanding the geographical extent of the conflict, we might avoid the necessity of strategic nuclear retaliation. But can we reasonably hope to acquire a capacity for local ground defense in this area?

When we consider the present number of troops that would be available to fight a war in the NATO area, it appears that, from a total of more than a hundred combat-ready divisions, the Soviet Union could at least draw upon the sixty or so Russian divisions stationed in eastern Europe, excluding the sizable satellite forces, whose reliability for offensive purposes is doubtful;[11] whereas the NATO countries have at the most thirty-five divisions available for the defense of western Europe, only a fraction of which are combat-ready and at full strength, and about seventeen nominal divisions (actually more like regimental combat teams) in Greece and Turkey, which can offer little aid outside the southern flank. Even more important than Russia's advantage in mobilized manpower are her huge trained reserves (about 200 divisions), which are a great many times larger than NATO reserves.

At the Lisbon meeting of the North Atlantic Council in February, 1952, military planners set a goal of ninety-six divisions (excluding Greek and Turkish forces) as the minimum amount necessary to defend Europe with conventional forces. It seems unlikely that fewer troops could serve the same purpose with tactical nuclear weapons if the aggressor had these weapons also. Yet since 1952 one European nation after another, pleading domestic economic needs, has drastically scaled down its defense goals; and short of a revival of the immediate threat of Russian invasion, it is unrealistic to expect these nations to increase their military contribution substantially. The involvement of British and French troops in the Middle East threatened to make even the decreased number of divisions contributed to European defense merely nominal. At the same time, the United States obviously has no intention of redressing the discrepancy between the Lisbon goals and actual force levels by expanding its own ground force substantially or allotting more than the present five divisions, among the nineteen scattered around the world, to the European theater.

Ever since the Korean War—more precisely, since September, 1950—the United States has persistently sought a German contribution to NATO, fixed at twelve divisions at Lisbon in 1952, in order to rectify the existing deficiency in ground troops and permit the defense of Europe as far east as possible. But it should be obvious that twelve divisions are not going to make the difference between ineffective and effective local ground defense. Moreover, it is not certain that, if or when the Germans raise these divisions, SHAPE will be able to control them for NATO's purposes. From the German standpoint the integration of these divisions with the NATO forces would erect a prohibitive obstacle to the pre-eminent political objective of national unification, since the Russians will certainly not grant the reunion of East Germany with West Germany under conditions that would be tantamount to the military integration of all Germany into the western alliance.[12] The Germans, at least, are acutely aware of this fact.

For these reasons it is hard to escape the conclusion that, if the United States wants to acquire a capacity for local defense in Europe, it will have to furnish the troops itself. But although this is within the realm of physical possibility, the idea of the United States maintaining a large army in Europe for an indefinite period is out of the question on political and psychological grounds. Therefore, undesirable as the situation may be, the containment of communism in the NATO area must, evidently, continue to depend primarily upon two military factors: (*a*) America's capacity for strategic nuclear retaliation; (*b*) sufficient local ground troops to prevent a small-scale military coup, to compel the troop concentrations and maneuvers that will give advance warning of a larger attack, and to slow down the progress of such an attack so as to enable our nuclear air power to strike back. Given the existence of these two factors and a modicum of economic and political stability within the NATO countries, the defense of Europe must be largely a political problem, centering upon the role of a resurgent Germany, and not excluding the possibility of a general agreement to secure the withdrawal of Russian troops from eastern Europe. For Germany holds the balance of power in Europe, and the way it disposes this power could have far more effect upon the strategy of containment in Europe than any military policies the United States might adopt.

For the protection of the flanks of NATO, where local defense is somewhat more feasible, the creation and maintenance of additional mobile ground troops in a strategic reserve, highly skilled in tactical nuclear warfare, would serve as a useful deterrent and might considerably enhance the opportunities for limiting wars not initiated by a large-scale

Russian assault. Certainly, we should not automatically respond to such flanking incursions as though they were inevitably the prelude to total war. If the aggression can be contained locally, it would be foolish to make it the cause of a general European war. But here, too, the importance of the strategic stakes and the technical difficulties of applying practical target restrictions compel us to place our primary reliance upon a capacity for retaliating against the center of aggression. That being the case, there is more need for mobile troops in other parts of the world, notably the gray areas, where the threat of limited aggression is much greater and strategic retaliation is relatively ineffective.

As for the application of the policy of graduated deterrence to the NATO area, the general policy is still a good one. However, it is probably unwise to announce our adherence to specific reciprocal restraints in advance of a war, since this might only reduce the deterrent effect of our strategic retaliatory power while giving no added assurance that both sides would find it to their advantage to observe such restraints when the chips were down. Even after the nature of an attack becomes known, the establishment of weapons and targets restrictions that all belligerents will find to their advantage to observe will be extremely difficult in the NATO area. Of course, whether we expected the aggressor to observe certain limitations or not, we might announce our adherence to reciprocal target restrictions, designed to spare European ports and centers of production, in order to leave it up to the aggressor to bear the onus of mass obliteration if he chose to violate these restrictions. But in that case the purpose of graduated deterrence would be propagandistic rather than military, and it would probably not be very effective propaganda at that.

Even though it may prove impossible to confine a war within a small segment of the NATO area, it will not necessarily be impossible to prevent a war from extending beyond the area or impossible to save major cities from obliteration within the area.[13] Certainly, both the Soviet Union and the United States would have a compelling interest in avoiding an all-out contest to destroy each other's economic foundations, and neither would profit by the indiscriminate devastation of Europe. But whatever minimum mutual restraints might be applied to a nuclear war extending throughout a large portion of the NATO area, they would not spell the difference between a small-scale war of the Korean variety and a large-scale holocaust of the dimensions of World War II, even if they prevented a holocaust from becoming a complete catastrophe for civilization. Actually, the chief hope of keeping such a war from degenerating into an unmitigated catastrophe lies, not in the field of reciprocal military restraints, but rather in the realm of diplomacy; for where the potentialities of destruction are so immense, the indispensable condition for maintaining a rational relation between war and national policy will be a political settlement that limits the duration of the struggle.

Limited War in the Middle East

In the "underdeveloped" lands of the Middle East the physical possibility of limiting a war in area, weapons, and targets is far more promising than in the highly integrated industrial areas of Europe. But the political context in which a Middle Eastern war involving substantial Communist forces would occur is little more congenial to limitation than in western Europe. Just as the immense immediate value of western Europe to potential belligerents virtually precludes the possibility of a limited war in that vital area, so the almost equal importance of the Middle East —and especially the Near East, from which western Europe gets three-quarters of its oil—makes it hard to conceive of a Middle Eastern war in which substantial Communist forces participated remaining long a local struggle fought by limited means. Certainly the West could not afford to restrict such a war in area, weapons, or targets at the risk of surrendering it to hostile control, if by lifting such self-imposed restrictions it might prevent hostile control. In the pressure of battle the risk of total war that such removal of restrictions would entail might understandably be considered not out of proportion to the value of the objective at stake in the eyes of our Western allies, especially the United Kingdom, which is crucially dependent on Near Eastern oil and enjoys an independent nuclear capacity.

However, the most likely form of war in this area is not, initially, a general Middle Eastern war involving large Communist contingents but rather an indigenous revolution on the Soviet border—say, in Iran or Afghanistan—supported by Soviet economic aid, equipment, and agents or a war between Middle Eastern states, possibly involving Western powers on one side and Soviet economic and material assistance, supplemented by "volunteers," on the other side. In either of these two contingencies it should be feasible for the United States and the Soviet Union to keep the conflict localized and limited by stringently restricting their participation and fully utilizing their diplomatic influence. However, in the case of the second contingency, if we assume that Western powers were directly involved, then even limited and indirect American or Soviet participation would carry grave risks of producing a general Middle Eastern war that would grow into a general total war. Therefore, the effective limitation of such a war would seem to depend largely on a quick termination by negotiated settlement. In such a termination American diplomacy, backed by a capacity for limited as well as total war, could play a central role. Regardless of whether a war involving substantial Communist forces occurs, if we do not have this kind of flexible capacity, we shall run the very serious risk of promoting Russian political and economic penetration in this vital area by failing to dispose our power and acceding to nuclear blackmail because we fear our inability to meet indirect Soviet military intervention without precipitating total war.

In the light of the most probable military contingencies in the Middle East there would seem to be little military advantage to be gained by supporting an alliance like the Baghdad Pact (formed by Pakistan, Iran, Turkey, Iraq, and Great Britain), which the United States sponsored but failed to join. For this defense pact purports to establish a line against direct Soviet invasion, whereas the real deterrent to an invasion, as in western Europe, must be America's capacity for strategic retaliation. (There may be political advantages in supporting the Baghdad Pact, in terms of promoting a particular balance of power in the area; but there are also political disadvantages. So far the Pact seems only to have strengthened the ambitious hand of Egypt and facilitated Soviet penetration.)

Limited War in the Gray Areas

It is in the gray areas, extending along the Sino-Soviet periphery from Iran to Korea, that military and political conditions are most inviting to piecemeal Communist aggressions that we would be unwilling to oppose at the risk of total war. In these areas neither the immediate importance of the political objectives at stake nor the physical difficulty of imposing geographical, weapons, and targets restrictions constitutes such a serious obstacle to the limitation of war as in the NATO area.

The Communist threat in the gray areas, far more than in Europe, arises from internal political, psychological, and economic factors, interacting with external Communist pressure. But the external military threat is connected with the internal non-military threat in such a way that it is quite ambiguous to call one or the other primary. Thus if the inhabitants of a country contiguous to the Communist sphere lack the will and the economic and political stability to resist Communist political penetration, external military defense will probably be ineffective. That is certainly one of the lessons of the war in Indochina. On the other hand, it is difficult for a country to develop the requisite economic and political stability without a minimum level of security from external aggression; and even if a nation exhibits a vigorous determination to resist Communist control, it will be vulnerable if it does not have the military means of defending itself. The Republic of Korea would have passed into the Communist orbit in spite of outside military aid if it had lacked internal strength and cohesion and the will to resist communism. But, actually, although the Republic checked all attempts at infiltration and subversion and displayed a powerful will to defend itself, this did not save it from the North Korean invasion (perhaps it was the very thing that determined this form of aggression), and it would not have prevented the unification of Korea under Communist auspices without American military intervention and the determination of South Korea's own tough troops.

A realistic appraisal of the Communist threat to the gray areas must recognize that the long-run danger springs, in large part, from the Communist attempt to capture an indigenous Asian revolution, which feeds upon a desire for political and economic independence from the West, combined with a yearning for the West's material power. But this long-run political and ideological danger exists concurrently with the short-run military threat. Whatever other methods the Communists may employ to extend their power among the unsettled peoples of Asia, they will not abandon their reliance upon military force. They have amply demonstrated this fact, in different ways, in China, Korea, the Philippines, Malaya, Burma, and Indochina. The Chinese Communists may manage to present themselves in the eyes of Asians as social and economic reformers, concerned with military matters only to the extent of resisting Western imperialism; but they nevertheless give top priority in their planning to the construction of a huge modern army; they cast covetous eyes upon the resources of Southeast Asia as the means of sustaining an ambitious program of internal development; and they regard the contiguous nations of this area, as well as Korea, Formosa, and Tibet, as their legitimate sphere of control.

Allowing for the interdependence of military and non-military factors and the diverse Communist tactics, there are three general requirements of containment in the gray areas:

a) The existence within indigenous regimes of a minimum internal cohesion and stability and a minimum ability to satisfy social and economic demands to prevent Communist ideological and political penetration.

b) The existence of indigenous military establishments capable of combating local insurrection and guerilla activity.

c) The ability of indigenous troops, acting as nuclei of resistance in conjunction with American forces and American military and economic assistance, to defeat larger military incursions on a local basis.

A study of the role of military power cannot deal with the first requirement, which would reach into the obscure and complex subject of the economic, political, cultural, and ideological consequences of economic and technical assistance. Probably it is in this realm of the non-military prerequisites for effective military defense that the most difficult and challenging problems of American national strategy lie, although it is the more easily visualized military problem that seems to have absorbed most of American attention and energy. If we can provide the necessary margin of economic and technical assistance and establish the proper political and psychological context in order to help the nations of the gray areas defend themselves against internal and external enemies, then we may find that the purely military task of containment is less formidable than we have imagined.

Given a modicum of internal cohesion, an indigenous policing capability should be within the power of most of the nations of the gray areas, with little outside aid. The task of subduing guerilla activity may be long and trying; but the success of the anti-guerilla campaigns in Burma, the Philippines, Malaya, and, under somewhat different circumstances, Greece, proves that the Communists can be beaten at this game. The more difficult military problem confronting a strategy of limited war is the problem of checking larger attacks, directly or indirectly supported by China or Russia, that are beyond the power of indigenous forces to contain. Here, again, we must judge the feasibility of military plans in terms of the coincidence of the requirements of limitation with the requirements of military effectiveness.

As we have already observed, the localization of wars in the gray areas is technically feasible; and successful local defense presents no

insuperable military obstacles, considering the actual physical characteristics of the area, its internal political alignments, its geographical position with respect to the sea, and our superior mobility, firepower, and
logistical situation. Just as the relatively undeveloped and unintegrated
state of the economy of this region facilitates area restriction, so it
facilitates the discrimination between tactical and strategic targets and
a working distinction between tactical nuclear weapons and super-
bombs. Although we must be prepared to initiate the use of tactical
nuclear weapons against conventional aggression, one can envision situations in which it will be wise and feasible to accept mutual exclusion of
all nuclear weapons, either because such weapons will be ineffective or
because the side with atomic superiority—presumably the United States
for at least the next five years—is more vulnerable to them.

Therefore, in order to facilitate a strategy of limited war, as well as
to minimize the political and psychological disadvantages of our military
policies, it may be wise to announce our adherence to a policy of graduated deterrence in the gray areas. The advantages to be gained from such
a course outweigh the possible disadvantage of reducing the deterrent
value of our capacity for strategic retaliation, since this capacity is ineffective anyway in deterring limited aggressions in the gray areas.

However, we still have not answered all the controversial questions
raised by our self-imposed limitations in the Korean War. In the event of
a Communist Chinese or Chinese-supported aggression, should we strike
at tactical targets within China? The correct answer is impossible to determine in advance of the actual situation; the most we can do is make
ourselves aware of the considerations that should enter into a decision
when the situation arises. For where it is not only feasible but essential to
preserve a wide range of responses to Communist aggression, it would be
unwise to reduce our strategic flexibility by determining our response in
advance, when this would contribute little or nothing to deterrence. As in
the case of the Korean War, our response should depend upon an accurate estimate and judicious balancing of at least the following factors:
the importance of the objective at stake and of the political consequences
of defeat; the military efficacy of the contemplated measure; the military
consequences of possible Chinese counter-retaliation; the risk of Russian
intervention, both direct and indirect; and the effect upon our relations
with allied and uncommitted nations. In estimating these factors and
weighing them against one another, we need not assume that the same

kind of restrictions that existed in the Korean War must be applied to other parts of the gray areas or even to Korea itself. However, it remains true that in proportion as we can avoid the resort to the kind of measures that we rejected in the Korean War, we shall minimize the risk of warfare expanding beyond the bounds of political control. To minimize this risk, the requirements of limitation must coincide with the requirements of military effectiveness, for only insofar as we can resist aggression effectively on a strictly local basis can we avoid extending our military operations to targets outside the area, except at the price of military defeat.

The prospect of reconciling the limitation of military operations with the requirements of military success is much brighter in the gray areas than in the NATO area. Yet here, too, we must take account of the possibility that, rather than acquiesce in the loss of some position, we shall be driven to take measures that may lead to total war; and we face the likelihood that, whether or not things come to a showdown, our political position will suffer merely from having to anticipate choosing between total war and acquiescence. As in the NATO area and the Middle East, the best protection against this contingency is a capacity to contain aggression locally without resorting to tactical and strategic air strikes beyond the combat area; and here, too, this capacity depends, preeminently, upon adequate ground troops. In 1956 America's ground strength was almost as inadequate for local defense in the gray areas as in the NATO area. On the other hand, it was considerably more feasible to remedy the former deficiency than the latter.

There could be little doubt of the inadequacy of America's capacity for local ground defense in the gray areas six years after the Korean War began. Except in Korea and Formosa there were no ready combat troops capable of checking any aggression larger than a police action, and there was no prospect that indigenous forces would obtain any such capacity.[14] Yet this weakness was not inevitable. In the gray areas America's superior mobility, training, equipment, and firepower most readily compensate for numerical deficiency in manpower. Even if Chinese manpower were really "inexhaustible," as we commonly assume, China's supply of trained and equipped manpower and its ability to sustain them in combat are certainly limited, as the latter stages of the Korean War clearly demonstrated. If we anticipate a "war of attrition," that would be precisely the kind of war in which our superior production and economic base would give us the greatest advantage. As one writer has observed, "A war of attrition is the one war China could not win."[15]

Exactly how many divisions of ground troops, supported by how many wings of tactical aircraft and how many combat and transport ships, would be needed to put teeth into containment in the gray areas is obviously a highly technical question that the layman is in no position to answer. But recognizing, as our public spokesmen have often observed, that there is no such thing as absolute security anyway, one can infer from the statements of the military experts that an expansion of our combat-ready ground forces by ten divisions would be a very useful, perhaps indispensable, contribution to a flexible military capacity.[16] These troops ought to be a truly mobile reserve capable of coming to the aid of indigenous forces in "brushfire" wars before the aggressor could consolidate his gains. Furthermore, they ought to be an active reserve stationed in key areas near the Communist perimeter, not in a central reserve inside the United States. The United States performed a remarkable feat in transporting troops to Korea, but it took two weeks to bring the first full division from Japan to the battlefield and more than a month for divisions of the central reserve in the United States to arrive; and Korea was relatively accessible.

The military problem of defending the gray areas cannot properly be considered apart from the political problem of securing the co-operation of the inhabitants in defending themselves, but we cannot wait for the ideal political arrangements to materialize before we fulfil the military prerequisites essential for our immediate security. The mere presence of mobile American ground forces near the Sino-Soviet periphery would be a salutary deterrent; and, if clearly associated with a defensive strategy of limited ends and means, it would be an assurance to the peripheral nations of our intention to co-operate with them in their self-defense rather than to use them as an instrument of total war.

However, a tightly organized military alliance, like NATO, does not seem desirable, even if it were possible. We have already suggested that such an alliance would tend to increase the difficulties of limiting a war. But a more serious objection is that the attempt to form it would create serious political disadvantages without producing any compensating military advantages. The gray-area nations have neither the economic capacity nor the political stability to raise military forces beyond what they need for internal security. In addition to this military weakness, they lack at present the political will to form an alliance for containment, since they have neither the requisite sense of a community of interests nor a sufficient awareness of the external threat of Communist power. The nations in southern Asia that could be persuaded to join such an alliance would do so less from a common conception of the threat of Communist power than from a desire to promote their special interests within the area, which would not necessarily correspond with our own. Consequently, their membership, instead of consolidating a community of interests, would be more likely to exacerbate national antagonisms, just as our military alliance with Pakistan seems to have intensified the conflict between Pakistan and India, and between the United States and India as well.

Added to these obstacles to collective defense, and shaping the whole pattern of our relations with Asia, is the deep-rooted suspicion of Western intentions, which is seemingly confirmed in Asian eyes by any emphasis on military schemes, as opposed to economic and technical assistance. And closely associated with this subjective element is the fact that most of these nations find compelling reasons of national self-interest, however short-sighted they may seem to us, for avoiding rigid alignments with either of the antagonists of the cold war.

Where such inhospitable motives as these govern the policies of nations, we could only antagonize the uncommitted governments of Asia by pressing them to enter into a military alliance that would so clearly contravene their conception of national interest. In other parts of the world where the sense of the external threat is more keen and the distrust of the West is less compelling, military alliances can serve a useful purpose. But in southern Asia the best way to create a political atmosphere conducive to local defense may really be to place our diplomacy in accord with neutralism rather than in opposition to it. Then, if in the course of their release from a preoccupation with Western "colonialism" and their growth to political maturity in the world of power politics, these governments, which have so recently gained their independence, come to perceive a common security interest, they may more readily enter into defense arrangements on their own initiative than if we had prematurely intruded our special conception of their interests upon them. In any case, as long as the Communists present themselves as the champions of neutralism, we shall do better to encourage these nations to exhibit a strong, independent position, for what deterrent value it may have, than to seek them as partners in the cold war and so incur the onus of "imperialism" while permitting the real imperialists to pose as their protectors.

The Economic Limits of National Strategy

Implicit in this outline of American strategy is the assumption that such a strategy is within our economic resources and what one might call our psychological resources or our national will. The relationship between the two is closer than we realize. Every strategy makes a claim on the human and material resources of a nation, a claim that must be met by economic expenditures. These expenditures, in turn, demand a share of the individual citizen's means of livelihood, more immediately in the form of taxes but ultimately in terms of real goods he is able to consume with the money he earns and the great variety of governmental services he has come to expect. At a time when foreign-policy and defense expenditures comprise about 70 per cent of the national budget, the individual share is consequential. Its psychological significance lies in the fact that, aside from military service, economic sacrifice may be the only medium through which the average citizen actually experiences the impact of national strategy, which is otherwise something remote and nebulous at best. Only through his individual economic sacrifice may the citizen in time of cold war be directly cognizant of a relationship between foreign commitments and national resources.

One may doubt that the hypothetical average taxpayer is as acutely conscious of the direct connection between foreign policy and his personal livelihood as his elected representatives, who control the nation' purse strings, claim in his behalf. But from the standpoint of what is acceptable and unacceptable in national strategy the important point is that the representatives act as though he were—and so, in various degrees, does the whole hierarchy of elective and appointive officials extending down from the President at the apex. In a market-oriented society, openly dedicated to increasing the individual's material welfare and his enjoyment of private pursuits, the men who are charged with the responsibility of translating strategy into monetary terms must always be somewhat apologetic for expenditures designed to meet remote and uncertain contingencies abroad; and they can never forget the great variety of domestic benefits competing with defense for a share of the national budget. The market mechanism, after all, is a method of meeting by economic means certain goals established by society. However, since it is by its very nature an impersonal arbiter of selfish, individual pursuits, the subordination of individual pursuits to collective social goals for the sake of national security requires, in the long run, an alteration of the individual consumer's value preferences. No one likes to ask the public for such an alteration; it is easier to act as though the collective goals and the individual goals were perfectly compatible.

This means that the nation's ability to sustain a defense program is not only a matter of the gross national product, per capita income, and the other objective criteria of economic strength but, just as much, a reflection of what the citizenry, its political representatives, and government officials are willing to sacrifice in terms of competing values for the sake of a particular national strategy. Thus, ultimately, America's strategic economic potential is determined, in some inexact fashion, by a diffuse process of weighing the security value of particular military, economic, and political policies against the individual, group, and national benefits that have to be sacrificed in order to support them. If the people and their leaders do not perceive the need of a particular strategic program or are unwilling to make the requisite sacrifice to support it, then that program is economically unfeasible even though the nation may have the productivity, the income, and the financial structure to support a program three times as expensive. But, clearly, at this point economics merges with national attitudes, political processes, and a host of intangibles that are beyond quantitative measurement.

In terms of the objective criteria of national defense potential there can be no doubt that the United States is capable of supporting the strategy of limited war outlined here, even though it would be expensive by current "peacetime" standards. The expansion of the ground forces, the acquisition of a large and diversified arsenal of low-yield atomic weapons, the development of new ground and airborne equipment for mobile tactical operations, and, at the same time, the support of an adequate system of conventional weapons and the maintenance of our capacity for strategic retaliation and total war—a military program like this could not be sustained without a substantial increase in defense expenditures. Such expenditures might amount to $60 billion, as compared to average annual defense expenditures of $35 billion (excluding foreign aid) since the Korean War. Yet there is every reason to believe that with an annual gross national product of over $400 billion and an annual accretion of about 3.5 per cent—a product three times larger than Russia's and a large multiple of any other nation's on either an absolute or per capita basis—the United States could easily maintain such a program without dislocating the economy, overburdening the taxpayer, or imposing comprehensive controls of materials, prices, and wages.[17]

Of course, when examining the nation's economic capacity for a strategy of limited war we must recognize that the objective economic limits of a national security program differ fundamentally in a protracted period of cold-and-limited war from the limits that apply to a transitory crisis of total war. During a total war a nation mobilizes for the single purpose of survival in a conflict of arms; all normal economic goals— consumer welfare, expansion of productive capacity, raising the standard of living—are subordinated to the overriding objective of total mobilization. In such a period of crisis the economic limit to the defense effort is set by the resources that can be used effectively for the conduct of the war. However, in a period of cold-and-limited war a nation undertakes partial mobilization over an indefinite period of time in order to prepare for the contingency of war; but at the same time it tries to maintain the vitality of all sectors of the economy, not just the defense industries, by satisfying consumer demands, providing incentives for increasing labor productivity and business expansion, and promoting a healthy world economy. The practical economic limit to this kind of defense effort is the indefinable point at which it diverts so much resources from investment and consumption, requires such levels of taxation, imposes such drastic controls, or results in such disruptive inflation as to weaken the social and economic fabric of society over a prolonged period.

In terms of the economic limit of partial mobilization the truism that a strong defense depends upon a "sound domestic economy" has some practical implications, but the levels of defense expenditures compatible with a sound domestic economy far exceed the limits that have commonly excited apprehensions of "bankruptcy." We are currently supporting a level of expenditure several times as large as the one before the Korean War, which, as the object of an "economy" drive, was said to be the limit that the nation could bear without courting bankruptcy. During the Korean War itself the annual rate of purchases of goods and services under the national security programs increased $32 billion in three years. Nevertheless, the economy was strengthened, not weakened, during the defense buildup. Public and private expenditures for all purposes continued to mount; per capita consumption rose; the increase in total production almost doubled the increase in the defense program; while tax increases stabilized prices and obviated the necessity for comprehensive controls.

A notable analysis of the capacity of the American economy to support major national security programs, published by the National Planning Association in October, 1953, concluded that an expansion of total defense spending from the existing $52 billion to $65 billion by 1956 would neither interfere with a continuing increase of investments and per capita consumption nor necessitate higher levels of taxation.[18] The association found that only a defense program approaching an upper limit of an annual $75 billion within the next three years would require additional taxes or controls on public and private spending, but even this level of expenditure would still permit increases in investments and the standard of living, compatible with a strong economy. Within this limit, the study concluded, "We believe that the decision as to the size of the defense program, under conditions short of full mobilization or major war, should be made on the basis of clear military and political strategic needs in the light of the international situation; and not on the basis of assumed economic limits that are not present."[19]

Unless the American government has grossly underestimated this nation's objective economic capacity, one must conclude that it has consistently determined the economic limits of defense expenditure by domestic political criteria and then tried to devise defense programs that would give as much security as possible within arbitrary budget ceilings. Only during the crisis of the Korean War did it act in accordance with the advice of the National Planning Association by determining the size of the defense program "on the basis of clear military and political strategic needs in the light of the international situation" rather than "on the basis of assumed economic limits." The economic limits of defense programs that government leaders have claimed the United States is incapable of exceeding have not been the ones the nation *could* support but rather the ones they believed the nation *would* support, or at least not vigorously oppose.

This in itself should not surprise us. Every democratic government must accommodate its strategic program to the levels of expenditure it thinks the nation, especially its legislature, will accept, since no program will be feasible unless the people and their political representatives believe that its benefits in terms of national security are worth the personal sacrifices it entails. However, this process of accommodation ought to work both ways, so that the government not only makes concessions to public opinion but also strives to educate the public to make concessions to the realities. The process becomes dangerous only when the government confuses the nation's *objective* defense potential and its *objective* security needs with the *subjective* limit of expenditures the nation will tolerate and compounds the error by estimating this subjective limit in terms of national attitudes formed on the basis of inadequate knowledge about the realities. For by this circuitous process the government is likely to fix the economic limits of strategy on the basis of popular assumptions and expectations concerning national security, which the government itself has created by presenting defense needs purely in terms of what it thinks is palatable instead of what is objectively required. Thus "economy" may become the excuse for a lack of political courage, which dangerously obscures the real economic potentialities and limits of national strategy.

The disposition to judge the economic limits of national strategy in terms of the lowest common denominator of expenditures believed to be palatable to the public is bound to be particularly pronounced when that strategy demands an indefinite period of sacrifice and promises no psychological compensation in terms of the moral and emotional satisfactions Americans have traditionally sought from their active intervention in the struggle for power. Clearly, the strategy outlined in this chapter is of this nature. To examine the economic requirements of a strategy of limited war objectively and to announce them candidly would entail a direct recognition of some disturbing realities and a direct confutation of some comforting popular illusions about the adequacy of American strategy and the prevailing military policies. It would mean frankly acknowledging the government's adherence to a conception of containment and limited war which political leaders have persistently sought to escape by taking refuge in generalities more compatible with America's conception of its national mission in the world. Thus it is apparent that at the bottom of the problem of economic capacity, like all other aspects of American strategy, there is a fundamental question concerning America's psychological capacity to adapt its thoughts and actions to the very idea of limited war.

The Challenge to American Opinion

This study began with the recognition that an American strategy capable of meeting the threat of limited war must depend, ultimately, upon a transformation of the traditional American approach to war and to the relation between force and policy. We have come full circle. The fundamental question concerning the ability of this nation to sustain such a transformation remains unanswered.

It is only too evident that a strategy of containment by limited war lacks the moral and emotional appeal that Americans have been accustomed to expect of foreign policy. Even if the strategy succeeds in attaining its objectives, it does not promise much more than a stalemate. One must wonder if a proud and aggressively idealistic nation can find within the somber prospect of indefinite containment sufficient incentives for enduring the frustrations and sacrifices of a protracted period of cold-and-limited war. In the trying process of harnessing a natural exuberance and moral enthusiasm to prosaic purposes, in the unending tedium of adjusting national power and will to the shifting demands of a strategy of limited objectives, might the nation not even lose the vitality that has made America great and creative? And one must wonder if any democratic people today can be expected to sacrifice life and happiness, without ever exerting the full military strength of which it is capable, in order to preserve a balance of power in remote portions of the globe. A smal professional army, a colonial garrison, could be expected to perform this chore; but when a whole nation is materially and emotionally involved in foreign affairs, will it permit its sons to die for the sake of holding some secondary position on the rimlands of Asia? Does not the very conception of a strategy that would require the United States to exert force here or there and to withhold force in another instance, to retreat in some circumstances and acquiesce in others, all the while carrying on a delicate and circumspect diplomacy with allies, neutrals, and Communist nations in order to manipulate the configurations of power—does not this conception imply a flexibility of tactics and a dissociation of foreign policy from ordinary moral and emotional considerations that is beyond the capacity of any democratic nation to sustain?

There are no unconditional answers to such questions. So much would depend upon political leadership, even if the nation at large were to exhibit all the requisite qualities of character and understanding. Certainly, if the authorities responsible for the conduct of American strategy take the position that Communist power can be opposed merely by the weight of world opinion, the collective will of the United Nations, and the threat of massive nuclear retaliation, if they take the position that the United States suffers a hopeless disadvantage in trying to contain Communist advances by local defense, then the nation as a whole will not of its own accord insist upon making a concerted effort to meet the challenge of limited aggression in peripheral areas. If the American government approaches the task of countering the threat of Communist expansion as though containment were indecent, and limited ends and means a subject for apology, then the American people cannot be expected to accept the sacrifices and frustrations of a strategy of limited war with good grace or resolution. And if they should actually become involved in limited war, they will not then be disposed to tolerate the galling but indispensable restraints for keeping military means commensurate with political ends.

But what if the government should explain the existing strategic alternatives candidly, with neither embellishment nor apology? What if the responsible leaders should present the prospects of containment as neither more nor less distasteful and perplexing than they really are? And what if they should then appeal to the nation to support a program, well within its resources, which would prepare the United States, for once in its history, to meet military crises before they occur and so enhance the possibility that they will not occur? Would the nation then refuse to listen? Would it lapse into a morbid paralysis of fear? Would it rise up in anger and throw the scoundrels out of office? Or might it not surprise the skeptics by exhibiting the very qualities of common sense and maturity to which its leaders had appealed?

Perhaps the prevailing popular assumptions and predispositions concerning military power and policy are so antithetical to the requirements of a strategy of limited war as to be beyond the power of public explanation and persuasion to alter. This may be true, but in the absence of explanation and persuasion how can one know? The prevailing state of opinion does not excuse the responsible authorities from spelling out the concrete alternatives so that the "public" can make up its own mind about what is acceptable and unacceptable. After all, the "public" is only a convenient abstraction of an extremely complex and diversified collectivity. "Public opinion" is not a monolithic entity with concise and immutable views on foreign policy. It is a heterogeneous mass of fluctuating opinions and predispositions, partial information and misinformation, together with a large measure of ignorance and apathy, filtered through a vast variety of institutions, pressure groups, and other media of expression. If it is possible at all to determine what constitutes public approval or rejection of foreign policy, one cannot assume that approval or rejection is a predestined and unalterable verdict; for opinion is a mutable and malleable thing, arranged into an endless succession of kaleidoscopic patterns under the impact of events and the weight of political leadership, acting upon each other.

Elective officers are understandably reluctant to challenge prevailing assumptions and predispositions. They prefer to play safe by appealing to known opinions and prejudices rather than to incur the risks of hazarding new thoughts on the basis of a conjectural public response. But might it not be that the unprecedented events of the last decade have dulled the luster of the old clichés and already prepared a receptive audience for a candid education in the realities of limited war, even while our political leaders have been vainly struggling to reconcile new events with outmoded images of the past? If this has happened, then great rewards of statesmanship await the men who are venturesome enough to act upon the fact.

Perhaps it is unrealistic to expect the American people to accept new international positions so contrary to their basic predispositions until catastrophes like the fall of France or the bombing of Pearl Harbor galvanize them to action. There is much to substantiate this view in the history of our foreign policy. Perhaps, in the absence of such catastrophes, the people must be artfully cajoled into undertaking new courses of action by indirection—by disguising new imperatives in terms of traditional principles. On the other hand, it may be that candor—where candor expresses the realities—is in these times a more effective prod to public opinion than the rhetorical generalities upon which we have largely relied until now. The continual efforts of public officials to dramatize national strategy in bold and unambiguous terms seem to spring, in part, from an assumption that the American public is so spoiled and immature that it will not support the imperatives of cold-and-limited war on modest and prosaic grounds. Yet the real case may be just the opposite.

Admittedly, this supposition rests largely upon intuition, because it depends upon an interpretation of something as nebulous as the American mood. The most that one can hope for is that intuition will be informed by a sound perception of the sources of American conduct, as revealed in the record of the national response to a changing international environment. The response of the last two decades is a remarkable record of pragmatic adaptation to novel and unpalatable circumstances. After all, it was the public grasp of the hard choice of evils imposed by the threat to American security and not any extravagant expectations of untrammeled initiative or national glory that produced the momentous revolution in the American outlook from isolation to intervention in the short span of a troubled decade of Fascist aggression. And what transformations have been wrought in the few years since the cold war set in! Surveying the evolution of the American outlook from the entrance into World War II through the latest developments of the cold war, one finds it hard to believe that the nation could have adjusted its international perspective with such equanimity if the public mood had not been one of self-restraint and moderation and a sober acceptance of what is necessary, rather than a mood of congenital knight-errantry or spineless rejection of personal sacrifice and national responsibility.

Projecting these speculations to the present, one suspects that the American people sense that the current time of troubles is too serious and too complicated to be reduced to facile slogans, empty platitudes, and grandiloquent pronouncements. They are bewildered; but they are not, fundamentally, either rash or complacent. They want the facts; they can do without the ornamentation. For Americans have grown suspicious of the rhetoric by which they have traditionally rationalized their policies to themselves and to the rest of the world. They have grown suspicious and a bit weary because they sense its incongruity and irrelevance under existing circumstances. One suspects that by intensifying the conflict between wish and fact this rhetoric only prolongs the fundamental ambivalence that has characterized America's conduct of the cold war. If we could quietly abandon the pretense that the policies we are compelled to pursue are a perfect manifestation of America's traditional approach to the outside world, the task of adjusting to unprecedented circumstances might be a good deal easier than it will be if we are continually conjured to envision ourselves as crusaders.

If these assumptions about the American mood and character are correct, then it is not improbable that this nation would accept far greater sacrifices of men and money for limited ends than its leaders have dared to ask of it—if they would only ask in terms of feasible concrete political objectives. Moreover, even on the narrowest political grounds there is something to be said for such moderation. The irresponsibility of a policy which purports to achieve more than it can actually achieve may well turn into a political boomerang in the long run, for the American people are not slow to compare promise with performance. They are no longer children in the world; in the long run, they will resent being treated like children. At least an adult approach is worth trying and one that has been tried too seldom.

It is true that a strategy of limited ends and means will not satisfy a yearning for the millennium, but the American people have long since ceased to expect the millennium. They know from experience that great expectations in international politics are more often than not great illusions. However, they need not on this account lose the dynamism that springs from a faith in ultimate aspirations. They need not abandon their traditional moral enthusiasm just because it has been freed from utopian expectations. For at this stage of the game of world politics they should be perfectly capable of understanding that great goals are reached only by a series of small steps; that the limited objectives of national strategy embrace only the necessary conditions of national security and not the larger aspirations of humanity, which, so far as the cold war is concerned, will remain in the province of a prolonged political and ideological competition with the Communist system. The great moral achievements remain where they have always been, in the realm of the cultural, political, and social conditions of existence, not in the realm of force and coercion. And surely in the present period of dramatic change there are plenty of exhilarating tasks in this realm to satisfy the most ardent practical moralists.

Moreover, even the military tasks of this period of cold-and-limited war are not devoid of moral challenge. It is sheer bellicosity to regard the pursuit of total destruction in the name of universal principles as being on a higher moral plane than the deliberate restraint and control of force for moderate political ends. It is a peculiarly irresponsible form of self-righteousness to regard general renunciation of force as more virtuous than the planned disposition of military power as a rational instrument of policy. Intelligent morality is superior to capricious moralism. If intelligence demands the steady, scrupulous discipline of military force, then it is more creditable to endure the sacrifices and frustrations of limited war and preparation for limited war than to reject them merely for the sake of gratifying superficially moral instincts. This kind of abdication of nerve and reason amounts to an admission that the United States and its allies lack the material and spiritual resources to better the Communist powers in a protracted struggle; but every exercise of foresight and restraint that gives rational direction to military power affirms faith in the proposition that time can be made to work for the side of freedom.

Surely, a sound strategy of limited war would impose novel and severe demands upon American patience, wisdom, and maturity. All the buoyant sentiments and aspirations that have traditionally sustained America's active intervention in the world arena would have to be subordinated to the discipline of responsible power politics. Yet the acceptance of this discipline would constitute a kind of practical idealism, even a kind of heroism, surpassing any moral heights this nation attained when the responsibilities of power were less pressing.

NOTES

NOTES TO CHAPTER ONE

1. I have grappled with this broader problem in *Ideals and Self-interest in America's Foreign Relations* (Chicago: University of Chicago Press, 1953). See especially the Introduction.

2. Karl von Clausewitz, *On War*, trans. O. J. Matthijs Jolles (Washington, D.C.: Combat Forces Press, 1953), p. 596.

3. *Ibid.*, p. 16.

NOTES TO CHAPTER TWO

1. Alexis de Tocqueville, *Democracy in America*, trans. Bradley (New York: Vintage Books, 1954), II, 292–93.

2. Ernest R. May, "The Development of Political-Military Consultation in the United States," *Political Science Quarterly*, LXX (June, 1955), 161–80.

3. Quoted in William T. Stone, "The National Defense Policy of the United States," *Foreign Policy Reports*, VIII (August 31, 1932), 151.

4. George F. Kennan, *American Diplomacy, 1900–1950* (Chicago: University of Chicago Press, 1951), pp. 65–66, 84.

5. Hearings before the Joint Senate Committee on Armed Services and Committee on Foreign Relations, *Military Situation in the Far East* (82d Cong., 1st sess.), Part I, p. 145; cf. pp. 223–24, 302.

6. *Ibid.*, pp. 39–40.

7. "The Rivalry of Nations," *Atlantic Monthly*, CLXXI (February, 1948), 19.

8. The Declaration on Liberated Peoples, part of the Yalta settlement, applied the principles of democratic self-determination to the peoples of Central Europe, who were liberated from German occupation. The image of diplomacy transcending power politics gleams through President Roosevelt's report upon the Yalta settlement shortly after his return: "The Crimean Conference was a successful effort by the three leading nations to find a common ground for peace. It spells the end of the system of unilateral action and exclusive alliances and spheres of influence and balances of power and all the other expedients which have been tried for centuries—and have failed. We propose to substitute for all these a universal organization in which all peace-loving nations will finally have a chance to join" (Address on March 1, 1945, *Department of State Bulletin*, XII [March 4, 1945], 361).

9. A good explicit expression of assumptions which are ordinarily only implicit in the American distrust of diplomacy appears in C. Hartley Grattan's book *The Deadly Parallel*, which was written in the atmosphere of disillusionment following World War I: "Diplomacy is one of the black arts. Its practitioners are

always a select minority, even of the governmental bureaucracy. Out of the mumbo-jumbo of a highly formal and specialized vocabulary, they snatch at advantages for the nation they represent. The line between victory and defeat is so narrow—so dependent upon interpretation of ambiguous statements—that it flickers before the eyes of the uninitiated to their utter bewilderment. The language employed is so specialized that the possibility of saying one thing and meaning another is always present. Vast consequences flow from the order of 'weasel' words in a sentence; the lives and fortunes of men are juggled within subordinate clauses. The influence of diplomacy on their destiny is something ordinary men are quite unable to control. Its results are a fatality like weather" (Grattan, *The Deadly Parallel* [New York: Stackpole Sons, 1939], p. 74).

NOTES TO CHAPTER THREE

1. Cited by Timothy A. Taracouzio, *War and Peace in Soviet Diplomacy* (New York: Macmillan Co., 1940), pp. 25–26.

2. V. I. Lenin, *Selected Works* (New York: International Publishers, 1936–38), VIII, 33.

3. Cited by Taracouzio, *op. cit.*, p. 26.

4. *New York Times*, February 15, 1956, p. 10.

5. Cited in Raymond L. Garthoff, *Soviet Military Doctrine* (Glencoe, Illinois: Free Press, 1953), p. 38.

6. Theoretically, the Russian national interest is inseparable from, and superior to, the national interest of any other Communist state. In the case of Communist China there is, apparently, a close accommodation of interests rather than a subordination of Chinese to Russian interests. However, the national interest, in some form, remains the practical criterion of the justness or unjustness of a war; and Mao Tse-tung has adopted Stalin's ideological rationalization of this criterion: "There are only two kinds of wars in history, just and unjust. We support just wars and oppose unjust wars. All counter-revolutionary wars are unjust, all revolutionary wars are just. . . . A war which will be waged by the overwhelming majority of mankind and of the Chinese people will undoubtedly be a just war . . . and will form a bridge leading world history into a new era" (Mao Tse-tung, *Selected Works of Mao Tse-tung* [London: Lawrence and Wishart, 1954], I, 179). See also *ibid.*, II, 199.

7. Lenin, *Selected Works*, XX, 104.

8. Kennan, "The Sources of Soviet Conduct," *American Diplomacy, 1900–1950* (Chicago: University of Chicago Press, 1951), p. 118. It should be noted that Kennan entered an important qualification to this interpretation a paragraph later: "While the Kremlin is basically flexible in its reaction to political realities, it is by no means unamenable to considerations of prestige. Like almost any other government, it can be placed by tactless and threatening gestures in a position where it cannot afford to yield even though this might be dictated by its sense of realism."

9. Garthoff discusses the influence of Clausewitz on Communist leaders in *Soviet Military Doctrine*, pp. 53–56.

10. Stalin's letter was published in February, 1947, in the magazine *Bolshevik*. It is reproduced in Byron Dexter, "Clausewitz and Soviet Strategy," *Foreign Affairs*, XXIX (October, 1950), 44–45.

11. This work appears in the *Selected Works of Mao Tse-tung*, II, 157–243.

12. *Ibid.*, pp. 202, 203.

13. *Ibid.*, pp. 191–92, 241.

NOTES TO CHAPTER FOUR

1. Cited in Hoffman Nickerson, *The Armed Horde, 1793–1939* (New York: Putnam's, 1940), p. 45.

2. De Saxe, *Reveries on the Art of War*, trans. T. R. Phillips (Harrisburg, Pa.: Military Service Publishing Company, 1944), p. 121.

3. According to Hans Speier, expenditures for military purposes amounted to more than two-thirds of the total budget in France, Russia, and England (*Social Order and the Risks of War* [New York: George W. Stewart, 1952], p. 241).

4. Johannes Janssen, *History of the German People at the Close of the Middle Ages*, trans. A. M. Christie (London: Kegan Paul, Trench, Trubner, and Co., 1900), III, 100.

5. Contemporary statistics indicated that as much as three-quarters of the population of the Germanies died, but modern historians believe that these statistics are exaggerated. C. V. Wedgwood estimates that losses were about one-third of the total population (Wedgwood, *The Thirty Years' War* [New Haven: Yale University Press, 1939], p. 516). In chap. xii Wedgwood examines the impact of the war on Germany in the light of modern scholarship and concludes that social dislocation and disintegration proved more devastating than immediate material and economic damage.

6. Guy Stanton Ford, *Stein and the Era of Reform in Prussia, 1807–1815* (Princeton: Princeton University Press, 1922), pp. 122–23.

7. Freiherr vom Stein, *Staatsschriften und politische Briefe*, ed. Friedrich Thimme (Leipzig, 1921), p. 57, cited in Gordon A. Craig, *The Politics of the Prussian Army, 1640–1945* (London: Oxford University Press, 1955), p. 47.

8. Otto von Bismarck, *Bismarck, the Man and the Statesman*, trans. A. J. Butler (New York: Harper's, 1898), II, 42–43.

9. Speech delivered in the House of Commons in February, 1871 (*Hansard's Parliamentary Debates* [Third Series], CCIV, 81–82).

10. Foch, *The Principles of War*, trans. J. de Morinni (New York: H. K. Fly, 1918), p. 27.

11. *De la Conduite de la Guerre* (4th ed.; Paris: Berger Levrault, 1918), p. 1, cited in Hoffman Nickerson, *op. cit.*, p. 207.

12. *The Principles of War*, p. 31.

13. *The Works of Lord Bolingbroke* (Philadelphia: Carey and Hart, 1841), II, 291.

14. Gibbon, *The Decline and Fall of the Roman Empire* (New York: Modern Library, 1932), II, chap. xxxviii, 94.

NOTES TO CHAPTER FIVE

1. Murray, "A Victorian Looks Back on Twenty-five Years," *The Listener*, November 13, 1947, p. 839.

2. Churchill, *The World Crisis* (New York: Scribner's, 1923), I, 199.

3. Sidney B. Fay, *The Origins of the World War* (2d ed.; New York: Macmillan, 1947), II, 548.

4. Churchill, *op. cit.*, II, 1.

5. See Raymond Aron's discussion of the material, as compared to the non-material, impact of the two world wars in chap. iv of *The Century of Total War* (New York: Doubleday, 1954).

6. Earle (ed.), *Makers of Modern Strategy* (Princeton: Princeton University Press, 1943), p. xi.

7. Hajo Holborn, *The Political Collapse of Europe* (New York: Alfred A. Knopf, 1951), p. 156.

8. John W. Wheeler-Bennett, *The Nemesis of Power* (New York: Macmillan, 1953).

9. In this scheme Russia was assigned 90 per cent "preponderance" in Rumania, 75 per cent influence in Bulgaria, 50 per cent in Hungary and Yugoslavia, and 10 per cent in Greece. Churchill did not regard this division of influence as a permanent political agreement but only as a means of preventing clashes of interest during the war. He has provided no clear explanation of how the percentages were to be translated into policy and action. Nor do we know how Stalin interpreted them. (Winston S. Churchill, *Triumph and Tragedy* [Boston: Houghton Mifflin, 1953], pp. 227–28, 231–33.)

10. General Omar Bradley made the estimate of 100,000 troops upon Eisenhower's request (Bradley, *A Soldier's Story* [New York: Holt, 1951], p. 535). The fact that the National Redoubt proved to be far weaker than the military estimates is irrelevant to the illustration of the kind of issues involved. That both Eisenhower and Bradley interpreted the political reason for occupying Berlin before the Russians as merely a matter of "prestige" must be attributed, in part, to the fact that neither Churchill nor the British Chiefs of Staff, who presented this argument, spelled it out as clearly as they might have—perhaps because they were sensitive to the American distaste for mixing power politics with war and the American distrust of the British for doing just that.

11. Robert J. C. Butow has presented a thorough account of the struggle between the Japanese peace advocates and the militarists in *Japan's Decision To Surrender* (Stanford: Stanford University Press, 1954).

12. Winston S. Churchill, *The Hinge of Fate* (Boston: Houghton Mifflin, 1950), p. 689.

13. The phrase was first used publicly on January 24, 1943, when President Roosevelt told a press conference at Casablanca that the Allies were determined to demand the unconditional surrender of Germany, Italy, and Japan. A week before this conference the American Chiefs of Staff had discussed and approved this stand. The announcement was almost universally hailed in the United States.

Churchill, after some initial opposition, had approved the formula in advance, although he took no part in its pronouncement. The British cabinet unanimously indorsed it.

Although the phrase received various interpretations, only a few officials questioned its wisdom at the time. Secretary of State Hull thought it would solidify Axis resistance and that it logically required the United States to take over the Axis governments (Cordell Hull, *The Memoirs of Cordell Hull* [New York: Macmillan, 1948], II, 1571). Secretary of the Navy Forrestal believed that the formula would lead to the destruction of Germany and Japan and "seriously unbalance the international system in the face of Soviet power" (Walter Millis [ed.], *The Forrestal Diaries* [New York: Viking Press, 1951], p. 24). Later opposition to the unconditional surrender formula came chiefly from those concerned with psychological warfare and from a few military leaders, such as General Eisenhower, who believed the enemy should have some incentive to surrender short of his annihilation.

14. For example, in an address in February, 1943, Roosevelt described the United Nations' policy toward the Axis as "a policy of fighting hard on all fronts and ending the war as quickly as we can on the uncompromising terms of unconditional surrender." In this policy, he declared, "We mean no harm to the common people of the Axis nations. But we do mean to impose punishment and retribution in full upon their guilty, barbaric leaders" (*Department of State Bulletin*, VIII [February 13, 1943], 146).

15. The reasoning behind this decision was first set forth in a Joint War Plans Committee memorandum early in June, 1944. This memorandum recognized that Japan might be defeated by "aerial bombing and blockade, accompanied by destruction of her sea and air forces"; but it advised against relying on this strategy on the grounds that it "probably would involve an unacceptable delay in forcing unconditional surrender." Therefore, it recommended that "our concept of operations against Japan . . . should envisage an invasion of the industrial heart of Japan" (Ray S. Cline, *Washington Command Post: The Operations Division* [Washington, D.C.: U.S. Department of the Army, 1951], p. 338).

16. Henry Stimson and McGeorge Bundy, *On Active Service* (New York: Harper's, 1948), pp. 618–19, 632–33.

17. Ambassador Joseph C. Grew, as early as May, 1945, urged that the war could be ended more cheaply if the United States would give clear assurances that the Emperor could remain as a constitutional monarch. For this he was called an "appeaser." However, Stimson, Forrestal, and Assistant Secretary of War McCloy favored Grew's approach. On July 2, 1945, Stimson presented a memorandum to the President suggesting that the United States offer the same imperial status Grew had suggested—but in the form of an ultimatum, combining an appeal for capitulation with a warning of dire things to come. However,

Secretary Hull opposed inclusion of any reference to the Emperor as "appeasement of Japan." The Potsdam ultimatum of July 26, 1945, was based upon Stimson's memorandum, but it made no mention of the Emperor's status. After the bombs were dropped on Hiroshima and Nagasaki, the Emperor brought about surrender on the terms of the Potsdam Declaration—but only after the American government implicitly recognized his status (Joseph C. Grew, *Turbulent Era*, ed. Walter Johnson [Boston: Houghton Mifflin, 1952], II, 1421 ff.; Stimson and Bundy, *op. cit.*, pp. 617 ff.; Millis, *op. cit.*, pp. 68–71; Hull, *op. cit.*, II, 1593–94).

18. The difference in political awareness underlying Anglo-American disputes over military strategy is fully documented in Forrest C. Pogue, *The Supreme Command* (Washington, D.C.: U.S. Department of the Army, 1954), as well as in Churchill's volumes on World War II, especially *Triumph and Tragedy*.

19. Pogue, *op. cit.*, p. 445.

20. Bradley, *op. cit.*, pp. 535–36.

21. Pogue, *op. cit.*, p. 468.

22. The *Survey*'s findings on the military effectiveness of strategic bombing are summarized and evaluated in W. F. Craven and J. L. Cate (eds.), *The Army Air Forces in World War II*, Vol. III (Chicago: University of Chicago Press, 1951), chap. xxii.

23. On a number of occasions the Army Air Force objected to these raids, proposed by the RAF and sometimes SHAEF, on the grounds that they were inconsistent with American ideals and historic policy. The AAF's resistance weakened progressively, however (*ibid.*, pp. 284, 638–40, 726–28, 732–33, 801–2). Those responsible for psychological warfare objected a few times to indiscriminate attacks on German cities, but their objections were ineffective (*ibid.*, p. 639).

24. Cited *ibid.*, p. 792.

25. By March, 1945, the Allies were sure of victory; and even German transportation, which had shown remarkable powers of recovery, collapsed. Yet not until the middle of April was the strategic air war closed in order that air power might be concentrated on tactical support of the armies advancing to the Elbe (*ibid.*, pp. 739, 746, 754).

26. Pogue, *op. cit.*, p. 446; see also Dwight D. Eisenhower, *Crusade in Europe* (New York: Doubleday, 1948), pp. 80, 194, 284.

NOTES TO CHAPTER SIX

1. Karl von Clausewitz, *On War*, trans. O. J. Matthijs Jolles (Washington, D.C.: Combat Forces Press, 1953), p. 18.

2. *Parliamentary Debates* (5th series; Hansard), DXXXVII, 1899.

3. Address delivered on January 7, 1953, *U.S. Department of State Bulletin*, XXVIII (January 19, 1953), 94.

4. Eisenhower made this extemporaneous statement in the context of a discussion of the implications of weapons of mass destruction. Since his administra-

tion on several occasions recognized the possibility of "small wars," I assume that this widely quoted sentence was not intended as a literal assertion that there is no alternative to total war except peace. In any case, it was interpreted in the United States and abroad simply as an expression of the irrationality of all-out nuclear warfare (*New York Times*, October 20, 1954, p. 16).

5. *U.S. State Department Bulletin*, XXVIII (January 19, 1953), 94.

6. *New York Times*, February 15, 1956, p. 10.

NOTES TO CHAPTER SEVEN

1. The article is reproduced in Kennan, *American Diplomacy, 1900–1950* (Chicago: University of Chicago Press, 1951), pp. 107–28. Excerpts from Kennan's original memorandum appear in Walter Millis (ed.), *The Forrestal Diaries* (New York: Viking Press, 1951), pp. 135–40.

2. Kennan, *op. cit.*, p. 119.

3. "Collective security," strictly speaking, is an arrangement whereby all nations combine to commit themselves in advance to oppose any nation that is found guilty, according to impartial rules and procedures, of aggression. According to this conception, nations are pledged to oppose all aggression, regardless of their interests, not just particular aggressions—just as policemen are pledged to resist crime rather than particular criminals. However, as commonly used since World War II, "collective security" actually refers either to an alliance of mutual self-interest, whose members agree under certain well-defined circumstances to oppose aggression by outside powers, or else simply to a temporary combination of powers who seek mutual security against other powers. Americans have repeatedly invoked the noble sentiments of collective security in the strict and pure sense in order to provide actions in the latter sense with an aura of morality they would not otherwise enjoy. The illusion of genuine collective security has been enhanced when political circumstances have permitted self-interested actions to be undertaken with the sanction of the United Nations, as, for example, the Korean War or regional security arrangements under Article 51.

4. In an address on June 29, 1951, Secretary of State Acheson said, "What we are working toward is a situation in which the normal course of settling disputes will be negotiation," but at other times he implied that no useful agreements could be reached with the Soviet Union until certain situations of weakness were overcome. At a press conference in February, 1950, he said that to make an agreement with the Russians not to "fish in troubled waters" would be like dealing with a force of nature. "You can't argue with a river, it is going to flow. You can dam it up, you can put it to useful purposes, you can deflect it, but you can't argue with it." We might reduce the opportunities for trouble by remedying situations of weakness. "But so far as agreement per agreement is concerned, I think we have discovered that even the simplest thing growing out of the war, which is to make peace . . . has become impossible." President Truman had presented a similar view in a speech on June 12, 1948, when he said, "There are

certain types of disputes in international affairs which can and must be settled by negotiation and agreement. But there are others which are not susceptible to negotiation. There is nothing to negotiate when one nation disregards the principles of international conduct to which all members of the United Nations subscribed. There is nothing to negotiate when one nation habitually uses coercion and open aggression in international affairs" (*Department of State Bulletin*, XVIII [June 20, 1948], 805; XXII [February 20, 1950], 273–74; XXV [July 23, 1951], 127).

5. Kennan, *op. cit.*, pp. 120, 126. Kennan did not interpret these words as literally as some of the critics of containment. He certainly did not envision containment as an automatic military reaction to every Communist incursion. Nevertheless, his general thesis raised the problem of meeting aggression locally instead of by retaliation on the center of aggression.

6. *Department of State Bulletin*, XVI (March 23, 1947), 534–37.

7. Joseph M. Jones, *The Fifteen Weeks* (New York: Viking Press, 1955), pp. 152–53. President Truman changed a few words in the central passages in order to provide additional emphasis (Harry S. Truman, *Memoirs* [New York: Doubleday, 1956], II, 105).

8. Jones, *op. cit.*, pp. 154–55.

9. A dozen of Lippmann's articles criticizing what he took to be Kennan's conception of containment, originally published in his syndicated column, were collected in *The Cold War* (New York: Harper's, 1947).

10. *Ibid.*, pp. 190 ff.

11. *New York Times*, May 11, 1947, p. 3.

12. *New York Herald Tribune*, March 29, 1947, p. 13.

13. *New York Times*, December 22, 1949, p. 1.

14. *Ibid.*, December 8, 1949, pp. 1, 3.

15. *Ibid.*, November 6, 1949, p. 29.

16. House Committee on Armed Services hearings, *Investigation of the B-36 Bomber Program* (81st Cong., 1st sess.); *ibid.*, *The National Defense Program— Unification and Strategy*.

17. *Ibid.*, *The National Defense Program*, p. 77.

18. *New York Times*, April 7, 1948, p. 4.

19. According to estimates made in a *New York Times* survey of the armed forces of the major powers (*ibid.*, May 12, 1947, pp. 14, 39).

20. House Committee on Foreign Affairs hearings, *Mutual Assistance Act of 1949* (81st Cong., 1st sess. [July 28, 1949]), p. 16. Six years later, when Western forces in Europe were three or four times larger, General Alfred M. Gruenther, Supreme Allied Commander in Europe, said: "We are still not strong enough to resist an all-out attack. . . . However, we could resist a surprise attack launched by Soviet forces in East Germany and the satellites" (statement made on March 26, 1955, in Senate Committee on Foreign Relations hearings, *NATO and the Paris Accords Relating to Germany* [84th Cong., 1st sess.], p. 2).

21. During the MacArthur hearings in June, 1951, General Hoyt S. Vandenberg, Air Force Chief of Staff, called attention to America's "shoestring air

force" (then some eighty-seven wings) and said that an effective strategic bombing against Chinese bases outside Korea would require "roughly, double the strategic air power that the United States has today," and might not achieve its end even then (Joint Senate Committee on Armed Services and Foreign Relations hearings, *Military Situation in the Far East* [82d Cong., 1st sess.]).

22. President Truman's and Secretary of State Acheson's statements on the Russian explosion appear in the *New York Times*, September 24, 1949, pp. 1, 2. Congress and the press generally shared the administration's depreciation of the event. Moreover, writing six years later, Truman reiterated his position in his *Memoirs*: "The Government of the United States was not unprepared for the Russian atomic explosion. There was no panic, and there was no need for emergency decisions. This was a situation that we had been expecting to happen sooner or later. To be sure, it came sooner than the experts had estimated, but it did not require us to alter the direction of our program" (*Memoirs*, II, 307).

23. *Ibid.*, II, 308 ff. The Russian explosion did lead some men in the State Department and the higher military echelons to argue for an increase in ground troops, as well as in retaliatory air power, on the supposition that, otherwise, Russia's atomic capacity would in five years or so enable her to utilize her great superiority in conventional forces to pursue a bold and aggressive policy of pressure upon various positions on the periphery of Communist power in Eurasia. Some of the men in the State Department Policy Planning Staff, at least, reached the conclusion that American strategic planning should anticipate the contingency of limited war. However, budgetary restrictions and the prevailing confidence in the atomic and the "super bomb" prevented the views of this group from carrying any weight until after the Korean War, when the heightened fears of Russian or Russian-inspired military adventures in Europe finally relieved the budgetary restrictions upon defense.

24. The pressure for a "super bomb" after the Russian explosion and the thinking behind it were brought out in the hearings on J. Robert Oppenheimer's eligibility for security clearance that would permit access to restricted data under the Atomic Energy Act. The hearings were conducted during the spring of 1954 by a special personnel security board under the chairmanship of Gordon Gray (*In the Matter of J. Robert Oppenheimer* [Washington, D.C.: United States Atomic Energy Commission, 1954]).

25. *Survival in the Air Age* (Washington, D.C.: President's Air Policy Commission, January 1, 1948), p. 22.

26. The term "gray areas" was coined by Thomas K. Finletter in his book *Power and Policy* (New York: Harcourt, Brace, 1954), pp. 83 ff.

27. Of course, one can argue that there were legitimate reasons for not applying the same policy to China that was applied to Greece. Among these reasons, spokesmen of the Truman administration later pointed to the ineffectiveness of the Nationalist government, the great magnitude of the task of successful intervention, the absence of sufficient American troops or administrative personnel, and the possibility of Russian counter-intervention. The Truman administration made its most complete case in defense of its China policy in the so-called China White

Paper, officially designated *United States Relations with China with Special Reference to the Period 1944–49* (Washington, D.C.: Department of State, 1949). However, to the official explanations for America's failure to apply the Truman Doctrine to China on a scale commensurate with the Communist threat one must add the American government's misconception of the nature of the Chinese Communists and of their ties with Moscow and its serious underestimation of the political and military importance of China.

28. In a memorandum to Mr. Jessup on July 18, 1949, Secretary of State Acheson stated, "You will please take as your assumption that it is a fundamental decision of American policy that the United States does not intend to permit further extension of Communist domination on the continent of Asia or in the Southeast Asia area." The text of this memorandum, as read into a Senate Foreign Relations Subcommittee hearing, is reproduced in the *New York Times*, October 5, 1951, p. 1. Subsequently, Acheson warned China that attempts to extend its control beyond its borders would be considered a violation of the UN Charter (Letter of Transmittal, *United States Relations with China* [Washington, D.C.: Department of State, 1949], p. xvii). See, also, address to the Commonwealth Club, San Francisco, March 15, 1950, *Department of State Bulletin*, XXII (March 27, 1950), 469.

NOTES TO CHAPTER EIGHT

1. This conclusion was set forth in a memorandum of the Joint Chiefs of Staff, dated September 25, 1947, which is reproduced in Harry S. Truman, *Memoirs* (New York: Doubleday, 1956), II, 325–26.

2. Contrasting America's current defensive position with its former position, MacArthur told a reporter in March, 1949, "Now the Pacific has become an Anglo-Saxon lake and our line of defense runs through the chain of islands fringing the coast of Asia. It starts from the Philippines and continues through the Ryukyu Archipelago, which includes its broad main bastion, Okinawa. Then it bends back through Japan and the Aleutian Island chain to Alaska." He further expressed the view that, although the Red Armies of China were on the flank of this position, "this does not alter the fact that our only possible adversary on the Asiatic continent does not possess an industrial base near enough to supply an amphibious attacking force"; and here he was speaking of the Soviet Union and its base in the Urals (*New York Times*, March 2, 1949, p. 22).

3. Acheson's "defensive perimeter" included only America's direct security commitments. "So far as the military security of other areas in the Pacific is concerned," Acheson said, "the initial reliance must be on the people attacked to resist it and then upon the commitments of the entire civilized world under the Charter of the United Nations" (*Department of State Bulletin*, XXII [January 23, 1950], 115–16).

4. Joint Senate Committee on Armed Services and Foreign Relations hearings, *Military Situation in the Far East* (82d Cong., 1st sess.), p. 382; cited hereafter as *MacArthur Hearings*.

5. See, for example, President Truman's explanation of the decision for intervention (*Memoirs*, II, 333–34).

6. *Ibid.*, p. 345; see also pp. x, 346, 416.

7. *Ibid.*, pp. 331, 341, 343, 346, 420, 432.

8. *Ibid.*, pp. 437, 456.

9. *Ibid.*, p. 420.

10. *Ibid.*, pp. 335, 337, 464.

11. *Ibid.*, pp. 359–60.

12. *Ibid.*, pp. 373–82.

13. Statement on June 26, 1951, House Committee on Foreign Affairs hearings, *Mutual Security Program* (82d Cong., 1st sess.), pp. 24–25.

14. See, for example, *MacArthur Hearings*, pp. 146, 167–88.

15. Truman, *Memoirs*, II, 415, 433–34.

16. This portion of the Joint Chiefs of Staff memorandum to the Secretary of Defense, dated January 12, 1951, was cited in the MacArthur hearings. Secretary of Defense Marshall explained that the improved military situation had made it unnecessary and inadvisable to put most of the memorandum into effect (*MacArthur Hearings*, p. 324).

17. *Ibid.*, p. 731–32.

18. *Ibid.*, pp. 1718–19.

19. *Ibid.*, pp. 39–40.

20. *Ibid.*, p. 45.

21. *Ibid.*, pp. 83, 120.

22. Admiral C. Turner Joy, Commander of Naval Forces in the Far East and Senior Delegate and Chief of the United Nations Command delegation to the Korean armistice conference, has written, "I know of not a single senior military commander of United States forces in the Far East—Army, Navy, or Air Force—who believed that the U.S.S.R. would enter the war with the United States because of any action we might have taken relative to Red China" (*How Communists Negotiate* [New York: Macmillan, 1955], p. 176).

23. When General Van Fleet relinquished his command of the UN ground forces, he said that the Communists were defeated in the spring of 1951 and implied that the UN forces then in Korea could have overwhelmed the Chinese forces if the United States had not agreed to an armistice (*New York Times*, February 10, 1953, p. 2). However, General Clark, who took command of the UN forces in May, 1952, has made more moderate claims, asserting that during his period of command we could have "obtained better truce terms quicker, shortened the war and saved lives," but only if there had been more trained divisions and more supporting air and naval forces available, if the ban on attacks north of the Yalu and on using Nationalist Chinese had been lifted, and if, "in the event of a decision by my government really to win the war," use of the atom bomb had been authorized (Mark W. Clark, *From the Danube to the Yalu* [New York: Harper's, 1954], pp. 2–3). Admiral C. Turner Joy, who was in charge of the UN's armistice negotiations, has written that elimination of "artificial restraints" imposed on UN forces, coupled with the imposition of an effective blockade

against China "probably would have resulted in military victory in less time than was expended in truce talks" and at less cost in men (Joy, *op. cit.*, pp. 166, 176, 177).

24. Matthew B. Ridgway, *Soldier: The Memoirs of Matthew B. Ridgway* (New York: Harper's, 1956), pp. 219–20.

25. While the United States maintained a force of several hundred thousand combat ground troops in Korea, and the South Koreans eventually had sixteen combat infantry divisions in the battle, the maximum contribution of the other UN members at any one time was 33,000 ground soldiers.

26. Address delivered on May 30, 1951, *Department of State Bulletin*, XXIV (June 4, 1951), 936.

27. Answering the complaint that American policy in Korea was a policy of stalemate, Secretary of Defense Marshall said, "For the last five years our supreme policy has been to curb Communist aggression and, if possible, to avoid another world war in doing so." After citing America's actions in Iran, Greece, Turkey, Trieste, Berlin, Indochina, and Korea, he said, "It is therefore our policy to contain Communist aggression in different fashions in different areas without resorting to total war, if that be possible to avoid" (*MacArthur Hearings*, p. 366).

28. *Ibid.*, p. 68.

NOTES TO CHAPTER NINE

1. *Department of State Bulletin*, XXII (January 13, 1950), 116–17.

2. *Ibid.*, XX (January 20, 1949), 125. The act to provide foreign economic assistance under the Point Four Program did not go into effect until June 5, 1950.

3. *New York Times*, July 11, 1952, p. 8.

4. *Ibid.*, May 6, 1952, p. 3; May 13, 1952, p. 8.

5. "A Policy of Boldness," *Life*, XXXII (May 19, 1952), 146.

6. *New York Times*, February 23, 1952, p. 4. For earlier statements of Dulles' conception of the dynamic and the static and of the moral law, see his book *War, Peace, and Change* (New York: Harper, 1939), p. 138; *A Righteous Faith for a Just and Durable Peace* (New York: Federal Council of Churches, 1942), p. 7; "The Christian Citizen in a Changing World," in *Man's Disorder and God's Design* ("Amsterdam Assembly Series," Book IV [New York: Harper, 1948]), pp. 100, 104. See also "A Policy of Boldness," *op. cit.*, p. 154.

7. Address on February 16, 1952, *Congressional Record* (82d Cong., 2d sess.), p. 1802.

8. In the hearings on the troops-for-Europe controversy in February, 1951, Senator Wiley complained that he had been unable to win the government to a plan for an organization of political penetration—a plan which he called the "new atomic bomb." "We have the opportunity all over Europe, and it will save us millions of dollars," he said. "To me it is the big hope." Governor Dewey exclaimed, "Behind that iron curtain everybody knows we all have friends in

Czechoslovakia, in Poland, and many of us in other countries there, and we know that there are millions of people all over the world just waiting to have a 100-to-1 chance to revolt successfully. We know that if the free world will evidence that it is aware of the danger, that it is prepared to make whatever sacrifices are necessary to remain free, and be intelligent and united, I have the greatest confidence that Stalin's empire will start to crumble" (Senate Committee on Foreign Relations and Committee on Armed Services hearings, *Assignment of Ground Forces of the United States to Duty in the European Area* [82d Cong., 1st sess.], pp. 256–57, 567).

9. "A Policy of Boldness," *op. cit.*, p. 154. Before the 1952 campaign Dulles had occasionally indorsed a program of clandestine activities. In 1948 he proposed to Secretary of State Marshall the formation of an international counter-Cominform organization (*New York Times*, April 8, 1948, p. 12). In his *Life* article he referred vaguely to the creation of political "task forces" for each captive nation. In the campaign, however, he omitted all such references, perhaps, as some reported, in deference to Eisenhower's more cautious approach.

10. See C. L. Sulzberger's report on "retaliation" and the Republican platform in the *New York Times*, July 9, 1952, p. 21. For some of Eisenhower's campaign criticisms of retaliatory air power, see *ibid.*, June 24, 1952, p. 21; *New York Herald Tribune*, June 25, 1952, p. 12.

11. *New York Herald Tribune*, May 16, 1952, p. 8.

12. *New York Times*, May 6, 1952, p. 3.

13. *Ibid.*, June 4, 1952, p. 23; October 30, 1952, p. 26.

14. *Ibid.*, October 3, 1952, p. 16.

15. See President Truman's statements to the American Hungarian Foundation and to a group of Rumanian exiles, *ibid.*, October 13, 1951, p. 6; May 29, 1952, p. 10. See also Acheson's statement over the Voice of America, *ibid.*, May 27, 1951, p. 1.

16. *Ibid.*, May 1, 1953, p. 1.

17. *Ibid.*, February 19, 1953, p. 1.

18. *Department of State Bulletin*, XXX (January 25, 1954), 107–10.

19. *Documents on American Foreign Relations, 1953* (New York: Harper, 1954), pp. 432–33.

20. *Department of State Bulletin*, XXIX (September 14, 1953), 339–42.

21. Address of August 4, 1953, *New York Times*, August 5, 1953, p. 10.

22. *New York Herald Tribune*, May 16, 1952, p. 8.

23. "How Dulles Averted War," *Life*, XL (January 16, 1956), 71. Dulles disclaimed responsibility for the parts of this article that were not direct quotations of his words, but he did not deny the authenticity of the factual statements. Joseph C. Harsch reported Dulles' interpretation of the Nehru incident in his column in the *Christian Science Monitor* on April 21, 1955. However, Robert J. Donovan's account of these events, written on the basis of his access to cabinet officers and the minutes of cabinet meetings, states that "at no time . . . did the President make a formal decision to enlarge the war," although "some of those who were closest to him at the time are convinced that he would certainly

have done so if the stalemate had dragged on" (*Eisenhower: The Inside Story* [New York: Harper, 1956], p. 119).

24. "How Dulles Averted War," *op. cit.*, p. 78.

25. Donovan has reported that in the spring of 1953 the United States moved atomic missiles to Okinawa "as a warning of what might come if the Communists did not end the stalemate" (*op. cit.*, p. 116). Neither Admiral Joy nor General Clark, who were in command in Korea at the time of the armistice, has mentioned the specific warning Dulles described. However, Admiral Joy has written that the most important consideration inducing the Communists to acquiesce in the principle of voluntary repatriation, which led to the armistice, was their fear of an expansion of the war to Red China. According to Joy, serious consideration was being given to this course, and "the threat of atom bombs was posed" (*op. cit.*, p. 161). General Clark has written that on May 23, 1953, Washington authorized him to break off the truce talks if the Communists rejected his final offer and made no constructive proposal of their own "and to carry on the war in new ways never yet tried in Korea." However, he attributes the armistice as much to exhaustion of the Chinese troops and to the Communist "peace offensive" that followed the death of Stalin as to the threat of expanding the war (Mark W. Clark, *From the Danube to the Yalu* [New York: Harper, 1954], pp. 2, 241, 267). Actually, it is probable that early in the truce negotiations the Democratic administration had already reconsidered the policy of preserving the privileged sanctuary in Manchuria with a view to enlarging the war if the negotiations failed. In a radio interview in November, 1951, General Hoyt S. Vandenberg, Air Force Chief of Staff, indicated that Manchurian bases might be bombed if current Korean cease-fire negotiations should fail (*New York Times*, November 23, 1951, p. 3). On December 21, 1951, Roscoe Drummond wrote in the *Christian Science Monitor* that it could be "authoritatively reported" that a far-reaching decision was being made to accompany whatever truce conditions might be reached with a stern warning to the Chinese Communists that violation of the truce would mean enlargement of the war.

26. Senate Committee on Foreign Relations hearings, *Foreign Policy and Its Relation to Military Programs* (83d Cong., 2d sess.), p. 4.

27. *New York Times*, March 17, 1954, p. 5; Dulles, "A Policy for Security and Peace," *Foreign Affairs*, XXXII (April, 1954), 360.

28. "A Policy for Security and Peace," *op. cit.*, pp. 359, 358.

29. On March 28, 1953, the American and French governments issued a joint communiqué warning that if the Chinese took advantage of an armistice in Korea to pursue aggression elsewhere, "such action would have the most serious consequences for the efforts to bring about peace in the world and would conflict directly with the understanding on which any armistice in Korea would rest" (*Documents on American Foreign Relations, 1953* [New York: Harper, 1954], pp. 269-72). In a notable address on April 16, 1953, setting forth the American government's peace program, President Eisenhower said that peace in Korea should mean "an end to the direct and indirect attacks upon the security of Indochina and Malaya. For any armistice in Korea that merely released aggressive armies to

attack elsewhere would be a fraud" (*Department of State Bulletin*, XXVIII [April 27, 1953], 601).

30. See Premier Laniel's report to the French National Assembly on April 9, 1954, and Secretary Dulles' speech of March 29, 1954 (*New York Times*, April 10, 1954, p. 2; March 30, 1954, p. 4).

31. *New York Times*, February 25, 1954, p. 2.

32. *Department of State Bulletin*, XXX (April 12, 1954), 540.

33. *New York Times*, April 8, 1954, p. 18.

34. *Ibid.*, April 17, 1954, pp. 1, 3; April 18, pp. 1, 2.

35. Statement at a press conference on February 10, 1954 (*ibid.*, February 11, 1954, p. 16).

36. Statement at a press conference, March 10, 1954 (*ibid.*, March 11, 1954, p. 1).

37. *Ibid.*, February 12, 1954, p. 2. Senator Knowland's statement, like President Eisenhower's, was made in response to the congressional apprehensions that were raised by the revelation that the government planned to send aircraft and air technicians to Indochina. Knowland later, on April 17, agreed with Vice-President Nixon that American troops should be sent to Indochina if that were necessary to keep Southeast Asia from falling into Communist hands, but he did not believe that the necessity would arise (*ibid.*, April 18, 1954, p. 1).

38. It may be that some members of the administration, like Vice-President Nixon, were prepared to employ American troops under some conditions, but their views did not prevail. James Shepley's article in *Life*, based upon a recorded interview with Dulles, reported that on April 4 Dulles and Radford proposed to Eisenhower that the United States try to get Great Britain and France to join in opposing the Communist forces "on the ground in Indochina, just as the UN stepped in against the North Korean aggression in 1950" (p. 72). However, the only specific measure the article mentioned as having been under consideration was air-atomic attacks, launched from two American carriers in nearby waters; and the only decision which it claimed the President approved involved air strikes against staging bases in South China if the Chinese were to intervene openly. As for Nixon's off-the-record statement of April 16, the press generally regarded it as a "trial balloon." If it reflected any serious official plan, the government soon abandoned it in an attempt to allay popular apprehensions, as the State Department gave assurances that intervention was "unlikely" and affirmed its confidence that the French would not withdraw. On April 20 Nixon restated his views. "The aim of the United States," he said, "is to hold Indochina without war involving the United States, if we can." But he added, "We have learned that if you are weak and indecisive, you invite war. You don't keep Communists out of an area by telling them you won't do anything to save it" (*New York Times*, April 21, 1954, p. 4).

39. *Department of State Bulletin*, XXX (June 28, 1954), 972. These conditions were the same ones that Eisenhower had prescribed on April 4, when he had agreed to submit Dulles' and Radford's plan for united action to Churchill (Donovan, *op. cit.*, p. 265).

40. As of 1956 public knowledge of the details of America's policy concerning intervention during the Indochina crisis comes largely from four sources, which were in substantial agreement with one another: James Shepley's account, *op. cit.*, pp. 70 ff.; Robert Donovan's book, *op. cit.*; the report of Chalmers M. Roberts, diplomatic correspondent for the *Washington Post and Times Herald* which appears in its most detailed form in "The Day We Didn't Go to War," *Reporter*, XI (September 15, 1954), 31–35; and the contemporary account of another correspondent, Marquis Childs, *The Ragged Edge: The Diary of a Crisis* (New York: Doubleday, 1955).

41. Donovan's account states that on April 4, 1954, Eisenhower agreed to submit Dulles' and Radford's plan for united action to Churchill for his approval but laid down the following conditions that would have to be met before the United States would intervene militarily:

"1. Britain must participate. Implicit in this, in the American view, was participation also by Australia and New Zealand.

"2. France and the Associated States . . . must invite the United States and the allies to join them in their struggle.

"3. France must agree to stay in the war and see it through.

"4. France must go beyond her previous efforts in granting unequivocal independence to Vietnam, Laos, and Cambodia so that American entry into Indochina would not have the taint of colonialism" (Donovan, *op. cit.*, p. 265).

42. According to Shepley's, Roberts', and Childs's accounts, Dulles believed that a clear threat of American air strikes from the two carriers in adjoining waters would probably be sufficient to achieve America's purpose. He sought both a congressional resolution and some form of British and French approval as a means of giving force to such a threat. However, his talks with the representatives of Great Britain and France, as well as of Australia, New Zealand, the Philippines, Thailand, and the Associated States of Indochina, which took place in the first half of April, were directed merely toward the formation of a Southeast Asian Treaty Organization, as far as the public reports indicate. On his return to Washington Dulles called a meeting of the ambassadors of the states concerned with the formation of SEATO for April 20, but two days before that meeting the British ambassador, who may have been influenced by Nixon's off-the-record comments about the employment of American troops, notified the State Department, after cabling London for instructions, that his government would not participate in the discussions. According to Shepley's report, Dulles had envisioned this meeting as the means of obtaining joint support for a threat of military intervention.

43. The account appears in Matthew B. Ridgway, *Soldier: The Memoirs of Matthew B. Ridgway* (New York: Harper, 1956), pp. 276–77.

44. *Ibid.*, p. 277. Marquis Childs, like other columnists writing contemporaneously with the events Ridgway describes, corroborates his account. According to Childs, Eisenhower followed the unusual procedure of having Ridgway state his views before the National Security Council. Ridgway's presentation, Childs reports, was believed to have been the chief factor in persuading Eisen-

hower to reject Radford's view and adopt a more cautious line (Childs, *op. cit.*, pp. 153–59).

45. Herbert Luethy, *France against Herself* (New York: Praeger, 1955), p. 459.

46. See, for example, the editorial in *Life*, XXIV (January 19, 1953), 18.

47. For example, in an address on December 8, 1955, Dulles said: "We have developed, with our allies, a collective system of great power which can flexibly be used on whatever scale may be requisite to make aggression costly. Our *capacity* to retaliate must be, and is, massive in order to deter all forms of aggression. But if we have to *use* that capacity, such use would be selective and adapted to the occasion" (*Department of State Bulletin*, XXXIII [December 19, 1955], 1004).

48. *New York Times*, January 13, 1955, p. 14.

49. *Ibid.*, July 16, 1955, p. 1.

50. On June 27, 1950, shortly after the outbreak of the Korean War, President Truman ordered the United States Seventh Fleet to prevent either a Communist attack on Formosa or a Chinese Nationalist attack on the mainland. On February 2, 1953, President Eisenhower—as a measure of psychological warfare, in an effort to put pressure upon the Communists to end the stalemate in Korea—said that there was "no longer any logic or sense in a condition that required the United States Navy to assume defensive responsibilities on behalf of the Chinese Communists," and he announced that he was revoking the instructions to the Fleet to restrict the Nationalists (*Department of State Bulletin*, XXVIII [February 9, 1953], 209). This move was generally interpreted as the "unleashing" of Chiang Kai-shek. However, on December 10, 1954, in an exchange of notes a month after the signing of a mutual defense treaty with the Formosan government, the Nationalists agreed that offensive military operations from Nationalist-held territory would be undertaken only as a matter of joint agreement. The mutual defense treaty limited America's defensive commitments to Formosa, the Pescadores, and "such other territories as may be determined by mutual agreement" (*ibid.*, XXXI [December 13, 1954], 899). Subsequently, the American government induced the Nationalists to evacuate the Tachen Islands but said that the United States would defend the Nationalists on Quemoy and Matsu if it appeared that a Communist attack on these islands were part of a general offensive aimed at taking Formosa. On January 29, 1955, Congress passed a joint resolution authorizing the President to use American forces to defend Formosa and the Pescadores and leaving the defense of "related positions and territories" to presidential discretion.

51. Testifying before the Senate on SEATO in November, 1954, Dulles said that the United States was not dedicating any major elements of American ground forces to defense in the area. "We rely primarily upon the deterrent of our mobile striking power. . . . I believe that if there should be an open armed attack in that area the most effective step would be to strike at the sources of aggression rather than try to rush American manpower into the area to try to fight a ground war" (Senate Committee on Foreign Relations hearings, *The*

Southeast Asia Collective Defense Treaty [83d Cong., 2d sess.], p. 17). In a news conference on December 21, 1955, Dulles, in defending the withdrawal and reduction of military forces in the Far East, explained the role of indigenous forces, a central strategic reserve, and retaliatory air power (*Department of State Bulletin*, XXXII [January 3, 1955], 12–14).

52. Donovan, *op. cit.*, pp. 115–16.

53. See Dulles' nationwide address on March 8, 1955 (*Department of State Bulletin*, XXXII [March 21, 1955], 459–64).

54. *New York Times*, March 16, 1955, p. 9.

55. See President Eisenhower's statements on January 12 and March 16 and 23, 1955, and Dulles' statements on March 8 and 16, 1955 (*New York Times*, January 13, p. 14; March 9, p. 4; March 16, p. 1; March 17, p. 18; March 24, p. 18).

56. These remarks were reported in an unofficial transcript, phrased in indirect discourse, according to conference rules against direct quotation (*ibid.*, December 16, 1954, p. 24).

57. In July, 1956, it was reliably disclosed that Admiral Radford, chairman of the Joint Chiefs of Staff, proposed to reduce the armed forces by 800,000 by 1960 in order to keep the defense establishment within budget ceilings. The great bulk of the reduction, it was reported, would fall on the Army— some 450,000—with the Navy, Marine, and Tactical Air Command absorbing the remainder (*ibid.*, July 13, 1956, p. 1; July 14, p. 1; July 15, p. 1; July 17, p. 1). A month later Secretary of Defense Charles E. Wilson told a news conference that he had rejected initial budget estimates submitted by the service chiefs for fiscal year 1958, which had amounted to an aggregate sum of $48.5 billion, because this sum represented an "unconscionable burden on the American taxpayer and was completely out of range of the nation" (*ibid.*, August 8, 1956, p. 1).

58. *Ibid.*, August 5, 1956, p. 34. The italics are mine. Several weeks later Secretary Quarles somewhat qualified the implications of this statement by saying that, although the United States would use atomic weapons in a limited war, it would avoid "excessive action," choose its weapons carefully, and employ them on military targets. However, after expressing his fear that a limited war would grow into a total war, he said that the best way to prevent this was to end the war quickly with atomic weapons (*ibid.*, September 27, 1956, p. 19).

59. In this instance, however, the additional funds were voted by an almost solid Democratic bloc, with the help of only a few dissident Republicans (*ibid.*, June 27, 1956, p. 1).

NOTES TO CHAPTER TEN

1. Thomas R. Phillips has pointed out that on the basis of UN statistics the 15 NATO nations have a population of 436,060,000, whereas Russia and her European satellites have only 278,125,000 (*St. Louis Post-Dispatch*, November 21, 1954, p. 3 C). However, because of foreign policies and domestic economic

and political considerations, the free world clearly suffers a great numerical disadvantage in terms of the troops it is willing to mobilize and maintain.

2. The possibilities of local ground defense are assessed in greater detail in the discussion of the application of a strategy of limited war to the NATO area and to the gray areas on pp. 259–73.

3. See, for example, the observations of Roger Hilsman and William W. Kaufmann in Kaufmann (ed.), *Military Policy and National Security* (Princeton: Princeton University Press, 1956), pp. 182, 250.

4. As of 1956, the less powerful nuclear weapons suitable for tactical use depended upon atomic fission for their explosive power. However, the general term "nuclear" is used so as not to exclude suitable hydrogen or fusion weapons that may be developed.

5. Kaufmann, *op. cit.*, pp. 72–73.

6. Matthew B. Ridgway, *Soldier: The Memoirs of Matthew B. Ridgway* (New York: Harper, 1956), pp. 296–97.

7. A. T. Hadley deals with the characteristics, the potentialities, and the cost of these weapons in "Low-Yield Atomic Weapons: A New Military Dimension," *Reporter*, XIV (April 19, 1956), 23–25. As against Hadley's hope that tactical nuclear weapons might be a boon to our capacity for limited war, Hanson Baldwin concluded on the basis of Exercise Sage Brush—in which a theoretical total of 275 tactical atomic projectiles, ranging from two to forty kilotons' power, were expended in a war game in western Louisiana during October and December, 1955—that such large-scale devastation would have resulted that "there probably can be no such thing as a limited or purely tactical nuclear war," at least not in similar areas. However, he did not say what proportion of low-yield weapons were expended or how much of the theoretical devastation was caused by the twenty- to forty-kiloton bombs (*New York Times*, December 5, 1955, p. 12). The theoretical results of Operation Carte Blanche the NATO tactical air force exercises held in western Europe during June, 1955, were similar to the results of Exercise Sage Brush. According to unofficial calculations 1,700,000 Germans were "killed" and 3,500,000 "wounded." However, these calculations were based on the explosion of 335 bombs, presumably of the same power as the ones "dropped" on Louisiana, in the area between Hamburg and Munich (*ibid.*, June 29, 1955, p. 4; Kaufmann, *op. cit.*, pp. 225–26).

8. Rear Admiral Sir Anthony Buzzard has, perhaps, done the most to publicize the policy of graduated deterrence. See his articles in the *Manchester Guardian Weekly*, November 3, 1955, p. 5, and in *World Politics*, VIII (January, 1956), 228–37. For an earlier and fuller expression of a similar idea, see Colonel Richard S. Leghorn, "No Need To Bomb Cities To Win Wars," *U.S. News and World Report*, XXXVIII (January 28, 1955), 79–94. Both Buzzard's and Leghorn's plans are based upon a distinction between tactical and strategic targets, and both would rule out bombing cities unless the enemy bombs ours first. Both plans recognize that target and weapons restrictions must be contingent upon the enemy's observing similar restrictions.

9. Henry A. Kissinger has observed that "forces will have to deploy as if

nuclear weapons might be used, because the side which concentrates its forces might thereby give its opponent the precise incentive he needs to use nuclear weapons. But if forces are dispersed, they will not be able to hold a line or achieve a breakthrough with conventional weapons, because the destructive power of conventional weapons is so much smaller" ("Force and Diplomacy in the Nuclear Age," *Foreign Affairs*, XXXIV [April, 1956], 356-57). Roger Hilsman believes that as nuclear weapons are integrated more closely with fighting units, "it is also likely to become more difficult for a unit to switch from one kind of war to another" (Kaufmann, *op. cit.*, p. 192). Thomas R. Phillips has argued that in our adaptation of equipment, transportation, and tactics to nuclear weapons we may be approaching the point beyond which we shall be unable to fight anything but a nuclear war ("Our Point of No Return," *Reporter*, XII [February 24, 1955], 14-18).

10. Churchill, evidently, had such considerations in mind when he contended in a major defense speech before the House of Commons on March 1, 1955, that Great Britain should develop its own nuclear bombing capacity. "Unless we make a contribution of our own," he said, "we cannot be sure that in an emergency the resources of other powers would be planned exactly as we would wish, or that targets which would threaten us most would be given what we consider the necessary priority, or the deserved priority, in the first few hours. These targets might be of such cardinal importance that it would really be a matter of life and death for us" (*Parliamentary Debates* [5th series; Vol. DLXXV (Hansard)], p. 1898).

11. From 1946 to 1956 the Russian order of battle included 175 to 200 divisions (about 4,500,000 men), 60 to 100 of which were maintained at full strength. In 1955 and 1956 the Soviet Union announced two cuts in its armed forces, cuts of 640,000 men and 1,200,000 men, respectively. It said that 63 "divisions and independent brigades" would be "disbanded."

12. There are other reasons for questioning the reliability of German divisions. Among them is the German dissatisfaction with NATO's strategy of fluid defense in depth, which would use Germany to absorb a Russian blow and turn it into a nuclear battlefield. Gordon A. Craig deals with this problem and others concerning the integration of German troops into NATO strategy in "NATO and the New German Army," Kaufmann, *op. cit.*, chap. vii.

13. Arnold Wolfers deals with the possibilities of establishing limits upon a nuclear war in Europe in "Could a War in Europe Be Limited?" *Yale Review*, XLV (December, 1955), 214-28.

14. As of 1956 military plans called for 1 American division and 23 ROK divisions in Korea; about 300,000 Nationalist Chinese troops for the protection of Formosa; 3 American divisions and 1 regimental combat team supplementing the local "police force" in Japan; 1 American division in Hawaii and 1 regimental combat team in both Okinawa and Alaska, as a Far Eastern reserve; 6 Army divisions and 2 Marine divisions in the United States, as a central reserve for both Asia and Europe. Communist Far Eastern troops were believed to number

115 divisions (2,500,000 men) in China, 25 North Korean divisions (400,000 men), and 16 Vietminh divisions.

15. Henry A. Kissinger, "Military Policy and Defense of the 'Gray Areas,'" *Foreign Affairs*, XXXIII (April, 1955), 425.

16. General Matthew B. Ridgway and his successor as Army Chief of Staff, General Maxwell D. Taylor, who have both pointed to the need for ground troops capable of meeting small wars, have both supported an Army of twenty-seven or twenty-eight divisions, instead of the present nineteen. This would require about 500,000 more men. See Taylor's statement of February 12, 1956 (*New York Times*, February 13, 1956, p. 1).

17. As defined and computed by the Department of Commerce, the gross national product is the sum of the values at market prices of final goods and services produced. It is widely accepted as one of the most significant measurements of a nation's economic capacity.

18. Gerhard Colm, *Can We Afford Additional Programs for National Security?* (New York: National Planning Association, 1953).

19. *Ibid.*, p. ix.

INDEX

INDEX

Acheson, Dean, 167, 173, 191, 198, 200; on American "defensive perimeter," 164; on containment, 191–92; on military efficacy of NATO, 155–56; on Truman Doctrine, 149
Acton, Lord, on political power, 15
American Civil War, 65; as preview of World War I, 88
Angell, Norman, 89
Atlantic Charter, 38
Atomic stalemate, 125 ff.
Atomic weapons: end of American monopoly, 157 ff.; and limitation of targets, 248–49; and limited war, 248–49; policy of retaliation, 202 ff.; rational use, 131 ff.; tactical, 136; tactical, and limited war, 230 ff., 251 ff.; tactical, military efficacy, 251 ff.; tactical, restrictions in use, 253 ff.; see also Limited war; United States
Austro-Prussian War, 64
Austro-Sardinian War, 64

Baghdad Pact, 267
Balance of power: in age of Enlightenment, 80 ff.; and Congress of Vienna, 85–86; in eighteenth century, 77 ff.; in nineteenth-century Europe, 86–87; and "nuclear stalemate," 125 ff.; between United States and the Soviet Union, 117; after World War I, 95
Balkan Wars, 65
Berlin: blockade, 125; Congress of, 85
Bismarck, Otto von: foreign policy of, 72 ff.; operation of European alliance system, 86–87
Boer War, 65
Bolingbroke, Henry St. John, on operation of the balance of power, 77–78
Bolshevik Revolution, 47
Borodino, Battle of, 33
Bradley, Omar N.: on expansion of Korean War, 175; on military strategy and political considerations, 113

Carnot, Lazare, 67, 70
Castlereagh, Viscount, 72, 96
Charles VI, 80
Chiang Kai-shek, 229
China: intervention in Indochina, 215 ff.; and Korean War, 171 ff.; policy toward gray areas, 268 ff.; policy toward Vietminh, 215 ff.
Churchill, Winston S., 109, 156; on "balance of terror," 126; on diplomatic atmosphere before World War I, 90; and negotiated settlement with Germany, 105 ff.; policy toward Soviet Union, 105 ff.; on unconditional surrender, 110 ff.; on World War I, 93
Clausewitz, Karl von, 28, 74, 132, 176; Communist adaptation, 54 ff.; on war, 21, 23, 53 ff., 123
Communism: approach to war, 46 ff.; concept of international society, 49–50; conception of war, 100; flexibility of tactics, 52 ff.; limited-war strategy, 4 ff.; revolutionary approach to war, 53 ff.; see also Soviet Union; War
Communist Party, and Communist morality, 46 ff.
Concert of Europe, 84–85
Containment: genesis, 146 ff.; and geographical limitation, 243 ff.; and gray areas, 269 ff.; before Korea, 141 ff.; and limited political objectives, 237 ff.; logical implications, 143 ff.; methods, 150 ff., 235; and military means, 241 ff.; Republican policy, 199 ff.; and shifts of Communist strategy, 160 ff.; see also Limited war; Soviet Union; United States
Crimean War, 64, 66, 85

Declaration on Liberated Peoples, 38
Dienbienphu, defense of, 216 ff.
Diplomacy: American conception, 38 ff.; Communist conception, 54 ff.; Wilsonian, 39

311